ENDURING

ROOTS

ENCOUNTERS WITH TREES, HISTORY,

AND THE AMERICAN LANDSCAPE

ENDURING ROOTS

GAYLE BRANDOW SAMUELS

RUTGERS UNIVERSITY PRESS
NEW BRUNSWICK, NEW JERSEY, AND LONDON

Samuels, Gayle, 1943–
   Enduring roots : encounters with trees, history, and the American landscape / Gayle Brandow
Samuels.
      p.   cm.
   Includes bibliographical references (p.   ).
   ISBN 0-8135-2721-X (cloth : alk. paper)
   1. Trees—United States—Folklore.   2. Trees—Symbolic aspects—United States.   3. Trees—
Environmental aspects—United States.   4. Landscape assessment—United States.   I. Title.
GR105.S333   1999
398'.368216—dc21
                                                                                          99-14092
                                                                                          CIP

British Cataloging-in-Publication data for this book is available from the British Library

Frontispiece: Root, stem, and branch structure of a sixteen-year-old Cox's Orange Pippin apple tree.
(Horticulture Research International, East Malling, Kent, United Kingdom)

Manufactured in the United States of America
Printed on partially recycled paper

For Jennifer and Eric Samuels

For Nancy Gordon Hess

For Gertrude, Aaron, and Louis Brandow

And especially for my husband,

Stu

CONTENTS

ILLUSTRATIONS

PREFACE

Almost thirty years ago, around the time my husband and I bought our first home, there was a pop psychology quiz that was very much in vogue. It went like this: picture your perfect home; now describe the number of trees you see and where they stand in relation to the house. The trees, so it was said, represented friends and the house represented the self. The quiz claimed to reveal how many friends the test taker wanted and how close those friendships would be, all based on an imaginary placement of trees.

It worked for me. And it worked (as a measure of present desires, not future outcomes) for just about everyone I knew who took it. We seem to have had no difficulty with either anthropomorphizing trees or with imagining them as friendly. We didn't consider discussing why because we didn't need to. Our attitudes toward trees are as much a part of our cultural inheritance as our language. Both reflect a firmly rooted engagement with what William Gilpin, the eighteenth-century English parson and author of *Remarks on Forest Scenery,* called "the grandest and most beautiful of all the productions of the earth."[1] Or, what I have always thought of as my friends in high places.

The widespread use of everyday, nickel-sized words like root, tree, and branch and simple phrases such as "up a tree," "tree climber," "family tree," and "money doesn't grow on trees" serve as daily affirmations of this linguistic and imaginative heritage.

However distant, we are still the genetic offspring of ancestors who flopped out of the sea into a landscape made habitable by trees. And as the Eden story relates, these towering plants immediately evolved into potent symbols: of Life, as providers of shade, sustenance, and shelter; and of Knowledge, as repositories of faith, folklore, history, and more recently, science—for all humankind.

It is this universality of affection for trees, combined with their very individual meanings, that is so intriguing. Yes, we all love trees. But, not surprisingly, cultures and individuals differ on specifics. At a time when Europeans were beginning to look to their ancient trees as a cultural patrimony, for example, Americans still saw deforestation as a "civilizing" enterprise. Yet when we discovered the giant redwoods—very old trees in a very new country—we began to look to the natural landscape for some of the points of cultural unity that Europeans had found in their constructed landscape.

Our current complicated attitudes toward trees are revealed by our actions: from the spiking of trees by Earth First! to prevent their felling, to the activism of communities across the nation engaged in saving historic trees, to allowing old-growth forests to be logged. Our historic position is more clearly enunciated in our words—the stories that have been passed down from generation to generation imbuing specific trees with communal and individual meanings. It is these stories that form the substance of this work, stories that address our attachment to the land; that talk of our universal and eternal need to leave a legacy; that explain our creative and destructive impulses vis-à-vis the natural world; that speak to the unresolved problems surrounding native versus nonnative species; and that understand the landscape as a gift, to be both received and sometimes—as on one deadly cold night in 1991 when towns in eastern Colorado, western Nebraska, and Kansas lost up to 70 percent of their trees—almost instantly destroyed.

Like America's trees, America's tree stories are a lushly diverse expression that spans our continent and our pre- and postcolonial history. My selections were informed by both personal preference (I chose stories that intrigued me because they revealed aspects or concepts of trees that I had not considered) and by a desire to include tales that I felt exemplified many of the others. But in the same way that it is a joy to see a new tree, it is always a pleasure to read a new tree story. It is my hope, therefore, that this collection will be seen for what it is, a few trees selected from a great forest, and that readers will explore both—the trees and the forest—and find pieces of their own stories in each.

ACKNOWLEDGMENTS

My greatest obligation, as always, is to my husband, a sensitive reader of the many drafts of this work and a solver of the host of computer problems that I managed to generate while producing it. He has shared in this process day in and day out, been my enthusiastic companion on field trips near and far, and never wavered in his encouragement throughout. Other family members have also supported me with their love and unfailing interest in every aspect of the life and history of trees. Despite an enormously hectic schedule of her own, my sister Nancy has always found time to read drafts, make suggestions, and provide encouragement. My children have also taken a much-appreciated interest in this work, as have my parents and my brother. I thank them all here and, I hope, in all ways.

During the four years it took to write this book, I have been graced by the wisdom, expertise, shared memories, enthusiasm for this work, and just plain helpfulness of an extraordinary number of people. It is with a deep sense of indebtedness and appreciation that I thank some of them here. Because this work began as my master's thesis at the University of Pennsylvania, I want to first thank several faculty members who read this work in that earlier form and provided very useful comments: John Dixon Hunt, Roger Abrahams, Paul W. Meyer, Ann F. Rhoads, Ben Le Page, and most especially my thesis advisor, Peter Conn. Yael Zerubavel, now at Rutgers but formerly at Penn, was reader and midwife both. I owe her special thanks. Timothy Block always found time to answer my botanical questions, Janet Theophano made it possible for me to study as widely across the university as I did, and Linda Chance was helpful with Japanese sources. I am also grateful to Blair Birmelin; Delight W. Dodyk of Drew University; Sheila Cowing; Doris Friedensohn; Kirk Johnson from the Denver Museum of Natural History; Roland M. Jefferson of the U.S. National Arboretum, retired; and Joan Infarinato for their careful reading of various chapters.

I can never adequately thank all of the reference librarians and, in the smaller libraries, general librarians—those most helpful of all people on earth—who answered my myriad questions, tracked down sources, suggested local people to contact, and somehow found time to locate and send all the materials I requested. The list includes: Patricia Rayfield, Marcia Bass, Ken Trotter, and the rest of the fine reference staff at Ludington Library, Bryn Mawr, Pennsylvania; David Azzolina, at the University of Pennsylvania Library; Heidi Hill, Olana Library; Matthew Tiews, Yale University Map Collection; Milton Gustafson, National Archives; Martha Smart, Connecticut Historical Society; Linda Oestry, Missouri Botanical Garden; Joan Markam, Morris Arboretum; Jane Alling, Pennsylvania Horticultural Society; Cheryl Oakes, Forest History Society; Miriam Touba, New-York Historical Society; Carol David, Arnold Arboretum; Brian A. Sullivan, Harvard University Archives; Virginia Smith, Massachusetts Historical Society; Tom Graham, Alice Lloyd College; David Smith, Knott County Historical Society; Marjorie Neipert, Wilton Public Library, Iowa; Sylvia M. Coast, Franklin Public Library, Pennsylvania; Karen Furlong, Mansfield/Richland County Public Library, Ohio; Anne Rumsey, New York Botanical Garden; and Daryl Morrison, University of the Pacific.

Others who have provided invaluable assistance are: Jane Waldbillig, who shared a piece of her family legacy, the story of Mary Francis Garvey Cooley; Ferris Olin; Herman Katz; Judith Jahnke; Brigitte Regier; Philip L. Forsline, U.S. Department of Agriculture, Geneva, New York; P. David Searles; Paul Downs; Meghan Campbell, University of Illinois; Judith Lefevre, Hartford Steam Boiler Inspection and Insurance Co.; Troy Stewart, City of Hartford; Jim Ryan, Olana State Historic Site; Walter F. Gabel, retired Delaware State Forester; David Peercy, Kentucky District Forester; Jim Phelps, University of Kentucky; Barbara Hill, town historian, Summerville, South Carolina; Collin Proctor, Wilton, Iowa; James E. Ivey, National Park Service, Southwest Region; Kathleen Nelson and John Louth, Inyo

National Forest; George H. Ware, Morton Arboretum; everyone I met and spoke with in Colorado, especially Lucy Price, Butch Blockowitz, Mark Brown, Mike Jackson, Ron Gosnell, Phillip J. Hoefer, Damon Lange, and Carrie Krickbaum, Colorado State Forest Service; Gary K. Lancaster, Colorado Cooperative Extension Service; Susan Bartell Ford, U.S. Forest Service Rocky Mountain Region; David Mooter, Nebraska Forest Service; Joe Lohnes, Greeley City Forester, and Laureen Schaffer, City of Greeley Museums; also Mark Bays, Oklahoma Forestry Services; Rex Adams, University of Arizona Tree-Ring Laboratory; Robert Fogel, University of Michigan; and Robert DeFeo, National Park Service Capital Region.

Finally, but in a sense initially, I want to thank my Women's Project of New Jersey colleagues, perhaps the greatest group of women anywhere, and friends near and far who have shared in my fascination with trees and tree stories. And although I had great expectations when I entered into my relationship with my editor, Leslie Mitchner has exceeded all of them, as have the fine staff at Rutgers University Press, most especially Paula Kantenwein and Marilyn Campbell, as well as my indefatigable copyeditor, Robert Brown.

ENDURING
ROOTS

Tab. CCCLVII.

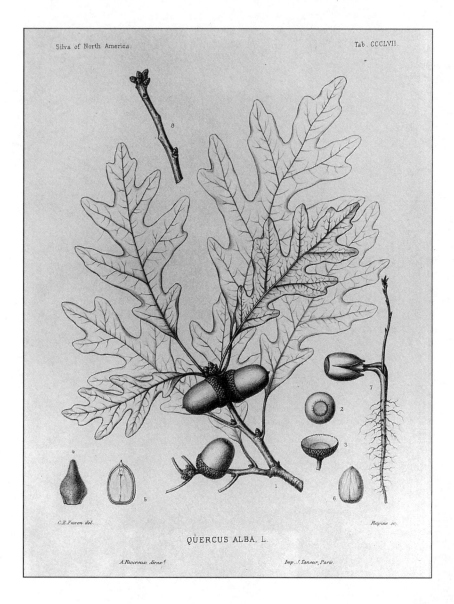

C.E.Faxon del.

Rapine sc.

QUERCUS ALBA, L.

A.Riocreux direx.t

Imp.J.Taneur, Paris.

CHAPTER ONE

TAKING ROOT: THE CHARTER OAK

ROOT: THE LOWER PART OF A PLANT, USUALLY UNDERGROUND, BY WHICH THE PLANT IS ANCHORED AND THROUGH WHICH WATER AND MINERAL NUTRIENTS ENTER THE PLANT.

MICHAEL ALLABY, *The Concise Oxford Dictionary of Botany*

I am openly polygamous when it comes to trees. My first love was a sycamore (*Platanus acerfolia*). The mottled bark, furry balls, and satisfying sound of its name attracted me. But what kept my affection was its presence on my grandmother's street: my favorite was directly in front of her house. After I married, when the paint was hardly dry on our first home and we were already moving again, we took a slip of the willow (*Salix nigra*) our toddlers had just begun to climb, tucked it in with the photo albums and finger paintings, and we planted it at our new home with the wish that all our roots would grow well in the new place we had found. Much later, on a trip to the West Coast, the eucalyptus (probably *Eucalyptus ficifolia*) caught my eye and my breath. It, too, had the "pied beauty" of the sycamore, but it also rustled soothingly when the breeze touched its leaves. It had a slightly pungent scent that perfumed the air and a seedpod so beautiful I secreted it in my suitcase so I could look at it and look at it on my windowsill at home. Thoughts of California still evoke thoughts of eucalyptus, and each sycamore, if I allow it, conjures up my childhood as certainly as Proust's madeleines did his.

These, then, are some of memory's trees: to paraphrase A. Bartlett Giamatti, the green trees of my mind. Over the years, they have had more than a few companions. So many, in fact, that I have lately felt a need to organize; to shape and cultivate my trees, to discover their preferences and their favored companions, and to learn their stories. So I have continued to look, but I have also been reading.

The choices are almost as varied and numerous as the trees themselves. I select from folklore and field guides, history, plant morphology, dendrochronology, news clippings, geology, forestry journals, paleontology, legal opinions, and family papers. I read botany to learn how trees work—this from the British botanist Oliver Rackham: "A tree does not have a predetermined life-span as we do. . . . The onset of old age is determined more

1. *Charles Sprague Sargent*, The Silva of North America, *vol. 8. (The McLean Library, Pennsylvania Horticultural Society, Philadelphia)*

by the size of the tree than by the number of its years; a tree that grows fast when young is likely to reach an early, middle, and old age." [1] And I read poetry to understand how trees make us feel:

> When dusky night do nearly hide
> The path along the hedge's zide . . .
> Then if noo feäce we long'd to greet
> Could come to meet our lwonesome treäce . . .
> However lwonesome we mid be,
> The trees would still be company. [2]

I travel, look, listen, and fill myself with stories that are as like mine as another face and as unlike mine as another face. I read essays. This from John Fowles: "trees are like humans: they need their pasts to feed their presents"; and this from Emerson: "All the facts in natural history taken by themselves, have no value, but are barren, like a single sex. But marry it to human history, and it is full of life." And I remind myself of what Annie Dillard says: "We are here on the planet only once, and might as well get a feel for the place." [3] Dillard wrote this about a trip to the Ecuadorian jungle, but I decide to visit Hartford, Connecticut, to get a feel for two different intersections—the intersection of Charter Oak Avenue and Charter Oak Place and the intersection of the past with the present.

Hartford is the home of the Connecticut Historical Society. Sitting there in a quiet room at a library table, I am reading about a funeral for a tree.

Centered between two items urging support for the newly formed Republican Party's antislavery candidate, the soldier-explorer John C. Frémont, a black-banded front-page obituary in the August 21, 1856, *Hartford Courant* proclaimed the tree's death. "The Charter Oak is Prostrate! Our whole community, old and young, rich and poor, were grieved to learn that the famous old CHARTER OAK, in which Wadsworth hid King Charles' Charter of the old colony of Connecticut, in 1687, at the time when . . . James 2nd, demanded its return, had been prostrated by the wind." The article went on to say that "no tree in the country has such legendary associations," and to tell of a dirge being played at noon by Colt's Armory Band and of the bells all over the city tolling at sundown "as a token of universal feeling, that one of the most sacred links that binds these modern days to the irrevocable past, had been suddenly parted."

At the time of its death the Charter Oak had been a Hartford institution for almost two centuries. The tree was fully mature when colonial Hartford was founded. It was then, according to the enduring tale alluded to in the obituary, that the colonists, finding their freedom threatened by their monarch's decision to revoke their liberal charter, had turned to the tree and hidden the cherished document in a cavity within its trunk. (Like my mother, who hid behind her corpulent grandmother when trouble was brewing, I always think.)

Newspapers across the country and as far away as England sympathetically reported the tree's death—from the *New York Times* to the *Louisville Journal, Springfield Daily Republican,* Washington *Daily Union,* and London *Times.* Grief, followed closely by a feeding frenzy among those eager to secure a fragment of the sacred relic, reached into Texas, Alabama, Georgia, the newly admitted state of California, and the Minnesota Territory. The president of Jefferson College in Mississippi requested a piece as did Hartford residents "bowed with age, and whose eyes were bleared with time [who] begged a sprig in commemoration." [4]

After its death, Nelson Augustus Moore photographed the fallen tree for posterity and, although greater artists had already depicted the Charter Oak, Charles De Wolf Brownell then painted what became the favored image. His painting was later selected for a 1936 U.S. postage stamp commemorating Connecticut's Tercentenary. Hartford and Connecticut chairs of state were fashioned from its wood, as were earrings, bracelets, goblets,

2. A 1936 postage stamp commemorating Connecticut's Tercentenary.

beads, Bibles, a lamp and screen depicting heroes of the Revolution, and three pianos, which, by using the new technique of veneering, combined a celebration of nineteenth-century technology with commemoration of the ancient oak.[5]

Hartford resident Mark Twain quipped that he had seen enough pieces of the Charter Oak made into "a walking stick, a dog collar, needle case,

3. John H. Most, Hartford Chair of State. (Wadsworth Atheneum, Hartford. Bequest of Elizabeth Hart Jarvis Colt)

three-legged stool . . . and toothpick . . . to build a plank road from Hart-ford to Salt Lake City": [6] based on the estimate of one newspaper editor that in 1856 10,000 pieces of the tree made their way across the country, Twain might have exaggerated only a wee bit. Although it amuses us to learn that some Charter Oak relics were actually made from elm, there was nothing counterfeit in the fervor that swept America in the wake of the tree's demise. Flag-draped, it had been given a hero's funeral, and the nation had responded with that mixture of respect and memento-gathering that it would dust off again less than nine years later as solemn onlookers placed pennies on the tracks when the train carrying Abraham Lincoln's coffin passed by.

Lincoln's presidency and the Civil War were still several years away when the Charter Oak fell, but the tree's death was clearly a national unifier during a time of increasing dissension. Portents of the coming conflict had been spewing forth like volcanic ash: the Missouri Compromise excluding slavery from a portion of the Louisiana Purchase; the publication of *Uncle Tom's Cabin*; the battle over Kansas, which had required federal troops to maintain order between pro- and antislavery factions; and the continuing drumroll of states declaring their slavery sentiments as they entered the union. Political issues hung heavy in the air, but economic and cultural matters also claimed national attention.

The Charter Oak fell during a time when market forces were changing the economics of farming. As early as 1814, writers such as Revolutionary War general Benjamin Lincoln bemoaned the lavish consumption of trees, which was creating timber shortages around coastal towns. Pessimistically he observed, "There is little hope these things will change for the better, since the tenure of our land cannot secure them in the family for any distant period. Thus is destroyed one great motive which would lead the grandsire to plant the acorn." [7]

It was a time when the advance of American industrialism, especially the extractive industries that depend on natural resources such as trees, was leaving an ever-greater mark on the common landscape and the collective consciousness. Industrialization created wealth much more rapidly than agriculture ever had, enriched a newly enlarged mercantile class, and populated factories and mills with immigrants, many whose ethnic roots differed from those of the early colonists. Home-based production was being replaced by newer industrial modes. "The capitalist revolution separated private from public life. The public sphere of marketplace and politics was dominated by men, the private sphere of home and family by women. Nature was also severed: science and technology became the instruments for economic development, spirit and emotion a counterpoint to competition."[8] There was a growing awareness that idealized the past—and glorified its symbols, such as the ancient trees.

The Charter Oak fell during a time when Americans were trying to establish a national culture. Europeans had been busily mining their pasts, searching out their "primitive, tribal, barbaric origin[s]." "Americans," the historian Perry Miller explains, "tried to answer by bragging about the future, but that would not serve . . . [so] many of our best minds went hard to work to prove that we too were a nation in some deeper sense than mere wilfulness." What emerged was an American culture that was "rooted in the soil." "We may have come to this land by an act of will [writers like James Fenimore Cooper were saying], but despite ourselves, we have become part of the landscape."[9]

Our forebears, then, sought their "identity in their relationship to the land they had settled" and looked to the wonders of the landscape to provide "points of mythic and national unity" not confined to any religion or sect. The genteel tourist pilgrimages of the 1820s and 1830s to places like Niagara Falls, Lake George, or the Catskills reflect that search for a nature-inspired cultural idiom by that part of the population with leisure, money, a broadly defined cultural literacy, and the ability to secure lodging in a network of inns and hotels not open to everyone. Others saw in the continuing trans-Atlantic trade in new and exotic American plant species an affirmation of the more-than-raw-material value of the American landscape.[10]

And by the 1850s, the entire nation was awed and energized by a specific piece of the American landscape—trees. Reports of Yosemite and the Big Trees (*Sequoia gigantea*) rippled from west to east. The realization that America had living monuments of its own—older by far than Europe's constructed landscape, reaching back beyond the beginnings of the Christian era—was a matter of national pride.

The Big Trees were not the only trees Americans marveled at. Tree stories were a well-developed regional art and claimed a national audience. In 1862, the popular *Harper's New Monthly Magazine* included a twenty-page illustrated article about the Charter Oak and sixteen other "grand old trees, about which memories cluster like the trailing vines." This was the same year that Thoreau's essay in praise of native apple trees, "Wild Apples," appeared in the *Atlantic Monthly*. The genre, which reveals an appealing emotional engagement with trees, includes narratives incorporating, though not limited to, various elements of my own tree stories and of the Charter Oak legend. These are: trees as witnesses to personal and national events, as memorials to people and places associated with them, as markers of the seasons, as landmarks, lighthouses, trail markers, and property boundaries, as soil indicators, as places of outdoor worship, as providers of shade, sustenance, beauty, and refuge, as public and private meeting places, as living legacies passed from one generation to the next and as the source of objects that have heightened interest and value because of the specific trees they were made from.

American scenery was also attracting the attention of serious artists. Influenced by European Romanticism, a school of American artists called the Hudson River School was celebrating the scope and scale of America's natural riches and, in the process, founding our first truly national school of art. Called "priests of the natural church" by the art historian Barbara Novak—such men as Thomas Cole, Frederic Edwin Church, Asher Brown Durand, Jasper F. Cropsey, and Albert Bierstadt—they converted "the [American] landscape into art" and, in the process, created an "iconography of nationalism."[11] They produced a body of work revealing the sweeping grandeur of the American continent in such monumental canvasses as Bierstadt's *Mount Whitney—Grandeur of the Rockies,* as well as its more intimate treasures, such as Cole's and Church's depictions of the Charter Oak.

Cole, who also wrote poetry condemning the widespread destruction of America's forests ("The Complaint of the Forest" and "The Lament of the Forest" for example), produced a sketch of the oak, and Church did several sketches and two paintings. As Gerald Carr, who has written the catalogue raisonné of Church's work, explains: "because it was situated only a few blocks from the family residence on Trumbull Street, Church must have passed by the Charter Oak many times during his youth, and doubtless he was nourished visually by images of the tree." Said to be "one of the first things a stranger visiting Hartford generally wishes to visit," in 1844 the tree that had preserved democracy was chosen as the backdrop for a Whig convention held "virtually beneath its branches."

4. Frederic Edwin Church, The Charter Oak, *1846, oil on canvas. Looking southwest. Including a mother and son paying homage to the tree. (New York State, Office of Parks, Recreation, and Historic Preservation, Olana State Historic Site)*

In his 1846 painting of the tree Church included two symbolic figures, presumably a mother and son, the former "passes on her knowledge of the tree to her young son who represents the next generation. The boy already has begun gathering fragments of the sacred tree." The painting was prescient. Church himself was among the collectors of the tree's fragments after it fell. The collection at Olana, his home in New York state's Hudson River Valley, includes "two partial cross sections, one of a branch and the other of a root, and a letter opener with a wooden handle, all inscribed 'Charter Oak.'" [12]

Church, Cole, and Brownell, however, were hardly the first, or the only, artists to produce renderings of the famous tree. Ralph Earl included the tree in a 1790s portrait of Mary Wyllys Pomeroy (the tree stood on the Wyllys property), George Francis painted it, and in the 1820s "when it

5. Frederic Edwin Church, The Charter Oak, *August-September 1846, ink and graphite drawing. Looking east. Inscribed with notes made by Church, including the word "character" in the upper left. (New York State, Office of Parks, Recreation, and Historic Preservation, Olana State Historic Site)*

became the custom to decorate earthenware with printed views of historical objects and places, the tree was celebrated on china." Another "group of images is clustered in the 1830s . . . [and] include[s] schoolgirl watercolors, professional oil paintings, two lithographs, and a skillful pen and ink drawing by a Hartford engraver made on the basis of exact measurements of the tree. The lithographs and the wood engraver's drawings are extremely important," decorative arts expert Robert Trent explains, "for they demonstrate that inexpensive prints of the tree were in demand among those who did not have access to a piece of it." [13]

Pruned of its images and artifacts, however, the Charter Oak emerges even more clearly as a storehouse of national memory. Its role in the 1687 myth of colonial legitimacy and freedom gave it fame and a new name; but this particular white oak had also served Native Americans as a council tree "under which they had met for generations," as a guide to the time for planting their corn, and as a landmark where "at flood time, they tied their canoes to its branches." Reaching even farther back, it stood as a primordial visitor, a living reminder of the vast woodlands that had once covered New England.[14]

Trees are the oldest and the largest of all living things. For the centuries before buildings exceeded their height, trees dominated the landscape. They still do in many places. Their long life, stature, and seasonal regeneration have made them objects of wonder and worship. Some believe that the tracery of arching branches against the sky inspired the design of Europe's great Gothic cathedrals and that the quality of filtered light experienced in the forest is what stained glass is meant to duplicate. Why not? What else negotiates the space between heaven and earth as felicitously as a mature tree? Most widely revered among the trees, the oak is called Jupiter's tree because of its status as king of the forest; it is also, as Michael Pollan points out, "the tree most often struck by lightning, and so may be thought to enjoy a special relationship with the heavens."[15] But it is a relatively recent addition to the New England ecosystem.

The oaks and other hardwoods we consider typical of the forest joined the spruce and white pines, which were their predecessors, only about seven thousand years ago.[16] "Based upon 162 sites with radiocarbon-dated plant-fossil sequences, [across eastern North America] late-glacial and postglacial migrations have been reconstructed for a number of important forest trees." These reconstructions reveal that the trees with smaller, lighter seeds that can be wind-dispersed, such as spruce and pine, moved north more rapidly than the heavier-seed trees, such as hickory and oak, which are typically dispersed by birds and small mammals. Contrast, for example, the annual rate of northward migration for the oaks—slightly more than 400 feet—with that of the spruce which was advancing at almost 550 feet a year.[17]

The Charter Oak was a white oak (*Quercus alba*), a deciduous tree that can grow to 100 feet and have a crown spread that exceeds its height. The *cognoscenti* speak of it in superlatives. "I have selected the *alba*," Thomas

Jefferson wrote to a French gardener to whom he was sending seeds, "because it is the finest of the whole family, it is the only tree with us which
disputes for pre-eminence with the Liriodendron [the tulip tree]. It may be
called the Jupiter while the latter is the Juno of our groves."[18] And in 1884
when Charles Sprague Sargent, a Harvard professor of horticulture and
director of the Arnold Arboretum, wrote the "first comprehensive synopsis
of North American trees,"[19] his *Silva of North America,* he had this to say
about the white oak:

> The great size that it attains in good soil, its vigor, longevity, and stately
> habit, the tender tints of its vernal leaves when the sunlight plays among
> them, the cheerfulness of its lustrous summer green and the splendor of its
> autumnal colors, make the White Oak one of the noblest and most beautiful
> trees of the American forest; and some of the venerable broad-branched
> individuals growing on the hills of New England and the middle states real-
> ize more than any other American tree, that ideal of strength and durability
> of which the Oak has been the symbol in all ages and all civilized countries.[20]

The first to describe the tree, according to Sargent, was the English apothecary and plantsman John Parkinson, who, in 1620, wrote of the tree as an
apothecary might: "They have in *Virginia* a goodly tall Oke, which they
call the white Oke, because the bark is whiter then of others . . . the
Ackorne . . . is not only sweeter then others, but by boyling it long, it giveth
an oyle which they keepe to supple their joynts."[21]

Natural historian Donald Culross Peattie writes, "if Oak is the king of
trees, as tradition has it, then the White Oak, throughout its range, is the
king of kings. The Tuliptree can grow taller, and the Sycamore in the days
of the virgin forest had gigantic boles, but no other tree in our sylva has so
great a spread. . . . Indeed, the fortunate possessor of an old White Oak
owns a sort of second home, an outdoor mansion of shade and greenery
and leafy music."[22]

A slow-growing tree, therefore not likely to reach old age quickly, as
Oliver Rackham made clear, the oak waits until maturity to really make a
statement. "Probably the largest of all the native oaks," according to *Taylor's Guide to Trees,* white oaks sometimes reach an exceptional size. The
Wye Oak in Wye Mills, Maryland, for example, has a circumference of

382 inches (at breast height, or 4½ feet above ground level) and measured 96 feet tall with a crown spread of 119 feet in 1996; its estimated age then was over 400 years. These measurements come from *American Forests'* National Register of Big Trees, a project initiated in 1940 to "identify and protect America's living landmarks." [23] For fifty-four of the fifty-eight years the list has been maintained, the Wye Oak has been the undisputed champion.

But there are older white oaks. At 515 years old, the Columbus Oak in Solebury, Pennsylvania—"so named because it predates Columbus' arrival in the Western Hemisphere" [24]—may be one of the oldest white oaks in the eastern United States. There are even older members of the larger oak genus, *Quercus,* such as the Angel Oak on John's Island, South Carolina. Named after the nineteenth-century owners of the property on which it stands, the Angel Oak is a live oak (*Quercus virginiana*—the tree often planted along the long drives leading up to plantation homes), believed to be the oldest living thing east of the Mississippi at about fourteen hundred years old. [25]

It is not size and age alone, however, that have made oaks especially admired among our trees, it is also their deep roots. Sargent comments on their "thick perpendicular tap-roots penetrating deep into the ground, stout wide-spreading horizontal roots and few thick rootlets." [26]

This is a subject that interests me a great deal: the subject of roots. That they are hidden, of course, adds to their mystery in the same way that Salome's veils added to hers. But it is also their eternal isolation and permanence, or rootedness, that are so intriguing.

There is much that we know. It turns out that the size of the seed dictates the form the initial root system will take. "Small seeds like birch produce a small root that grows downward." But, because the small root is not generally able to "penetrate surface leaves . . . [it] is easily deflected sideways." Large seeds like acorns, on the other hand, "produce large taproots . . . reminiscent of carrots . . . that can penetrate leaves and grow down for a long way using the stored food." [27]

It also turns out that trees have been classified into three categories—deep, intermediate, and shallow—based on the depth of their roots. Oaks, of course, are with the deep-rooters, those trees like osage orange (first described by Meriwether Lewis as the result of the Lewis and Clark Expedition), hackberry, mulberry, and honey locust, with roots that typically penetrate 10 to 20 feet below the surface. In *Growth and Development of Trees* the plant physiologist and forest biologist T. T. Kozlowski writes of a sixty-five-year-old oak (*Quercus macrocarpa*) with a "taproot which extended down to 14 feet and gave rise to 30 or more large branch roots. These main branches, which varied in diameter from 1 to 7 inches, extended outward for 20–60 feet." The roots of the intermediate group— "green ash, American elm, red cedar, and box elder"[28]—go down to 10 feet. Willow and cottonwood are examples of shallow-rooted trees.

Oak roots have another distinguishing characteristic: their volume. Measuring root development of pines versus oaks growing on sandy soil in central Wisconsin, scientists found that pure oak forests produced 44,200 pounds of roots per acre, while the pure pine forests only produced 12,300 pounds per acre.[29]

The interesting thing is that when it comes down to it, however, no matter how deeply or shallowly rooted a tree might be, two things are true: first, most roots grow horizontally, not vertically; and second, most roots are concentrated in the upper six inches of soil. "Measurements from all over the world show that in forests most of the roots are concentrated in the surface layers."[30]

So we can eliminate our mental picture of trees as barbells standing on end. Since they need to adapt to very different environments, roots and branches do not develop the same form or a necessarily equivalent size. Even trees considered to be deep-rooted, such as oaks, do not develop a root mass equal in height (or depth) to the trunk and branches. We can also, it seems, eliminate our mental picture of trees as isolated or "discrete physiologic units, often in competition with other individuals of the same or different species." Writing in *The Botanical Review*, B. F. Graham, Jr., and F. H. Borman reveal that "natural root grafts occur commonly among the roots of many forest-tree species. Parallel or intersecting contiguous roots, by continuous diameter growth, develop a pressure point of contact. Near this pressure point, the characteristic vascular union [graft] becomes established."[31] There they stand, it seems, holding hands underground.

This means a lot to foresters. It means, for example, that a substance which is put one place in the forest can wind up somewhere else. "Translocation between grafted trees of water, dyes, radioactive isotopes, silvicides, fungus spores, and antibiotics has been demonstrated." It also provides another explanation for spacing: "The possible involvement of natural root grafting in the establishment of patterns of natural spacing in the forest has been recognized relatively recently [1961]."[32]

But it also means a lot to all of us because it raises some very basic questions. "Where," Graham and Borman's paper asks, "is the line drawn between an individual and the rest of the community?"[33] Where indeed. It seems this has been a cooperative venture all along, and we were the last to find out.

On these shores Native Americans were the first to separate the trees from the forest. This was a task of more than philosophical interest to a farmer—creating fields generally means destroying forests—especially a farmer confronted with the once-dense forests of southern New England. Long before the first colonists arrived, as William Cronon points out in *Changes in the Land,* Native American farmers had established fields by repeatedly burning the fallen trees and underbrush. The colonists continued to use some burning to expand their fields, along with girdling and cutting of trees, and they added extensive cutting to support their lumbering. Still, remnants of the forest dotted even the cultivated landscape, and because fire had long been the method of choice for clearing, the more fire-resistant species of hickory, chestnut, and oak achieved a new dominance in the eastern countryside.

The Charter Oak, then, was first of all a survivor of the forest—trees do not stand alone unless they are made to do so—and secondly, a valued part of the Native American landscape. To the agricultural tribes of southern New England, where corn provided about 65 percent of their caloric intake, determining the correct time for planting was crucial to survival. The cultivators were women and, according to the historian of science Carolyn Merchant, they used a variety of ecological indicators as guides: the spring runs of alewives, the position of the stars, and "the spring growth of the leaves of the white oak to the size of a mouse's ear."[34] In the 1630s, when the land the tree stood on became the property of George Wyllys, a "deputation of Indians representing the former occupants of the place" came asking that the oak be spared. And it was. The tree, as the librarian of the Connecticut Historical Society, W. I. Fletcher, commented in 1883, thus "became an interesting link between the prehistoric and the modern."[35]

The request would not have seemed strange to the colonists. They, too,

were an agricultural people; they understood the importance of determining the correct time to plant crops. And they were familiar with the oak. It
is a tree of both the Old World and the New. Their worldview would also
have promoted an affinity for the oak because of their respective positions
of primacy within the Chain of Being, a philosophy that ordered their universe in a hierarchy from the lowest to the highest. "The lion we say is the
king of beasts, the eagle is the chief of birds . . . Jupiter's oak the forest's
king . . . and . . . shall we not acknowledge a nobility in man of greater
perfection . . . and prince of these?" [36]

The first Europeans to settle Connecticut were the Dutch. They bought
the land for their Hartford settlement from the Pequot, who claimed to
have acquired it in conquest, and built a trading post there in 1633. That
same year English members of the Massachusetts Bay Colony bought their
land from the Nawaas and established a settlement near Hartford. By
1635, when John Winthrop arrived with the first official claim to the land
on the part of the English authorities—a deed from the Earl of Warwick—
three English towns surrounded the soon-to-be-abandoned Dutch trading
post. Four years later these towns drafted and signed the Fundamental
Orders of Connecticut, incorporating provisions for governance, which
provided for the election of officials, the supremacy of the General Court,
and the collection of taxes. The Orders remained in effect until 1662, when
Charles II issued the Connecticut Charter, a liberal document, which su-
perseded but endorsed the limited self-government the colonists had already set up under their Fundamental Orders.

The colonists chose to have their authority and legitimacy rest on the
popular Charter for three principal reasons: first, it endorsed their own
arrangements; second, they were the subjects of a crown that did not recognize native rights to land, and thus their earlier purchases would have
been considered invalid; and third, they themselves had developed the
concept of *vacuum Domicilium,* which explained and justified their appro-
priation of much native land on the grounds that since the indigenous
peoples had not fenced or bounded their land it was "waiting to be inhabited by a more productive people." [37] These arrangements worked as long
as Charles II was on the throne, but when James II succeeded his brother,
he moved to scrap the Charter and subsume Connecticut, along with all
of New England, under the rule of Sir Edward Andros, his appointed governor of New York.

What followed has become the stuff of legend. On October 31, 1687, Andros came seeking the Charter. The colonists understood that its transfer into his hands would mark the end of their limited independence. In a moment that includes the best of theater, magic, and playground strategy, the document mysteriously disappeared at the moment when it was about to be handed over, having been secreted in the oak by Captain Joseph Wadsworth. Although the event itself was magical, without its sequel the colonial action would have been a minor skirmish and not a triumph. Because in 1689, after James II fled England and William and Mary assumed the crown, Andros was displaced and Connecticut's Charter, never having been officially rescinded, was considered still valid.

Sadly, no contemporary accounts of the event exist. The first recorded mention of the Charter Oak incident came in 1715 when the Connecticut General Assembly voted a stipend to Joseph Wadsworth for "securing" the charter "in a very troublesome season when our constitution was struck at, and in safely keeping and preserving the same ever since unto this day." Over the next ninety years the story was embellished by various accounts, most notably one in 1759 by Roger Wolcott, a former governor of Connecticut, which indicates that after the Charter was laid on the table "all the candles were snuffed out at once." In the time it took to relight the candles, the Charter had vanished. A 1797 account identified the location of the "ancient hollow tree on the property of the Wyllys family in Hartford" (had a decision been made not to go public with the location of the tree until after the Revolutionary War?), and by 1805 all of the elements of the legend were in place when Abiel Holmes, in *American Annals,* mentioned "the large hollow oak tree, which to this day is regarded with veneration, as the preserver of the constitution of the colony." [38]

Why might they have chosen the oak as a hiding place? First, the tree would have suggested itself because of its visibility, its dominance over the landscape, its ability to stand alone, outside the forest and outside the deforestation enterprise the colonists were engaged in. "Venerable" and "imposing" are overused, but nonetheless appropriate, descriptors of mature oaks. Visit the superb Wye Oak to experience "venerable" and "imposing" in a tree. The Charter Oak was a vigorous survivor of both native agricultural techniques that eliminated many of the trees and of natural processes that cause trees to die. Was their action, then, symbolic of a wish to survive hostile Indians and a sometimes equally hostile environment? If the tree was outside the wilderness, the pejoratively native world, was it inside the ordered and rational human community or did it inhabit some halfway house of its own? When deciding where to hide the Charter the Connecticut colonists must have considered possible reprisals by the crown against any individual found harboring the document. This would have made the choice of a home as a hiding place very risky: the oak (nature) was neutral. Yet even in selecting a tree, they would have chosen carefully. Was the oak on the Wyllys property chosen because its owner had served as one of the original custodians of the Charter? They would have heard about Charles II hiding himself in an oak after the disastrous battle of Worcester in 1651. Would it have seemed like poetic justice to hide Charles's Charter in the same genus of tree Charles himself had taken refuge in, uniting the Old World King symbolically with the New World country? In passing the Charter to the tree were the colonists symbolically placing what they believed to be their natural rights within the larger natural order established by God?

What is the truth? "As it happens," Pollan writes, "the etymology of the word *true* takes us back to the old English word for 'tree.' A truth, to the Anglo-Saxons, was nothing more than a deeply rooted idea." [39] The truth, then, is that more than thirty generations of Americans, both native and naturalized, have venerated this specific tree. The truth is that the European colonists who reached these shores had traveled far in the hope of establishing enduring roots. They encountered a population that had already done just that. I like to think there were two handshakes when the decision was made to preserve the tree: one above ground and another below.

Maps began to note the tree's location in 1846 (during that period of seeking a cultural idiom in the landscape), and soon after it fell the two roads that intersect at the corner where it stood were renamed Charter Oak Avenue and Charter Oak Place. If you visit that eponymous intersection you will find a very small enclosed park planted with a young white oak and featuring a treelike column erected by the Society of Colonial Wars with an inscription praising the former oak for its role "as the hiding place of the Charter." If you stay long enough you will know you are at a meeting place, a place where people come and go and congregate, next to the monument, in the scant shade of the young white oak planted as a reminder of those earlier deeds.

You and the locals and the young tree will be part of that larger natural order within which the colonists were placing their Charter, the elegant ecological order in which trees breathe out so that we can breathe in. Today America's forests are diminished, some say endangered, and almost daily bulletins remind us of the failing health of our planet. But in the City of Hartford someone has found that one way to move forward is to reclaim the past, that planting a "sprig in commemoration" is the most perfect arrangement of giving and getting in the same action.

Recent studies done at Chicago's Robert Taylor Homes by Frances E. Kuo and William C. Sullivan of the University of Illinois's Human-Environment Research Lab indicate "signs of stronger communities where there are trees." They also show that "in buildings with trees, people report a stronger feeling of unity and cohesion with their neighbors; they like where they are living more and they feel safer than residents who have fewer trees around them." And "we are finding less violence in urban public housing where there are trees."[40]

The Charter Oak, then, has served as the preserver of a limited democracy, as a symbol of national identity deeply rooted in the American soil, and as a place for us to come together, to find that evanescent ideal we call community or "company," as the poet said. "To plant trees," the gardener Russell Page wrote, "is to give body and life to one's dreams of a better world."[41] Exactly what the Charter Oak is all about.

Pl.30

P.J.Redouté del.

Gevain Sculp.t

Black Walnut.

Juglans nigra.

CHAPTER TWO

FAMILY TREES

BRANCH: A LATERAL STEM THAT ARISES FROM ANOTHER OF THE SAME FORM.

MICHAEL ALLABY, *The Concise Oxford Dictionary of Botany*

This is how I imagine the scene: a two-story white clapboard house sits off to the left, a fence—part stone, part whitewashed rails—separates the house from the wide dirt road in front. A couple, appearing to be in their late sixties, stands in front of the house, behind the fence. On a narrow strip of grass between the old Boston Road and that fence a young man stands near a newly planted tree. He is wearing what appears to be a military uniform, as are a group of young men who stand at a distance facing him, with their backs to me. Closer to the center of the canvas, near the young man and the tree, yet another group of young men has gathered. They seem to be listening carefully to something the man near the tree is saying to them. Off in the distance, far down the road, in the right rear of the image, a very young female figure stands alone, surrounded by silver and red maples, poplars, and champagne-flute–shaped American elms dotted with nosegays of furry-looking fringed flowers that signal spring. The image is framed in elm.

Facts support my fantasy. The year is 1725. "A very worthy and promising young gentleman,"[1] Jonathan Frye, is preparing to leave North Andover for the "Howling Wilderness." He is the eleventh child, and only surviving son, of Captain James and Lydia Osgood Frye. Twenty-year-old Jonathan also leaves behind his beloved, thirteen-year-old Susanna Rogers. Frye's contemporary tells us that "Young Frye . . . was Lead into war bye his Fathers Obstinacy to favour Him in a matter of Love." He has signed on to serve with Captain John Lovewell, an experienced Indian fighter with two successful expeditions to his credit, to fight the Pigwacket Indians along the frontiers of Maine and New Hampshire.

Jonathan's last act before leaving home was to plant a sapling elm (most likely *Ulmus americana*)—taken from the forest and placed along the roadside in front of his parents' home—"which he charged his friends to guard and cherish until his return." Evoking what the cultural historian Leo Marx

6. *François A. Michaux,* The North American Sylva, *vol. 1. (American Philosophical Society)*

has called a "metaphor of reciprocity . . . between man and not-man," Frye
has linked his well-being with the well-being of a tree.[2]

In contrast with his seasoned commander, Frye was a green recruit. A
member of Harvard's Class of 1723, Frye was among the majority in choosing the ministry as his profession. However, it was not as chaplain that
Frye received his commission—chaplains required the appointment of the
General Court—but as an ordinary soldier. Nonetheless, once away from
Massachusetts, he seems to have been equally employed with prayerbook
and musket. When the troop killed their first Indian, Frye is said to have
participated in the scalping, supporting one view of his possible reason for
enlisting, which suggests that he "joined the army to obtain scalp money
to enable him to marry." If so, he would have been following in the footsteps of his bounty-hungry grandfather, who was "conspicuous among
the community members [of Andover] for killing wolves, receiving five
pounds a head in colonial bounty." Later, when the forty-seven-member
company was decoyed into battle at Saco Pond by a Pigwacket force re-
putedly twice their size, Frye served as both chaplain and soldier—con-
fronting the enemy and comforting his comrades.

At the close of that May 9, 1725, battle about a third of Lovewell's company—including its commander—lay dead. The wounded crawled to the
pond "to slake their thirst and staunch their wounds; crimsoning the water
with their blood."[3] Four of those wounded, Frye among them, then joined
the survivors in retreat to the English fort at Ossipee, about twenty miles
away. When the wounded lagged behind, a mere mile and a half into the
journey, the uninjured party decided to leave them in the forest with provisions, hoping to reach the fort in time to send a fresh party to their
rescue.

Very soon, however, the quartet was reduced to a trio. Just after the
two groups separated, Jonathan Frye realized he was too injured to continue and urged his comrades to go on without him. As related by a contemporary, the Reverend Thomas Symmes, "he laid himself down, telling
them he should never rise more, and charged Davis [Frye's friend Eleazar
Davis of Concord], if it should please God to bring him home, to go to his
father and tell him that he expected in a few hours to be in eternity, and
that he was not afraid to die."

Both the battle and the circumstances of Frye's death attracted a good deal of attention. Cotton Mather spoke publicly to his "Worthy Friends, the Parents of Mr. Jonathan Frie, an Only Son, who after a Liberal Education, and a Temper and Conduct, which made him universally Beloved, and raised considerable Expectations of him . . . with Admirable Expressions of Piety, and Magnanimity and Resignation, Sacrificed his Life." Thoreau recalls "Lovewell's fight" during his travels on Maine's Allegash River, and Nathaniel Hawthorne took up the incident in "Roger Malvin's Burial," making the abandonment of a comrade the central moral dilemma of his tale. The Reverend Symmes also preached a sermon on the event a week after the battle, entitled "A Sermon Occasioned by the Fall of the Brave Capt. John Lovewell and Several of his Valiant Company in the Late Heroic Action," in which he exhorted his congregation not to be "Disheartened & cast down because a crew of Salvages [sic] have killed a few Brave Men . . . but . . . to Rally forth and come to March . . . to Recover if Possible our Dear Brethren that lie Wounded . . . and also to give Christian Burial to the Remains of our Departed Heroes."[4]

Frye's friend Eleazar Davis was one of the two wounded soldiers who did eventually reach home. Whether he conveyed Jonathan's message to his father is unknown, but it is certain that no one returned to bury Frye. In her "Mournful Elegy on Mr. Jonathan Frye," Susanna Rogers wrote of the "blooming youth":

there they left him in the wood
Some scores of miles from any food
Wandered and famished all alone
None to relieve or hear his moan.[5]

As the Hawthorne story opens, the author tells us he is "casting certain circumstances judicially into the shade." Roger Malvin, a man "past the middle age," is lying on a "bed of withered oak leaves" with a "young and vigorous sapling . . . close beside"[6] and encouraging his companion to leave him behind. Hawthorne has Malvin's companion "ben[d] the oak sapling downward" and tie a handkerchief to its "topmost branch" to help the presumed rescuers find their way in nature's trackless woods, suggesting that it takes human handiwork—in this case a colonial handkerchief or the saplings commonly bent by Native Americans to mark their extensive network of trails[7]—to make the natural world understandable.

Frye, in contrast, removed his tree from the forest and placed it within the human community, where it needed human intervention (Jonathan's friends) to thrive, reminding us that our preindustrial ancestors who lived cheek-by-jowl with the "hideous and desolate wilderness"[8] did not share our more recent Emersonian view of the woods as a place where "we return to reason and faith."[9] Long seen as fearsome places, forests were presumed to harbor all sorts of evil, including witches eager to swallow up children like Hansel and Gretel and wolves salivating over the tender flesh of Little Red Riding Hood. They were places of fear and confusion, places to be avoided. Today some of that earlier discomfort still lingers. It is why, for example, when we are uncertain of the future or see problems ahead we say we're not "out of the woods."

Individual trees are another matter entirely. Those of us who claim European roots are probably the progeny of ancestors who once lived in villages clustered around a central representation, sometimes hewn from a tree and sometimes in stone, symbolic of both the pagan tree-of-life—"viewed as a regulator of seasonal cycles and the forces of creation, destruction, and immortality"—and of the order imposed on the wilderness by early Christian agriculture.[10]

European customs associated with the May-tree or Maypole make this point. In *The Golden Bough,* James Frazer describes the annual event:

> In spring or early summer or even on Midsummer Day, it was and still is in many parts of Europe the custom to go out to the woods, cut down a tree and bring it into the village, where it is set up amid general rejoicings, or the people cut branches in the woods, and fasten them on every house. The intention of these customs is to bring home to the village, and to each house, the blessings which the tree-spirit has in its power to bestow.[11]

Later, Europeans, West Africans, and Pacific Islanders planted trees to commemorate life-cycle events such as birth and marriage.[12] The birth of a child, especially an heir, was an occasion English, French, German, and Italian parents sometimes marked with the planting of a tree—such as the poplar planted at Virgil's birth—whereas in Turkey, a platanus (sycamore) was planted at the birth of a son and a cypress at his death. In German and

Slavic countries twin or single trees were frequently planted on the occasion of a marriage "as a token of the happiness which is desired" for the new couple.[13]

In North America the Hidatsa Indians believed that the cottonwood, "the greatest tree in the valley of the Upper Missouri," could, "if properly approached," be helpful in some undertakings, and the Iroquois "believed each species of tree, shrub, plant, and herb had its own spirit, and to these spirits it was their custom to return thanks."[14]

Some Native American tribes also planted birth trees, and although colonial farmers were wary of trees too close to the farmhouse, from the seventeenth century on they frequently planted marker trees near their homes "to commemorate an auspicious event like the birth of a child, a marriage, the beginning of a dangerous enterprise, or the building of a house."[15] The 1797 *Encyclopaedia Britannica* wrote admiringly of those colonial farmers: "It may in truth be said, that in no part of the world are the people happier . . . or more independent than the farmers of New England."[16]

In planting guardian trees, those farmers and others—such as Jonathan Frye—were participants in a tradition with a long and rich history. Frazer, for example, relates a tale that is reminiscent of Frye's story. In that tale a Bengalee prince plants a tree in the courtyard of his father's palace before going off to a foreign country. The prince then tells his parents, "This tree is my life. When you see the tree green and fresh, then know that it is well with me; when you see the tree fade in some parts, then know that I am in an ill case; and when you see the whole tree fade, then know that I am dead and gone."[17]

The stories continue, each branching off a well-trodden path. In June 1985 Jim and Gloria Matthews planted a chokecherry in front of the Colorado middle school their thirteen-year-old daughter Jonelle had attended before her abduction, "in hope of [her] safe return."[18] And although this continuity alone is significant as an expression of an enduring need, it is the tree-by-tree planting of "new symbols of possibility" that resonates.[19]

These green alter egos—Frye's real elm, Hawthorne's fictional oak, the Jonelle tree as it is called, and the unnamed species planted by the prince—are portrayed as guardians of the lives with which they are linked, a custom that dates to the Middle Ages and binds the health and longevity of the traveler to the tree: for as long as the tree flourished, it was believed that the traveler would be safe.[20] This was centuries before scientists began to postulate theories such as the Gaia hypothesis, which suggests that "our planet's surface functions like a giant organism, one interconnected whole," to explain the very real interdependence of life on earth.[21] The elm that Frye planted and his friends assiduously cared for and loved seems to have failed as a guardian, but it might have been bound to Frye's life to its own detriment rather than his benefit. Like Frye, the tree lived an abbreviated life.

Favored as a council tree among the Native Americans (hence William Penn chose a large elm at Shackamaxon on Delaware River's west bank for the famous treaty site later immortalized in Benjamin West's painting), the American elm reaches maturity at about 150 years.[22] That is approximately when Frye's elm, like its namesake, died, entering its prime, long before Dutch Elm disease would rob America's main streets of their most graceful adornment.[23]

The first known planting of a memorial tree in America was the pear tree that Governor Peter Stuyvesant planted in 1644 "by which his name might still be remembered."[24] Although Stuyvesant's pear and Frye's elm are long gone, we can still reach out and touch the stories recorded in the rings of Mary Francis Garvey Cooley's spruce, Tom and Kim Sheridan's pines, Margaret Coleman's cypresses, Jim and Gloria Matthews's chokecherry, and Ashton T. Nelson's walnut trees, each of them a reminder that we are all, on some level, uprooted and that our enduring need to transform an anonymous space into a meaningful place requires that we mark it with the unique "moments of being"[25] of our individual lives.

Death, of course, is one of those moments. The impulse to provide dignity to one sadly abbreviated existence presumably led Mary Francis Garvey Coolley to plant a seedling Norway spruce (*Picea abies*) on the grave of an unknown infant who died on the westward journey. "If it is true that the nineteenth century knew death as a close companion," as Lillian Schlissel explains, "then it is also true that the Overland Trail intensified that experience." This first burial at Fairfield Cemetery was of a baby who died in 1855 as its family camped near Newman, Illinois.[26] Both the burial place and the marker would have been seen as luxuries. One of the anxieties frequently mentioned by families traveling west was that a grave—their own or a loved one's—would be dug up by Indians or wolves. (In *Women's Diaries of the Westward Journey*, Schlissel includes the example of sixteen-year-old Louisa Smith who, when she felt death approaching, implored her mother to dig "a Grave six feet deep for she did not want the

7. *Spruce planted by Mary Francis Garvey Coolley at Fairfield Cemetery to mark the grave of unknown infant. (Photo: Eric D. Hastings)*

wolves to dig her up and eat her." [27]) Marking the grave was another problem. Gravestones were expensive and carving them was time-consuming. So trees served as monuments "at a time when gravestones and similar memorials were largely confined to the socially privileged." [28] Today the tree, a monument to both Coolley and the child, towers above the nearby church.

In Norwalk, Connecticut, Tom and Kim Sheridan planted three pines in 1995 at a "Service of Prayer and Remembrance" for their triplets, who died as the result of a premature birth. Looking for a ritual that would bring some closure to their loss, the Sheridans decided on a service that included planting three seedling pines. Three years later, "Mrs. Sheridan will sit on a nearby bench and stare at the thriving evergreens, wondering how tall and mischievous her three . . . sons would have been." [29]

The happier occasion of a forthcoming marriage led a bride, Margaret Coleman, to plant bride-and-groom cypresses about 1813 at the couple's future home, where the trees still stand, along Kings Highway in Lewes, Delaware.[30] On May 23, 1992, a more recent pair of bride-and-groom trees—a male and female American holly—were planted at Woodburn, Delaware's governor's mansion, to commemorate the marriage of Governor Michael N. Castle and his wife, Jane.[31]

And, beginning in 1929, Ashton T. Nelson planted more than 550 walnut trees along a five-mile stretch of U.S. Highway 6 that links the towns of Wilton and Durant, Iowa. Born in 1867, Nelson was the grandson of a pioneer who had settled Durant in 1851 when the Sioux "relinquished their claim to 'Iowaland.'" As he grew, Nelson developed an interest in woodcarving, and the walnut from his grandfather's farm was his favorite material. When it was time to find employment, Nelson took a job at the local hardware store, later apprenticing to a tinsmith in nearby Wilton. When the Wilton store expanded, and Nelson's opportunities along with it, it became clear that "his future lay in Wilton, but his heart [and his sweetheart] had remained in Durant."

Thus began Nelson's nightly high-wheeled bicycle rides between the two towns, quiet hours during which he apparently conceived the idea of symbolically linking the two towns with a row of black walnut trees. Time passed. Nelson married his sweetheart, bought the Wilton store, raised two sons and two daughters, and became one of the town's leading citizens. Then, in 1929, he retired to his large garden with its more than

8. *A remaining stand of Ash Nelson's Walnut Bridge. (Photo: Nancy L. Peirce)*

550 walnut trees, ready to begin his planting. When Nelson's oldest son, the aviation pioneer Thomas Perry Nelson, died in a plane crash in December of that year, the row of walnuts took on the added meaning of a memorial to Perry. When a grass fire destroyed about thirty of his trees, Nelson simply dug up the dead ones and replaced them with new trees. When, in 1935, he learned that he had cancer, Nelson underwent surgery then returned to planting and caring for his trees. When he died in 1937 his tribute to two towns and his son was complete.

Today, fewer than half a dozen trees remain, but those that do are still a tangible link to Ash Nelson and his dream.[32] Had Nelson planted oaks instead of walnuts, however, according to Wilton resident Collin Proctor, the row would probably still be complete. Out on the Iowa prairie, walnuts generally need the protection of other trees, while oaks are better able to handle the prairie's bruising winter winds and summer sun. Even so, the local Boy Scouts had hoped to replant the missing trees, but the intervening years had seen more than the loss of the walnuts. The highway has been downgraded from a U.S. highway to a state highway, and the state now says the narrow shoulder is needed as a deceleration zone for runaway cars.[33]

The Machine in the Garden is how Leo Marx titled his work that explores the conflict between technology and our pastoral ideal between: for example, planting trees as an expression of our historic relationship to the landscape versus accommodating the newer needs of industrialization such as automotive traffic. However, after reviewing the unsatisfactory resolutions of this conflict—a conflict created by "the machine's increasing dominance of the visible world"—proposed by such writers as Melville, Twain, Thoreau, and Fitzgerald, Marx concluded: "The machine's sudden entrance into the garden presents a problem that ultimately belongs not to art but to politics."[34] To the body politic, then; to each of us.

It presents problems to Collin Proctor and Boy Scout Troop 151, for example, who have found another way to save Ash Nelson's Walnut Bridge. They collected the 1998 walnut crop from the remaining trees (numbering over 400 walnuts) and sent the seeds to American Forests, sponsors of the Famous and Historic Trees Program, which grows and sells the offspring of famous trees nationwide. The walnut trees will be ready for distribution in about two years. Although there may never be another two towns that are linked by a row of walnuts, many lives will now be linked to Ash Nelson and his dream.

"America," Wallace Stegner wrote, "was not only a new world waiting to be discovered; it was a fable waiting to be agreed upon."[35] It still is. We have mostly silenced the howling wilderness and put roads through the trackless forests. But we still plant trees. In cities and towns, alongside roads, in our yards, and in our cemeteries. As Wendell Berry writes:

> I return to the ground its original music . . .
> I have made myself a dream to dream
> of its rising, that has gentled my nights.[36]

We dig a deep hole and plant a story, over and over again.

Actually, the life span and size of an individual tree makes it more like a whole library than a single story. Two western species make the point: the gnarled, mountain-loving bristlecone pines (*Pinus aristata* and *Pinus longaeva*), which include individuals that have reached the 3,000- to 5,000-year mark (the *average* age of a bristlecone pine is 1,500 to 2,000); and the stratospheric sequoias (*Sequoia gigantea*) which have recorded more than 2,500 years of ecological history in their annual rings. Although these arboreal ancients might seem to be exceptions, even some familiar trees likely to be planted on a suburban property prove the rule; maple, spruce, oak, and Jonathan's elm, for example, can live about 300, 350, 450, and 300 years, respectively.[37] So whether you, like Frye, are descended from ancestors who arrived soon after the *Mayflower* or, like me, are the progeny of immigrants who arrived after the turn of the century, we could all be sitting in the shade of a tree planted by a family member. And, until about 1880 — the first census that records more Americans working off the farm than on it [38]—that would have probably been the case.

During that time when wealth was derived from the land, each generation took up the plow in its turn and planted its share of trees on both the anonymous woodlot and the storied front lot, fulfilling John Ruskin's dictum that "our part [is not] fitly sustained upon the earth, unless the range of our intended and deliberate usefulness include not only the companions, but the successors, of our pilgrimage."[39] For those successors, the ever-enlarging monuments that marked specific events came to complement other ways of knowing family history. To those who wielded the spade, and, in turn, welded tree to story, each tree was a bid for immortality, an attempt to "give meaning and dignity to our short existence on earth."[40]

When machines and market forces began to disrupt that settled agrarian way of life (did the *Encyclopaedia Britannica* then change its earlier views, I wonder?) and therefore "destroy one great motive which would lead the grandsire to plant the acorn,"[41] a counterforce grew, convinced that the United States needed to preserve and plant trees on a larger scale. The same decade that saw the demographic shift from farm to factory also saw the first celebration of Arbor Day (1872), the passage of the Timber Culture Act (1873, repealed with the passage of the Forest Reserve Act in 1891), the founding of the American Forestry Association, now American Forests (1875), the first state forestry association (1876, in Minnesota), and the appointment of the first federal forestry agent to study the state of the nation's forests (1876, Dr. Franklin B. Hugh).[42] The National Arbor Day Foundation reports that on that first Arbor Day approximately one million trees were planted in Nebraska, the first state to celebrate the holiday.[43] Make no mistake, though; impersonal forests will never replace the intimacy of our relationship to individual trees.

A stranger told me why. It was more of a monologue than a conversation. We were two women, random bus companions, traveling from London to Oxford at the end of a swelteringly hot July day in the record-breaking summer of 1994. I had gratefully collapsed into the last seat on the bus and was beginning to drift off into a much-needed nap when my companion began to talk about death. It was the death of her twenty-three-year-old niece, killed just a few months earlier in a car accident, that was on her mind. By reconstructing the details of the accident, the family had established that the young woman lay dying just as her mother was flying home from abroad. But it was what came next that caught my attention, the problem that was the constant subject of family phone calls and get-togethers: how to memorialize the young life they had lost.

For one reason or another, none of the memorial funds or scholarships that frequently grow out of these kinds of unhappy events appealed to this family. They had lost a member that was full of life, and in the fullness of life, and they were searching for something that would embody that spirit, now and into the future. Their search had just then led them to an organization that helped families in similar circumstances deal with their grief and loss by planting a tree to memorialize the missing family member. My bus companion said this felt right to her, and she hoped that this was what they would do.

I, too, hoped it was what they would do, but that is not why I tell this story. I tell it because a stranger's new, still undiluted emotion on a bus far from home reminded me why it is that where we are often looks so much like where we've been. As fate would have it, I had just been reading from the long line of paper-stories that are tucked behind the one she was telling—of trees planted by people like Jonathan Frye, Margaret Coleman, Mary Frances Garvey Cooley, Jim and Gloria Matthews, Tom and Kim Sheridan, and Ashton T. Nelson in other circumstances where human mortality sought consolation in the immortality of trees.

But consolation is only a piece of this whole, for them and for them in us. There is the binding of our fate to nature, the recognition that we are all branches of an interconnected tree, and the desire to give something back—in appreciation, perhaps, of the 21 percent atmospheric oxygen necessary for complex life that trees help to maintain. Two thousand years ago a man named Honi saw someone planting a carob tree. He asked how long it would be before the tree would bear fruit and was told it would take seventy years. Honi then asked the man why he would plant a tree that he might not live to enjoy, and the man replied: "Just as I found carob trees when I came into this world, so I am now planting carob trees for my grandchildren to enjoy." [44]

Part of what makes planting trees appealing is caring for them and making them part of our lives, parenting them, so to speak. When the motivations of urban forestry volunteers across the country were studied, it was found that people "were motivated to volunteer more by emotional, aesthetic, and psychological values of trees than by practical benefits (e.g., reduced temperatures or increased property values), indicating a predominance of 'deep values' for trees." [45] More participatory than the stewardship ecologists talk about, caring for a tree involves a one-on-one relationship to another life, a green one, a relationship and an act so significant that the ancient Jewish sages tell us:

If there be a sapling in your hand
When they say to you:
Behold the Messiah!
First plant the sapling, then go out
to greet the Messiah. [46]

As it happens, we are now moving less than we once did, so we can stick around and watch the trees grow. "The Census Bureau's figures show an overall decline in Americans' mobility. It said that about 16.7 percent of the population changed residences during a one-year period ending March 1994 . . . the second lowest level of mobility since 1948 when the Census Bureau began tracking such movement." [47]

Grandsires may begin to plant acorns (or carobs) again. Seeing the beauty of the thing, we might join in. And, in the process, we might create our own bond with the universe.

Aldo Leopold writes, "acts of creation are ordinarily reserved for gods and poets . . . [but] humbler folk may circumvent this restriction if they know how. To plant a pine, for example, one need be neither god nor poet: one need only own a shovel. By virtue of this curious loophole in the rules, any clodhopper may say: Let there be a tree—and there will be one."[48]

More than three hundred years ago, when the Englishman John Evelyn looked for ways to encourage his contemporaries to plant trees in a nation confronted with the scarcity of wood, he took a different approach. In his *Sylva, or a Discourse of Forest-Trees, and the Propagation of Timber in His Majesties Dominions* Evelyn wrote this very personal justification of tree-planting:

> Men seldom begin to plant trees until they begin to be wise, that is, till they grow old and find by experience the prudence and necessity of it. . . . 'Tis observed that such planters are often blessed with health and old age. . . . I am writing as an octogenarian, and shall, if God protract my years, and continued health, be continually planting till it shall please him to transplant me to those glorious regions above, the celestial paradise—for such is the tree of life, which those who do his commandments have right to.[49]

Such, then, are some of "the blessings which the tree-spirit has in its power to bestow."

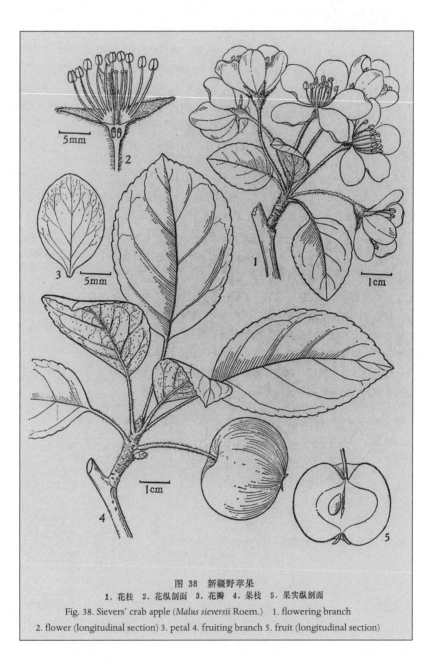

图 38 新疆野苹果
1. 花枝 2. 花纵剖面 3. 花瓣 4. 果枝 5. 果实纵剖面
Fig. 38. Sievers' crab apple (*Malus sieversii* Roem.) 1. flowering branch
2. flower (longitudinal section) 3. petal 4. fruiting branch 5. fruit (longitudinal section)

CHAPTER THREE

APPLES: CORE ISSUES

FRUIT: STRICTLY, THE RIPENED OVARY OF A PLANT AND ITS CONTENTS. MORE LOOSELY, THE TERM IS EXTENDED TO THE RIPENED OVARY AND SEEDS TOGETHER WITH ANY STRUCTURE WITH WHICH THEY ARE COMBINED, E.G., THE APPLE (A POME) IN WHICH THE TRUE FRUIT (CORE) IS SURROUNDED BY FLESH DERIVED FROM THE FLORAL RECEPTACLE.

MICHAEL ALLABY, *The Concise Oxford Dictionary of Botany*

A s we filed into the slightly apple-scented room, we were each given two sheets of paper. The first listed the thirty-six apple varieties we would taste. The second was for our ratings: "zero represents unpalatable and nine denotes an ecstatic taste experience." Swaar was my ecstasy. And Newtown Pippin, which my notes describe as sweet but interestingly complex, was my second choice.

I was with the majority in picking Swaar, a heavy American apple with a rich, some say nutty, taste. First raised along New York's Hudson River around 1804, it was ranked second by the almost fifty participants at the 1995 Monticello Apple Tasting. Virginia Gold was first. The Newtown Pippin, the apple that launched the American export industry when Benjamin Franklin introduced it in England along with its cousin the American Pippin, were ranked twenty-eighth and twenty-ninth, respectively (three places behind Mother, with its evanescent, aromatic taste). So much for one taste fits all.

Fortunately, however, with 7,500 apple varieties available, there is an ecstatic experience—probably several ecstatic experiences—awaiting every palate. Think of it. At the rate of the prescribed apple a day, it would take one person twenty years and two hundred days to try them all. Where to begin? With the sepia-tinted names like Westfield Seek-No-Further, White Winter Pearmain, Roxbury Russet, and Esopus Spitzenburg?

The Roxbury Russet, Esopus Spitzenburg, and the Newton Pippin were all grown at Monticello during Thomas Jefferson's lifetime. Our most horticulturally minded president, according to Allen Lacy, Jefferson wrote that "the greatest service which can be rendered to any country is to add a useful plant to its culture,"[1] and he worked to do just that, experimenting with Italian grapes and strawberries, Chinese silk trees, and French figs and endive. But not French apples. "They have no apple here to compare with our Newtown pipping," he wrote while in France.[2]

9. T. Ch. Yu, Taxonomy of Fruit Trees in China, *chapter 8. (From the collections of the Missouri Botanical Garden Library)*

Or start with the new? Pick a variety like the dark red Liberty, named for the "fruit breeders' goal of helping to liberate fruit growers from endless rounds of spraying."[3] Introduced in 1978, Liberty—like Empire, Cortland, Macoun, and Jonagold—was bred at Cornell's prolific New York State Agricultural Experiment Station in Geneva, New York, near the facility that houses the world's largest apple collection, the USDA Plant Genetics Resources Unit. Or just pick out the ones that sound fascinating? Granny Smith, for example, appeals to me because of the story. "Granny" Anne Smith emigrated from England to Ryde, Australia, in 1838. About thirty years later she discovered a young apple tree growing where she had "tipped out [the] last of some apples brought back from Sydney."[4] Smith tried the fruit, found it was good for both cooking and eating, and thus was born the apple that bears her name. Discovery as a household occupation.

For most of us, however, our association with apples began in infancy before we could make choices—apples are usually the first fruit introduced to babies. And so it is with the history of apples, which predates human evolution.

"It is remarkable," Henry David Thoreau wrote in *Wild Apples*, "how closely the history of the Apple-tree is connected with that of man. The geologist tells us that the order of the *Rosacea*, which includes the Apple, also the true Grasses, and the *Labiatae*, or Mints, were introduced only a short time previous to the appearance of man on the globe."[5] Although the product of outdated science (*Rosacea* does not include the Mints and Grasses, and the order significantly predates human evolution with the earliest fossil records of the family appearing in the mid-Cretaceous period, about 85 to 100 million years ago),[6] Thoreau's concept is entirely accurate: the versatile and adaptable apple has followed in our footsteps wherever they have led, endowing "a full store-House, out of which may be brought both Meat, Drink, and Mony [sic]"[7] as well as art, literature, and mythology. Two very different disciplines provide testimony; economic botanists point to the apple's significance as the most important tree fruit in the temperate regions,[8] and psychologists interested in cross-cultural studies demonstrate that children overwhelmingly produce apples when asked to draw a fruit tree, even in tropical climates where no apples grow.[9]

Most sources agree that the domestic apple, *Malus domestica,* originated in Asia Minor, in the Caucasus region somewhere near the boundaries of contemporary Kazakhstan, Uzbekistan, Kirghizia, and Turkmenistan.[10] "Even today," as Joan Morgan and Alison Richards write in their fascinating and comprehensive work, *The Book of Apples,* "large areas of wild fruit trees can still be found in the foothills of the Caucasus, in the Kopet-Dag mountains in Turkmenistan, in the Pamirs and especially in the Tien Shan range [between the former Soviet Union and western China], where whole valleys are filled with apple trees."[11] Kazakhstan's capital, Almaty (once called Alma-Ata, "literally the 'father of apples'"),[12] sits in one of those lush valleys in the foothills of the Tien Shans once traversed by the various trade routes, collectively known as the Silk Road, which linked Rome with China.

Negotiating the complexities of family relationships is (not surprisingly) considerably more difficult than locating the ancestral home: there is consensus around the idea that various species contributed to the complex hybrid *Malus domestica,* but its exact antecedents are uncertain. The most frequently mentioned possibilities are *Malus sieversii,* the Tien Shan apples; *Malus orientalis,* the Caucasus species; *Malus sylvestris,* the Northern European wild crab apple; and *Malus baccata,* a species found from North China to East Asia.[13] Each of these interfertile species (and probably many others) has contributed a bit of taste, size, hardiness, keeping qualities, blossom color (white to magenta), skin color (generally yellow, red, green, or some combination thereof, although we tasted the black-skinned Arkansas Black at Monticello), or disease-resistance to the genetic pool of the apple.

To understand something of the relationship between these ancestral species and the modern apple, look at drawings of *Malus baccata:* its yellow-red cherry-sized fruit superficially resembles a modern apple only slightly more than the famous fossil Lucy resembles a contemporary woman. Or examine the highly diverse *Malus sieversii,* the species that has "contributed the most genes to the domestic apple," according to Cornell/USDA curator/horticulturalist Philip L. Forsline. Its fruit can range in size from a little more than an inch to about three and a half inches, and though generally yellow-green with pink cheeks, it can span the spectrum from red, yellow, and green to white. Moreover, as Forsline explains, "each individual [apple] is very unique."[14] Apples, like many other fruits, have evolved to be self-incompatible, meaning they do not grow true from seed, because every seed is the product of two distinct parents. It follows then that every seed (or pip) represents a potentially new variety (hence the Granny Smith), sometimes inferior, sometimes superior, and that each of these varieties would, without intervention, last only as long as the individual tree on which they grow.

GRAFT: . . . A SHOOT OR SCION INSERTED IN A GROOVE OR SLIT MADE IN ANOTHER STOCK, SO AS TO ALLOW THE SAP OF THE LATTER TO CIRCULATE THROUGH THE FORMER.
GRAFT . . . THE OBTAINING OF PROFIT OR ADVANTAGE BY DISHONEST OR SHADY MEANS; THE ABUSE OF A POSITION OF POWER OR INFLUENCE.

Oxford English Dictionary

"Grafting is blackest magic," Tom Christopher wrote in a 1995 *New York Times* article. "It lets the gardener play Dr. Frankenstein, joining the dismembered parts of different organisms into a single, living whole." [15] Grafting, that is, binding a scion, or stem cutting, of one plant onto the rootstock of another is one of the two techniques used to clonally reproduce apple (and other fruit) varieties. Budding is the other. By careful selection of the rootstock, which determines the size of the tree and its resistance to climatic and soil conditions, and the scion (either a bud or a stem), which determines the variety of fruit, a grower can reproduce established favorites or propagate new varieties. All commercially available apples are produced by one or the other, grafting in the spring or budding in the summer and early fall.

Both techniques reach back at least to the Romans. Writing in the second century B.C.E. the Roman consul Marcus Porcius Cato, for example, treats the subject as a straightforward practical matter, which suggests he was offering improvements to an already well known art. By 1653 the almost unchanged practice had taken on a philosophical cast. It was seen as a metaphor for the relationship between God and the spiritually elect. As the Puritan divine and nurseryman Ralph Austen (considered the "greatest authority on fruit trees in his day")[16] explained in his aptly titled treatise *The Spirituall Use of an Orchard* (appended to his more practical *A Treatise of Fruit-Trees*), "The *Husbandman makes choice of what wild Plants he pleaseth, to bring into his Orchard there to Graft. . . . He leaves other plants in the Woods*

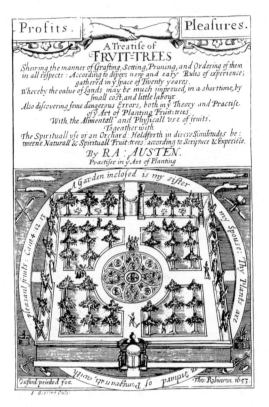

10. Title page of Ralph Austen's Treatise of Fruit-Trees *showing a perfectly ordered orchard. (Collection of Rachel Lambert Mellon, Oak Spring Garden Library, Upperville, Virginia)*

and waste grounds . . . and meddles not with them. . . . That God from all eternity made choice of what Spirituall Plants he pleased, to plant in his Garden the Church, and refused others." [17] (Austen's italics.)

Austen saw grafting as hopeful, a way to repair the world to its prelapsarian state. Cato saw grafting as helpful, a practical way of improving nature. But we are not quite as sanguine about Brave New World in the backyard, or in the nursery. Our concerns are perhaps revealed by our alternative use of the word, an Americanism introduced around Thoreau's day.

Thoreau's was a countervoice to the improvers of nature:

Apples for grafting appear to have been selected commonly, not so much for their spirited flavor, as for their mildness, their size, and bearing qualities,—not so much for their beauty, as for their fairness and soundness.

Indeed, I have no faith in the selected lists of pomological gentlemen. Their "Favorites" and "None-suches" and "Seek-no-farthers," when I have fruited them, commonly turn out very tame and forgetable. They are eaten with comparatively little zest, and have no real *tang* or *smack* to them.[18]

Is it wildness, then, not cultivation, that we should be seeking? Is "the fundamental issue of life in America . . . an irreconcilable opposition between Nature and civilization—which is to say, between forest and town, spontaneity and calculation, heart and head, the unconscious and the self-conscious, the innocent and the debauched"?[19] Is our only choice between the alternatives of a unique present with its *tang* and *smack* and a tame, forgettable, and reproducible past? If we could imagine a middle ground, what might it look like?

I believe it would look like an orchard. Orchards combine the seeming opposites of nature and civilization, forest and town, spontaneity and calculation. I, for one, found my ecstasy with Swaar. I see our choice more as a matter of ends than means. Not whether to graft or not to graft, but what to graft. But, then, I like a little past with my present.

I like to think, for example, about the one barrel of Franklin's Newtown Pippins that made their way aboard Captain Cook's *Endeavour*. Those apples were made into a pie when the ship "was between Tahiti and New Zealand . . . [which, after being stored for fourteen months] proved very good; if not quite the equal to the apple pies which our friends in England are now eating."[20] Or sample D'Eylau, which Morgan and Richards say is "claimed" to have been brought to France in 1812 from Eylau, Russia, by a soldier in Napoleon's Grand Army; or savor a Pippin (or Pépin) sold, we are told, at Rouen's markets in 1360 and introduced in England in 1533 from whence, presumably, they made their way eventually to Monticello; or maybe the Decio, served at a banquet given by the Duke of Ferrara in 1529.[21]

Thoreau's "wild" apples, as he must have known, were probably, like Granny Smith's, orchard escapees, the offspring of cultivated parents. Thoreau's great friend and patron Ralph Waldo Emerson was himself an avid orchardist (his orchard list includes an apple named "Thoreau"), who was inspired by the writing of the nurseryman and landscape gardener Andrew Jackson Downing. Downing, "arguably the greatest single figure in American horticulture" and "one of the teachers of Frederick Law

Olmstead and Calvert Vaux," was passionately lyrical on the subject of cultivation. To the individual, he wrote:

> who views with a more than common eye the crimson cheek of a peach, the delicate bloom of a plum, or understands the epithets rich, melting, buttery as applied to a pear, nothing in the circle of culture can give more lively and unmixed pleasure, than thus to produce and to create—for it is a sort of creation—an entirely new sort, which he believes will prove handsomer and better than anything that has gone before.

Downing's *Fruits and Fruit-Trees of America,* according to Emerson's biographer Robert Richardson, "invigorated Emerson and sent him back to his own proper projects refreshed . . . [the book provides] a practical vindication of the transcendentalist's emphasis on cultivation; it revives the concept of culture both as a process and as a metaphor by reconnecting it to its roots in agriculture and arboriculture. It calls attention to the efficacy of culture—of grafting, and pruning and training—and it offers itself as a vast metaphor for human culture." [22] The democratization of Ralph Austen.

Today's apples, with their long and rich history so closely allied to our own, taste of that imperfect but indivisible union between nature and culture. It is a taste that includes Delicious and Swaar and the one hundred and one varieties offered by Applesource. Take your pick (but be sure it is ripe). Make your choice (and tell your supermarket or greengrocer to stock it). Or learn to graft. Every seed still promises a new possibility. Nature and culture are a circle, not a line. And when you find perfection, please graft it—as Thomas Jefferson was still doing in the last spring of his life, sending off "a dozen cuttings . . . [of] the Taliaferro apple . . . [which] yield unquestionably the finest cyder we have ever known." [23] Then we all can have a taste.

Our first chance at perfection was Eden. Looking at that Biblical text, we have Adam to thank for naming the aardvark and the albatross, but apparently not the apple. Written around 800 B.C.E. (give or take several centuries), the Genesis story makes no mention of Adam naming any plants, nor does the original Hebrew version include the name of any specific tree or fruit other than the allegorical designation of two well-known trees—the tree of life and the tree of knowledge of good and bad. Regarding the latter, only the generic term for fruit, *peri*, is used to describe the famous forbidden fruit. Not until the second of two subsequent translations of the text appears is the apple conflated with the unidentified fruit of the tree of knowledge. It was the association of the apple with love-sickness and love in the Song of Solomon that "seems early to have led to the identification of the apple with sexual temptation and thus with the 'forbidden fruit' of the tree of knowledge . . . an association . . . firmly entrenched by the confusion of the [Vulgate] *malum* (apple) with *malum* (evil)."[24]

Long before the language of Rome was used to spread the word of Christianity, however, it transmitted the arts and sciences of Rome and Greece (with the apple figuring prominently in both cultures and both branches of knowledge) throughout the Roman Empire, including Europe and Britain. To some extent, as regards the apple, Rome was preaching to the converted. Europeans were already familiar with the fruit through their native crab apples and had myths of their own in which the apple figures prominently. Archaeological evidence indicates that Europeans used dried crab apples as early as the Iron Age, and both Celtic and Scandinavian mythology "link apples with paradise and immortality." The custom of bobbing for apples, for example, "was a means of divination among the Druids and survives in the folklife of countries influenced by Celtic culture." While in the "Norse legend Iduna kept a store of apples which the gods ate, thereby keeping themselves young."[25] Thus the numerous references in Greek and Roman literature and mythology to the role of the apple (sacred to Aphrodite, the Greek goddess of love, and her Roman counterpart Venus) in the rituals of courtship and marriage would not have been breaking entirely new ground in the way that Roman horticultural techniques did.

The horticulturally advanced Romans placed a high value on fruit trees and, like the Persians before them—whose fruit culture had "diffused through the Greek world" after the conquests of Alexander the Great— they encouraged the distribution of Roman varieties throughout their realms, preferring their sweeter, grafted varieties, to the tart, native crab apples. "Rome probably had more varieties of apple in cultivation than it did of any other fruit," according to Morgan and Richards. "Over 20 different varieties are mentioned by Pliny in his *Natural History* of the first century [C.E.]." And archaeological and mosaic evidence indicates that the

Romans introduced their techniques of grafting and pruning along with the trees. [26]

Cultivation of many kinds, including that of fruit trees, however, fell into general decline following the disintegration of the Roman Empire. But within the network of Christian monasteries a portion of Rome's intellectual and cultural knowledge was preserved, transmitted, and, in the case of orcharding, utilized. Also, secular evidence of a continued interest in horticulture is demonstrated by the undated *Capitularie de Villis vel Curtis Imperialibus,* presumably issued around the end of the eighth century, attributed to either Charlemagne or his son Louis the Pious. The document provides clear instructions regarding the plants and trees to be grown on crown lands, listing apples first among trees, specifying the following varieties: *"gozmaringa, geroldinga, crevedella,* [and] *spirauca"* and including the information that "there are sweet ones, bitter ones, those that keep well, those that are to be eaten straightaway, and early ones." [27]

Not until the Renaissance, however, did horticulture regain its classical stature. Propelled by the concentration of wealth in Italy, by more affordable sources of sugar in the New World (allowing for new techniques of fruit preservation, preparation, and presentation), and by the introduction of new species as the result of the voyages of discovery, enhanced fruit cultivation at first followed the earlier pattern of expansion under the Roman Empire with ideas originating in Italy then moving north to France and later to Britain. It was Henry VIII's fruiterer, Richard Harris, who established at Teynham (near the present site of Britain's National Apple Collection at Brogdale in Kent) what is considered England's first major fruit collection with cherry and pear grafts from the Low Countries and apples from France, "before which time there were no pippins in England." [28] (These pippins, presumably related to the ones sold at Rouen, were introduced in England in 1533, the same year that Henry married Anne Boleyn.) And though the trickle-down effect seems to have been an economic failure in our time, something like that worked in European and British fruit cultivation, as first monarchs, and later wealthy and prominent individuals, competed to serve the newest and the most unusual species and varieties.

The competition reached a new level in 1639 when England's French-Catholic queen, Henrietta Maria, was given Wimbledon Palace by her ill-fated husband, Charles I. Charles had recently (1637) sent the apothecary and plantsman John Tradescant to Virginia "to gather all rarities of flowers, plants, and shells." [29] At the same time, Charles had been impressed with his wife's transformation of the gardens and residence of his mother's un-finished palace at Greenwich,[30] worked ostensibly by the prominent English architect Inigo Jones, but also including ideas proposed by the French architects with whom Henrietta Maria consulted.

Henrietta Maria's appreciation of French style also extended to gardens. She brought the well-known French gardener André Mollet to England twice to design her gardens, first around 1629–1633 and later in 1642 to lay out the gardens of Wimbledon.[31] It was probably during Mollet's first visit that Henrietta Maria wrote to her mother, Marie de Medici, queen of France, that, "As I am sending this man into France to get some fruit-trees and some flowers, I most humbly entreat your majesty to assist him with your power, if by chance any one should do him wrong and hinder him." [32]

Her motivation might have been twofold. In addition to appreciating the style of her homeland, Henrietta Maria would have had firsthand experi-ence with the use of gardens as vistas of memory; her mother's creation of the Luxembourg gardens, for example, recalled the Boboli gardens of Marie's Italian childhood at the Pitti Palace. Likewise, Henrietta Maria. As Roy Strong points out in *The Renaissance Garden in England,* "the Wilder-ness and the Maze [at Wimbledon] must have been in the vein of the walks at the Luxembourg, which Henrietta Maria would have remembered from childhood," [33] "when she went there regularly with her mother to see how the work was proceeding." [34] This theme, of course, is not new. At least since the Hanging Gardens of Babylon, "built . . . by [Nebuchadnezzar (605–562 B.C.E.)] to please one of his concubines; for she [Amyhia] . . . being a Persian by race and longing for the meadows of her mountains, asked the king to imitate, through the artifice of a planted garden, the distinctive landscape of Persia," [35] gardens have been used to re-create beloved land-scapes. What is new is the way Henrietta Maria's story, and that of Wim-bledon, played out.

The woman who wrote of herself as "a country girl" and a "good coun-try lady" [36] was to spend more than half of her married life (some of it as a widow) in exile, with no real home of her own. She would never see those grand gardens she had commissioned. But "stories," as Wallace Stegner points out, "last better than the people who lived them." [37] Gardens are the same. More ephemeral even than their creators, gardens last longer in the mind (or imagination) than on the ground (as anyone who has left a garden untended for a brief summer vacation knows all too well); most importantly, their influence lasts longest of all. In the case of Wimbledon, that influence would cross political and geographical lines, providing momentum to an already established English interest in fruit, especially apple, culture.

A portion of the fascinating Commonwealth inventory, which values all the plant and construction materials in the gardens preparatory to their sale, provides a sense of the scale of the garden's fruit collections; "one hundred and fifty fruit trees, of divers kinds of apples and pears, pleasant and profitable . . . an hundred and nineteen Cherry trees . . . fifty three wall fruit trees of divers sorts of fruit . . . forty-two Oringe trees bearing fair and large oringes . . . 6 Pomegranet trees . . . two Apricot trees." [38]

It must have been a sight. Imagine spring at Wimbledon. Imagine the excitement of the new fruit to taste coupled with an explosion of available instructions on new techniques for managing the orchard and the storage room (one being the text by Ralph Austen mentioned above) and it becomes easy to understand the rush to join in, for join in they did. Both Royalists and Puritans became ardent orchardists. Following the religious wave originating in Germany and crashing down across northern Europe, "which eventually changed not only the moral and political geography of the Western world but also gave apples a new significance as the fruit favoured by 'God's Elect' . . . countries which were predominantly Protestant saw the apple as the fruit not only of God but of country, too." [39]

The Puritans took particular interest in orchards as Samuel Hartlib's 1652 work, *A Designe for Plentie, By an Universall Planting of Fruit-Trees*, makes clear, "for the relief of the poor, the benefit of the rich, and the delight of all." Hartlib and the "fruit lobby" [40] he headed in fact suggested legislation to Parliament that would make mandatory the planting of apples on every piece of spare land available throughout the country. As Alicia Amherst tells us, "It was not the Puritan party only who were occupied in the improvement of orchards. One of the great Royalist families took a prominent part in the work. . . . Lord Scudamore . . . occupied himself with planting and grafting apple-trees. He introduced the Red Streak Pippin, from which the choicest sort of cider was made." [41] And when people of both political persuasions—and those from other apple-loving Protestant nations—made their home in England's erstwhile colonies across the Atlantic (the Royalists generally in the south and the Puritans generally in the north), apples figured prominently in their imaginative and physical baggage.

I am not suggesting that Wimbledon was the *axis mundi* from which new apple varieties migrated out into the world, any more than I'm prepared to say that Almaty or Alma-Ata, terrific name notwithstanding, is the place to put up the plaque "Apples Originated Here." Recognizing that legacies are "ambivalent and complex, full of unconfessed wishes and unadmitted bequests . . . some of which contradict the rest," [42] it is still clear that Wimbledon was an oasis of fertility in the midst of an increasingly deforested nation.

Charles I continued to sell off the heavily treed crown lands to raise cash (and the elite buyers of those lands immediately proceeded to liquidate the valuable trees to increase their own wealth), just as Henrietta Maria was grafting England's most sophisticated fruit collection onto a personal landscape of memory. Like other immigrants, Henrietta Maria was staking her claim to her new country by cultivating the plants of her past (at a moment when the best minds were engaged in advancing horticulture her outstanding collection was put on the block to go who knows where).

Wimbledon was, like many gardens of its time, a walled garden, but in the case of this particular garden the symbolism of the walled garden as cut off from the outside world is sadly revealing. A monarchy busy collecting, displaying, and enjoying the beauty of the natural world within the wall was, at the same time, to its own peril, destroying the patrimony without. As Henrietta Maria was busy planting, Charles was cutting the very roots that nourished his rule.

THE FIRST ORCHARD IN MASSACHUSETTS WAS PLANTED BY WILLIAM BLAXTON (OR BLACKSTONE), A CLERGYMAN . . . [AND] BOOKISH RECLUSE, FOND OF FLOWERS AS WELL AS FRUITS, WHO CAME TO THE COLONY NOT LATER THAN 1625 AND BEGAN TO PLANT HIS GARDEN AT ONCE. HE IS SPOKEN OF BY SEVERAL EARLY HISTORIANS AS AN ECCENTRIC WHO TRAINED A BULL TO THE SADDLE AND FROM ITS BACK DISTRIBUTED APPLES AND FLOWERS TO HIS FRIENDS. . . .

IN 1605 A COLONY OF SPANIARDS FROM MEXICO FOUNDED SANTA FÉ AND PLANTED EUROPEAN CROPS. THE EARLIEST CONTINUOUS GARDENS IN AMERICA MAY HAVE BEEN THERE.

ULYSSES P. HEDRICK, *A History of Horticulture in America*

Mapping the introduction of European apples to North America would produce something visually similar to the maps of human migrations or military campaigns with their broad and curving arrow-headed shafts that arc across great swaths of landscape. One apple shaft would begin in Catholic France and cross the Atlantic to Canada and transport the sixteenth- and seventeenth-century fur traders and missionaries with their apple pips.[43] Another would come from Catholic Portugal and Spain to South America and Central America and then curve upward, reaching the pueblos, missions, and ranches of New Mexico early in the seventeenth century, according to the best estimates.[44] The widest shaft of all would originate in sixteenth- and seventeenth-century Protestant Europe (England, Germany, Holland, Scandinavia, and France) and wash across our eastern seaboard. A side shoot of the English shaft would travel the seas to western Canada and the state of Washington, to where the Hudson's Bay Company planted pips in the first quarter of the nineteenth century.

From the north, south, east, and west, European apples were being planted on the North American continent. The prize for first is still unawarded. Some, for example, believe the orchards of Manzano, New Mexico, might be the country's oldest. Although no definite proof exists, the settlers who established the town of Manzano in 1815 discovered extant apple orchards that possibly dated back to the Spanish ranches and farms established there during the first half of the seventeenth century.[45] The story is made even more enticing by the fact that *manzana* is the Spanish word for apple.

But the award for greatest impact is clear. It was the apples introduced in the east, in places like Monticello, the apples of Protestant Europe that eventually traveled across the continent and sowed the orchards of the eastern, midwestern, and western United States.

The first of the east coast orchards belonged to William Blaxton of Massachusetts. But, since Blaxton's residence in Massachusetts predated the Massachusetts Bay Colony and he was unwilling to submit to the newcomer's regulations—observing that "he had left England to escape the power of the lord bishops, but he found himself in the hands of the Lord's brethren"[46]—he moved to Rhode Island, on a farm near Pawtucket where he also established the first orchard in that state. There he grew an apple called Blaxton's Yellow Sweeting, "now grown as Sweet Rhode Island Greening . . . probably the first named apple to originate in the United

States." [47] The Anglican clergyman also, according to one account, "used to come to Providence and preach, and to encourage his hearers gave them the first apples they ever saw." [48] Whether, in fact, Blaxton was the first on these shores to initiate the custom of providing an inducement to get the customers in the door remains unclear, but the fame of his apples is certain.

Planting orchards was both a life-giving and a civilizing activity for the colonists, a claiming of the land in both a practical and a cultural sense, and a visible manifestation of the New Canaan they were creating in this New World. Familiar with European polluted water without understanding the scientific reasons for its ill effects, the colonists were likewise afraid to drink the water here so that "apples were grown in colonial New England almost wholly for cider. About one farmer out of ten had a cider mill." [49] Seed-grown apples were entirely satisfactory for cider, for providing a living reminder of the homeland, and also for providing cattle with shade and with forage from the grass grown beneath the trees. "Cattle browsed on the lowest branches of the trees and produced what farmers still call the 'browse-line,' the six-foot-high space empty of all limbs [which] horticulturalists and park superintendents unthinkingly adopted . . . for trees grown away from livestock . . . and carefully pruned trees, as they do today, so that the lowest branches just brush a man's head." [50]

The seed-grown orchards of New England, however, were not the rule throughout the colonies. Presaging the political differences that would later erupt into the Civil War, the north, south, and central seaboard states each cultivated different kinds of orchards. In the north, as already mentioned, the main form of apple cultivation was from seed; in the south, settled primarily by Royalists, the greater concentration of wealth and the desire to re-create the intensively cultivated gardens of England led to orchards such as that of Colonel William Fitzhugh, who was "said to have had, in 1686, an orchard of 2500 apple trees . . . most of them grafted and well-fenced . . . all of which probably came from England"; while the central states, which were organized around mercantile principles and settled by America's best gardeners and farmers, according to horticulturist Ulysses Hedrick, developed agriculture into an economically viable and enduring occupation.

England and the Low Countries were not the only beneficiaries of France's revocation of the religiously tolerant Edict of Nantes in 1685. Large numbers of French Protestants fled from Rochelle, France, for example, first to England, and then a portion continued on to New York in 1689, where they founded New Rochelle, a "center of orcharding and gardening." Also driven by religious persecution, the Germans who settled in Pennsylvania, the so-called Pennsylvania Dutch, "were particularly famous in the colonies for their orchard products . . . cider, applejack, apple-butter, dried peaches, and peach brandy . . . [and] it was [they] . . . who started a commercial industry in dried apples."

Native Americans also established orchards after contact with white settlers and missionaries. "The Spaniards," Hedrick reports, "early brought peaches to Mexico and Florida. The Indians liked them so well that long before Jamestown was settled there were Indian peach orchards from Texas and Arkansas eastward and as far north as peaches will grow. So abundantly were they found as escapees from Indian plantations that early American botanists looked upon the peach as native to America." During the Revolutionary War "40 [Iroquois] orchards of apples and peaches, one of which contained 1500 peach trees" were destroyed during Sullivan's raid and a famous Indiana apple tree, "doubtless [grown] from a seed planted by some [French] missionary explorer," [51] called the Miami apple tree after the local tribe that clustered their cabins around its three-foot-wide trunk, lived for more than a century and probably seeded a nearby orchard planted by the chief's white brother-in-law in 1804. The French had come from their Canadian territories, carrying fruit along the Great Lakes and into the Mississippi Valley. [52] When "Cadillac founded Detroit in 1701, he brought along a gardener from Quebec, one Pierre d'Argenteuil, to lay out gardens and orchards" [53] and by 1735 numbers of French families had settled near the trading post and fort at Vincennes, Indiana.

After independence from England, as American pioneers speaking many of the languages which share the linguistic root of the word apple—the German 'apfel,' the Swedish 'applen,' the Dutch 'appel,' and the Danish 'aeble'—continued westward, the American government required of them what they would have likely done on their own: in the Ohio lands (1787–1788), for example, "within three years the settler must have set out at least fifty apple or pear trees and twenty peach trees." [54] (It is interesting to note that the legislation proposed during the Interregnum to mandate the "universall planting of fruit-trees" failed in England, but managed to take root here.) The first Ohio orchards would have been grown from seed, but grafted apples reached Ohio in 1796 when Israel and Aaron Putnam established a nursery near Marietta. Grafted varieties soon became more widely available as "the first orchard of grafted trees planted in the south-central states seems to have been that of Captain James Stark, who came to Kentucky in 1785." [55] With scions from these trees his son, James Hart Stark, established in 1815 Missouri's first nursery, the still-thriving Stark Nursery.

And in 1847, Henderson Lewelling and William Meek established the first nursery in Oregon. Lewelling's nurseries had already been pioneer establishments in Indiana and Iowa when he decided to set off for Oregon, across the Oregon Trail. The Lewelling family left Iowa in April 1847, transporting 700 grafted trees and a "stock of fruit seeds" [56] in an ox wagon pulled by "three yolks of oxen" as part of a party of seven Henry County wagons, which were later augmented by a larger wagon train headed for the Pacific Coast. Troubles followed: the trees required daily watering, often meaning that water had to be carried a mile or more; Lewelling's partner and two of his oxen died; troublesome Indians appeared; and his fellow travelers insisted "that the trees should be thrown away." [57] Finally, Lewelling and his family continued on the rest of the way alone, reaching their destination on the shores of the Willamette River seven months after they had set out, with about half of their trees still alive.

> Lewelling planted the still living trees as well as the seeds. There was an unexpected bonanza. Among the seeds that Lewelling had brought . . . had been some cherry pits, and among the seedlings from these appeared a cherry tree with delicious fruit, large and dark colored, nearly black. Seth [Lewelling's brother] propagated the variety and named it after a Chinese workman called Bing. It was to become, and remains even today, the most popular cherry of the Far West. [58]

William Meek, another Iowan, had also arrived in Oregon the same fall with several varieties of fruit, so the two pooled their resources and founded the first nursery on the Pacific Coast. Several years later they grafted 20,000 apple trees, which were taken by Seth Lewelling to Sacramento, California, where they were sold for five dollars each. Then in 1854 the ever-restless Henderson moved his nursery to Alameda County, California, with Meek following in 1859. Henderson became wealthy in

California and built a mansion in Fruitvale, but felt the need to move again, this time to Honduras, where he lost all his money. Returning to California, he burned to death in 1878 while burning weeds on rented land in San Jose.

In marked contrast to fruit culture in Britain, where estate growing was still the rule and proliferating apple varieties were treated with the same discrimination as vintage clarets, the apple trees that crossed the American continent and established a still-flourishing industry were carefully chosen varieties, beneficiaries of a network of horticultural societies that promoted and highlighted the best American varieties. Among the favorites were the Rhode Island Greening and the trio still grown at Monticello, the Esopus Spitzenburg, Roxbury Russet, and Newtown Pippin. The Newtown Pippin "provided the basis not only for the early fruit industry of New York and New England, but under the name Albemarle Pippin, also for that of Virginia, and later Oregon." [59] Eventually, competition from American and Commonwealth apple growers would inspire the modernization of Britain's orchards, returning in a fashion the gift given several centuries earlier.

THERE IS IN THE WESTERN COUNTRY A VERY EXTRAORDINARY MISSIONARY OF THE NEW JERUSALEM. A MAN HAS APPEARED WHO SEEMS TO BE ALMOST INDEPENDENT OF CORPORAL WANTS AND SUFFERINGS. HE GOES BAREFOOTED, CAN SLEEP ANYWHERE, IN HOUSE OR OUT . . . AND LIVE UPON THE COARSEST AND MOST SCANTY FARE. HE HAS ACTUALLY THAWED THE ICE WITH HIS BARE FEET. HE PROCURES WHAT BOOKS HE CAN OF THE NEW CHURCH; TRAVELS INTO THE REMOTE SETTLEMENTS, AND LENDS THEM WHEREVER HE CAN FIND READERS, AND SOMETIMES DIVIDES A BOOK IN TWO OR THREE PARTS FOR MORE EXTENSIVE DISTRIBUTION AND USEFULNESS. THIS MAN FOR YEARS PAST HAS BEEN IN THE EMPLOYMENT OF BRINGING INTO CULTIVATION IN NUMBERLESS PLACES IN THE WILDERNESS, SMALL PATCHES (TWO OR THREE ACRES) OF GROUND, AND THEN SOWING APPLE SEEDS AND REARING NURSERIES. THESE BECOME VALUABLE AS THE SETTLEMENTS APPROXIMATE, AND THE PROFITS OF THE WHOLE ARE INTENDED FOR THE PURPOSE OF ENABLING HIM TO PRINT ALL THE WRITINGS OF EMANUEL SWEDENBORG, AND DISTRIBUTE THEM THROUGH THE WESTERN SETTLEMENTS OF THE UNITED STATES.

Manchester Society for Printing, Publishing, and Circulating the Writings of Emanuel Swedenborg: January 14, 1817

11. *An early rendering of Johnny Appleseed.* (Harper's New Monthly
Magazine, *November 1871*)

This first published account of the life of John Chapman, more familiarly
known as Johnny Appleseed, appeared in England almost thirty years before published American accounts began to crop up. When Americans did
finally adopt the subject, the claim was staked time and time again, as the
increasingly well-worn tale was patched with ever "new" bits of fact and
fancy. Given the transformative effect of the American soil on European
apple varieties, it is perhaps not surprising that the American imagination
would work similarly on the story of America's patron saint of orchards.

John Chapman (1774–1845) was born in Leominster, Massachusetts,
and migrated in 1797 to western Pennsylvania, where he established his

first orchard on Brokenstraw Creek, near Warren. In what was to be a lifelong pattern, the poorly clad and frequently shoeless bachelor would wash apple seeds out of the pomace left by cider mills and plant them in patches of land he had cleared and fenced for the purpose. He described himself (in an 1828 Ohio deed) as "by occupation a gatherer and planter of apple seeds," a description that accurately reflected a portion of his activities in the western Pennsylvania, Ohio, and Indiana locales where he is known to have lived. "The one unique thing about John's seedling tree business," Chapman's principal biographer Robert Price tells us, "was his scheme for moving it with the frontier. Few other nurserymen could adjust their lives and business to such a plan. So far as records now make known, no one else ever did."[60]

Chapman had an unerring notion of the way the frontier would move, and he always seemed to be enough ahead to have apple trees ready for sale when the pioneers arrived. He began his work in Pennsylvania during the second year of Thomas Jefferson's vice presidency and moved into Ohio and Indiana as Jefferson's Louisiana Purchase was pushing the frontier farther west. Although Frederick Jackson Turner, in his 1893 hypothesis about the American frontier, claims that the "frontier is the line of most rapid and effective Americanization,"[61] Chapman's apples, like most of the plants these pioneers and the earlier colonists and planters carried along and like many of the plants Thomas Jefferson cultivated, were the offspring of European cultivars.

At the same time that Chapman was moving ahead of the frontier, he continued to return to many of his former plantings, so he was simultaneously managing nurseries over a wide geographic area on land he sometimes owned and sometimes just used. At one time he "held rights to hundreds of acres of land in Ohio and later in Indiana."[62] Although the purpose of his planting was to generate apple trees for sale, Chapman also freely gave trees away to those who could not pay his standard fee of a fipenny bit—the unit of Spanish-American money that "circulated until after the first minting of U.S. coinage in 1783" and was worth about six cents.[63] He befriended Indians and children, planting trees in Indian villages and "never sit[ting] down to the table until he was assured that there was enough for the children."[64]

The apples, however, were only a part of his mission. Chapman was

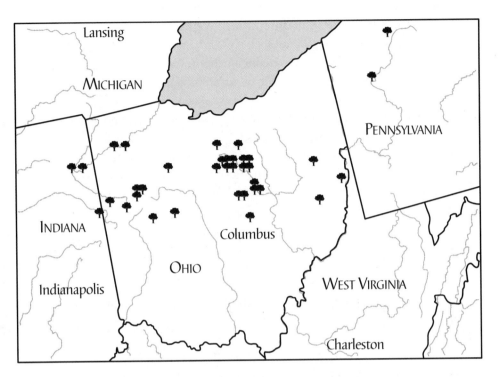

12. *Map showing locations of nursery sites established by John Chapman. (Map by Margaret Westergaard based on research by William Ellery Jones)*

apparently an ardent Swedenborgian who gave away Swedenborgian tracts as readily as apples and believed that "all things in the world exist from a Divine Origin . . . clothed with such forms in nature as enable them to exist there and perform their use and thus correspond to higher things."[65] When he was welcomed into a home he asked his hosts if they would like to hear "some news right fresh from heaven"[66] and then read to them from the New Testament and his Swedenborgian tracts. From 1820 to 1840 "all through the central and northern Ohio counties where Chapman spent his . . . middle years, a considerable number of small Swedenborgian societies sprang up and flourished vigorously for a time. . . . [He] is commonly credited with the sowing that sprouted into this sporadic crop."[67] From yet another perspective, it seems, apples were bound up with religion.

As regards the issue of grafting, where civilization seems to make its greatest inroads into the "natural" apple, Chapman was allied with Thoreau. Around 1801 Chapman is credited with the following remark during a conversation about grafting: "They can improve the apple in that way but that is only a device of man, and it is wicked to cut up trees that way. The correct method is to select good seeds and plant them in good ground and God only can improve the apples."[68] Thoreau was not as horticulturally naive as Chapman appears to be. He recognized that "*our* wild apple is wild only like myself . . . who belong not to the aboriginal race here, but have strayed into the woods from the cultivated stock."[69] Thoreau understood that his preferred apples probably sprang from the very trees he is arguing against, but he is encouraging us to see in wildness as much value as we find in cultivation and suggesting that we begin the task of reintegrating the positive meaning of the word "native"—banished in the first efforts of America's colonists to claim a land inhabited by others.

Though several earlier versions of the story existed, it was an article by W. D. Haley in the November 1871 *Harper's New Monthly Magazine* that made Johnny Appleseed a national hero. Again, as was the case with Chapman's ability to predict the route and the timing of the movement west, timing was a major factor. The article appeared shortly after the word "folklore" had first appeared in England, at a time when the United States was simultaneously reexamining the American experiment, in light of the recent Civil War, and searching for a uniquely American past. One of the places that search led was to the west, the presumed source of a self-sufficient pioneer vigor, of homespun values, and of the "American spirit" as defined by a belief in farming as the appropriate relationship of people to the land. A sense of loss was emerging even then about the disappearance of this "uniquely American" way of life.[70]

Haley makes his position clear in the first sentence of his article. "The 'far West' is rapidly becoming only a traditional designation: railroads have destroyed the romance of frontier life, or have surrounded it with so many appliances of civilization that the pioneer character is rapidly becoming mythical . . . [he continues, praising Chapman's selflessness and gentleness] . . . the early days of Western settlement witnessed sublimer heroisms than those of human torture . . . among the heroes of endurance that was voluntary, and of action that was creative and not sanguinary, there was one man whose name, seldom mentioned now save by some of the few surviving pioneers, deserves to be perpetuated."[71] And perpetuated it has been, along with another popular western tale, that of the forest-destroying Paul Bunyan.

B. A. Botkin's *A Treasury of American Folklore* includes both tales. Chapman can be found alongside Lincoln and Washington in the section entitled "Patron Saints"; Bunyan is placed with the steel-driving John Henry in a group called "Miracle Men." The title, of course, refers to his supposed deeds, but that Bunyan exists at all is a miracle of sorts. "Paul Bunyan . . . rest[s] on little or no oral tradition and on no historical prototypes," according to the historian Richard M. Dorson.[72]

The America that celebrated Bunyan was "ripe and self-confident after defeating the Kaiser and saving the world for democracy, [it] thirsted for a New World Thor, or Hercules, or Gargantua to symbolize her might. And so Paul Bunyan, bursting into public view in the 1920s, filled the psychic need."[73] The Bunyan tales celebrate "power without restraint [and] achievement without moral responsibility," but they, too, comment on our relationship to the natural world. We find Bunyan not only conquering nature with his physical prowess, but actually creating the features of the American landscape. The Mississippi River, for example, developed as the result of a leak in Babe's [Bunyan's blue ox] water tank, the Grand Canyon was formed by Bunyan dragging his spiked pole, and Puget Sound "exists because Paul dug it."[74]

We cannot, it seems, escape our role as agents of change—Bunyan reaped the past, as did Charles I, and Chapman planted an inheritance, as did Henrietta Maria—but we *can* choose what our changes will look like. We can *Designe for Plentie* "for the relief of the poor, the benefit of the rich, and the delight of all," as Samuel Hartlib suggested in his 1652 work on orchards. Our cities are full of vacant lots. We can choose, and it isn't easy in this land of the twice- and thrice-wrapped, to consume less and plant more. Who, after all, chooses a clear-cut hillside as the perfect view?

Not Jake Swamp. Swamp is a planter in the spirit of Chapman. But his crop is not apples, it is peace. Jake Swamp is a "dignitary of the Wolf Clan of the Mohawk Nation," a descendant of those long-ago Iroquois whose apple and peach trees were destroyed during Sullivan's raid, who travels the world planting trees of peace, an ancient Iroquois custom. The peace tree is a symbol of the Great Law, which "pierces the sky" with its "four white roots extend[ing] to the farthest parts of the earth" and beneath

13. *Chief Jake Swamp (center) receiving Arbor Day Foundation Media Award on April 25, 1998, in recognition for his work as founder of the Tree of Peace Society and as the author of* Giving Thanks. *Also pictured are John Rosenow and Mary Yeager of the National Arbor Day Foundation. (National Arbor Day Foundation)*

which are buried all the weapons of war. Swamp, who founded the Tree of Peace Society in 1983 "to promote peace through the planting of trees,"[75] writes that he has "planted peace trees all over the world like Japan, Germany, Netherlands, Australia, Italy, Israel, Columbia, France, England, U.S. and Canada. I estimate around two hundred million trees have been planted as a result of sharing the tree of peace ceremony."[76] Swamp's choice is clear.

The ever-versatile apple works both ways; it provides an inheritance at the same time that it can be used in the present. It is a symbol of cultivation and partnership with human society at the same time that it can grow without human intervention, in a more "wild" state. It can be eaten raw or cooked, hot or cold, liquid or solid, and states in between. It can stand on its own or support other dishes and perform both roles with that combination of sugar and acid, or art and nature, that is its defining characteristic. Moreover, it can negotiate the succeeding zones of indeterminacy created by the westward trek of America's population centers as easily as it settled into the carefully demarcated zones of intervention of the Renaissance garden.

We call our largest city the Big Apple. As Robert Hendrickson explains in *Ladybugs, Tiger Lillies and Wallflowers,* New York is "full of opportunity, ripe for plucking. . . . It may be that the 'big apple,' a dance craze of the swing era . . . influenced the coinage. A better guess is that jazz musicians in 1910 first used it as a loose translation of the Spanish *manzana principal,* the 'main apple orchard,' in reference to New Orleans's main city block downtown where all the action was." [77]

Finally, each of the 7,500 known varieties of apples in the world[78]— including Isaac Newton's Tree where, according to Voltaire, "the notion of gravitation came into his mind occasion'd by the fall of an apple"—can be cut horizontally to reveal the five fused seed-containing chambers of a single ovary. Their shape is the same as a star and their number is the same as our senses. Smell the apple after you cut it, really stick your nose in and think about our long connection with apples and what researchers at Yale's Psychophysiology Center are learning about smell: "they claim that the smell of spiced apples can reduce blood pressure in people under stress and avert a panic attack." [79] "Apples first, last, and always" is my motto: what's yours?

Pl. 33.

Bessa del.   Gabriel sculp.

Wild Cherry.
Cerasus virginiana.

CHAPTER FOUR

THREE
CHERRIES

FLOWER: THE REPRODUCTIVE PORTION OF THE PLANT, CONSISTING OF
STAMENS, PISTILS, OR BOTH, AND USUALLY INCLUDING A PERIANTH OF
SEPALS OR BOTH SEPALS AND PETALS.

JAMES G. HARRIS AND MELINDA WOOLF HARRIS, *Plant Identification Terminology:*
An Illustrated Glossary

From the winter of 1996 through late spring of 1997, I was consumed by cherries. It was a pleasant occupation, but not easy to explain. Which cherries, exactly, people would ask? The "three graces," I would answer: one is esteemed for the character of her wood, the second for the flavor of her fruit, and the third for the evanescent beauty of her blossoms. Or, "the glory of three continents." The wood is from our native wild black cherry (*Prunus serotina*), the fruit derives from the European sweet and sour cherry species (*Prunus avium* and *Prunus cerasus*, respectively), and the much-admired blooms that now adorn our nation's capital each spring are borne on the limbs of the Japanese flowering cherries (*Prunus serrulata*, *P. yedoensis*, *P. subhirtella*, and *P. incisa*, to name a few of the flowering cherry species).

I said this silently. It was too soon, then, to speak aloud of grace and glory.

But I could have said, "the rose family," since cherries, like apples, pears, strawberries, raspberries, blackberries, and our garden roses are all part of the same botanical family, *Rosaceae*, though not the same genus. *Rosaceae*, in fact, includes "about 115 genera [and] perhaps 3,200 species . . . in which are some of the major ornamental and pomological plants."[1] *Prunus*, for example, is the genus for cherries, *Malus* for apples, *Pyrus* for pears, *Fragaria* for strawberries, and *Rosa* for roses. The *Prunus* genus in turn "comprises 400 species growing naturally in the Northern Hemisphere. It is the genus," U.S. National Arboretum former director Henry M. Cathey goes on to say, "in which all of our stone fruits are found—almonds, apricots, cherries, nectarines, peaches, and plums."[2]

It is also the genus of our three cherries—as I did say, the American wood, the European fruit, and the Japanese flowers—exemplars of the agriculturally defined landscape of forest, orchard, and garden. I like their reach and the way they touch upon so many ways of knowing trees: the ways of craftsmen, botanists, planters and consumers of food, and spinners

14. *François A. Michaux, The North American Sylva, vol. 2. (American Philosophical Society)*

of stories, to, finally, the creators of and the pilgrims to a place of meaning-laden beauty—Washington's cherry trees.

The last had interested me first. But wanting to know about the one reminded me how little I knew about the others. In that way one grew to three, as growing things do, so before setting off for Washington, I tried to learn about them all, beginning where America began, with our wild black cherry.

I first went to Paul Downs Cabinetmakers, where every day is cherry day. The Philadelphia furniture maker explains the popularity of this "wood of the moment"[3] in generational terms. He believes his clients have chosen the warm mid-range color (that ripens with age) of our native American wild black cherry as a middle ground between the light-colored oak and ash of their parents' modern furniture and the dark mahogany of their grandparents'. Reaching back many more generations, they have chosen the wood of one of the cherries planted by George Washington at his Mount Vernon estate (Washington also planted sour cherries, *Prunus cerasus*) and admired by General Lafayette, who asked that seeds of the tree be sent to him.

Downs's clients have chosen well. In his autobiographical *The Soul of a Tree*, the internationally renowned nisei woodworker George Nakashima writes that "cherry and other fruitwoods produce material of great quality. . . . All woods have graining—patterns created by the trunk fibers. However, the grain of many woods, pine and maple for instance, is regular and comparatively uninteresting, while that of walnut, cherry and other fruitwoods is intricate and exciting."[4]

Black cherry's "satiny surface susceptible of receiving a beautiful polish"[5] also makes it a favorite of woodworkers and cabinetmakers, as does its stability. Stability indicates less reaction to humidity than some other woods—meaning less shrinkage during seasoning and less warping after seasoning—so Downs says he is more confident shipping cherry furniture to a foreign client than he might be with red oak or poplar, for example. It is also fairly hard, less brittle than the harder oak, but not as soft as pine, which dents when something is dropped on it.

And furniture makers and other woodworkers continue to find "good stocks available." (A Maine luthier told me that the growing interest in using native wood has resulted in some black cherry being used for the back, sides, and neck of steel-string guitars.) The botanist François A. Michaux, who traveled in North America with his father, André, personal botanist to Louis XVI, distinguished his work from that of his father as being not only interested in "the progress of botanical knowledge" but also the more practical "uses of the forest trees."[6] He reported cherry being "employed for bed-steads and other articles of furniture" sold in "planks 3 inches thick . . . at 4 cents a foot at Philadelphia, and at less than half this price at Pittsburgh and in Tennessee."[7] Today's black cherry, after a recent 20 percent increase in price, sells for a comparatively modest $5.00 a board foot. Modest, that is, compared to $.04 a foot, which, after factoring in a 3 percent rate of inflation, would be $8.18 in 1999 currency.

Downs talks warmly about his admiration for trees: about their adaptability ("we don't grow taller in a taller room," the way many trees grow taller in a forest, reaching upward for the light); and his recent reading about their ability to communicate ("when a tree senses an insect predator it relays that information to neighboring trees and those trees in turn change their chemical composition to help ward off the unwanted intruder"). But he also acknowledges that "the idea of wood is disassociated from the act of killing a tree." What he works with is lumber, not trees.

There are reminders though. Downs and his cabinetmakers sometimes find bullets, parts of fences, and mineral spots in the wood they work. All suggest the former tree. As does the need to plane with the grain, along the length of the trunk. ("The spirit of a tree," George Nakashima writes, "travels in and out through the grains and fibers and can often reveal great joy."[8]) And when they are planing or cutting the wood there is also a reminder of the specific species—its scent. Cherry exudes a sweetish smell that has a somewhat musty overlay, like the mustiness of the summer forest after a light rain.

The specific forests that produce Downs's cherry are in Sullivan County, in the Appalachian region of western Pennsylvania. Long known for its fine black cherry, this region was identified by Charles Sprague Sargent in *The Silva of North America* as a place where *Prunus serotina*, "one of the most valuable timber trees of the American forests," could be found "reaching its greatest size and beauty on the slopes of the high Alleghany [sic] Mountains,"[9] sometimes attaining a prominent 100 feet in height.

Timber was, and is, only one of its uses. The bark and leaves contain hydrocyanic acid, used from Sargent's day to the present in expectorants and cough syrups.[10] In some *Prunus* varieties, such as *Prunus caroliniana*, or mock orange, the concentration of hydrocyanic acid is considered dangerous to foraging animals, causing the city of Mobile to once pass an ordinance "prohibit[ing] throwing the trimmings of . . . [this] favorite hedge plant . . . into the streets where they might be eaten by cattle."[11]

Although none of the native American cherry varieties are cultivated for their fruit, the fruit of *Prunus serotina* is enjoyed by both bears and birds and, in its fermented state, is sometimes used to manufacture a liquor similar to the European kirschwasser. As the English writer William Wood, who emigrated to Massachusetts in 1629, observed of our native cherries in *New Englands Prospect:* "The Cherrie[s] . . . be much smaller than our *English* Cherrie, nothing near so good if they be not very ripe: they so furre the mouth that the tongue will cleave to the roofe, and the throate wax horse with swallowing those red Bullies. . . . *English* ordering may bring them to be an *English* Cherrie, but yet they are as wilde as the *Indians*."[12]

Wood's opinion of our native cherries was apparently widespread, so the colonists looked to Europe for their familiar fruit trees. Rather than bringing order to what they found, as Wood suggested, they simply ordered what they knew. Introductions of European species began quite early. As the Arnold Arboretum's well-known plant collector Ernest H. Wilson points out in *Aristocrats of the Trees:* "The native Apples and Cherries of this country have no value as fruit trees, and America's only contribution to the fruit trees of the world are her Plums. So small a part do these play even in American orchards that it is correct to write that this country owes all her fruit trees to Europe and Asia." In 1629 Francis Higginson wrote of Red Kentish cherries (originally introduced by the Romans, who "carried cultivated varieties of cherries to England . . . during their occupation") being cultivated in Massachusetts, and by 1641 a Massachusetts nursery offered cherry trees for sale.[13]

It is interesting to note that at the same time the early settlers were planting the familiar European cultivars of *Prunus avium* (so called, according to Wilson, because the birds favor its fruit) and *Prunus cerasus* in American orchards, English growers were planting our *Prunus serotina* in their gardens. Sargent says that "it was one of the first American trees cultivated in Europe," having been "established in English gardens before 1629."[14]

To seventeenth-century agricultural economies, money did grow on trees. These plant exchanges represented something more akin to contemporary technological or medical information swaps than our trips to the local garden center. They were pragmatic attempts to improve daily life, to add an important timber tree to the silva of a wood-dependent nation that was despoiling its own forests, or perhaps to find a tree that would bear a food crop to help to feed a family. From the American side of the Atlantic, the exchange was enormously successful. By adding European fruit cherries to our silva, those colonists secured for future generations both an important agricultural crop—the United States is the world's leading cherry producer[15]—and two early tales (subsequently augmented by the story of the Washington cherry blossoms).

Almost three-quarters of our cherry crop is sour cherries, the fruit planted by George Washington at Mount Vernon, and the fruit we use in pastries and pies, including the ones we bake to celebrate his birthday. Today's sour cherry cultivars have names like Early Richmond, Montmorency, and Meteor. Early Richmond "was brought to the lower St. Lawrence region as 'French,' and to Virginia before 1700, where it received its American name, its original English name being 'Kentish.'" Sour cherries grow on trees that are much smaller than their less acidic cousins, 15 feet tall versus 25 to 30 feet tall, and are also self-fertile (meaning a tree can be fertilized with its own pollen), unlike the generally self-sterile sweet cherry varieties. The color we call cherry-red is closer to the color of the sour cherry fruit. The sweet cherries have a more extensive palette, ranging from the yellow of Wood, through the yellow-with-a-red-cheek of Yellow Spanish ("the Bigarreau of the French, it goes back at least to the first century of the Christian Era; it was brought to America soon after the Revolution"), the purple-red of Windsor, the purple-black of Black Tartarian, to Schmidt, which *Taylor's Encyclopedia of Gardening* describes as black, and the black-red of Bing. Bing, which was named by Henderson Lewelling of apple fame for a Chinese workman, is the only cherry name I knew when I began this and the only variety I'm certain I know the flavor of.[16]

Our stories, however, do not differentiate sweet from tart or fact from fiction, for that matter. The first explains a crook in New York's Broadway. Apparently Broadway was originally conceived to be both broad and straight, but where Grace Church now stands a cherry tree grew. That tree was the special place where a local tavern keeper named Hendrick Brevoort enjoyed smoking his pipe on warm evenings. When Brevoort saw the original street plan, which would have required removing the cherry, he protested to the city fathers, who, "realizing that the city would never grow so far," [17] relented and diverted the street.

The second tale, familiar to every child in America, is Mason Locke Weems's legend of George Washington chopping down the cherry tree. "Widely known to be a fabrication," as Peter Conn writes, "America's most familiar myth . . . was first included in the fifth edition of Weems'" biography, *Life of Washington, the Great* (1806).[18] Weems tells us that the tree was "a beautiful young English cherry-tree."[19] It was especially

15. Grant Wood, Parson Weems' Fable, *1939, oil on canvas. Shows Mason Locke Weems pulling back a cherry-fringed curtain to reveal a representation of his famous fable. (Amon Carter Museum, Fort Worth, Texas 1970.43)*

favored by the elder Washington for presumably many of the same reasons we favor it today: for its delicious utility, its then scarcity, and as an irreplaceable addition to our native flora. That it was an English tree, however, would have also been important to the elder Washington and his fellow colonists. They were also English transplants, seeking a hospitable place to put down their own roots. Where an English tree flourished, they could have reasoned, so might Englishmen.

It was almost two centuries later that the other cherry trees made their way to the city named for the man who supposedly chopped down that earlier tree. Variously called ornamental cherries, Japanese flowering cherry trees, flowering cherries, or oriental flowering cherries, depending on the political season, these arboreal art forms were sent as the gift of a nation whose citizens we then excluded under the terms of what is called the Gentlemen's Agreement, an informal policy negotiated during the administration of Teddy Roosevelt (a few years after the birth of George Nakashima in 1905), whereby the Japanese government agreed to discourage "emigration of its subjects of the laboring classes"[20] to the United States. These cherry trees, then, represented a twist on that earlier formula: where a Japanese tree flourished, they could have imagined, so might a Japanese citizen—someday.

They were a gift and a guide. You can read it in their flowers. First look at the buttercup-like white flower of either the wild black cherry (if you are as fortunate as I am to have one growing in your yard) or the sweet cherry with their five petals. Then watch closely as each of the thirty clear pink petals of the Kwanzan (a popular double-flowering cultivar included in the Washington, D.C., planting) blossom unfolds from its rose-red bud and you will intuit much of the more than twelve hundred years of Japanese horticulture, history, and myth that has been written there so delicately.

Horticulture first. Arboreal cherries, as Henry Cathey pointed out, are found throughout the northern hemisphere. North America claims six distinct species while, according to Collingwood Ingram, Europe has five, Japan thirteen (Ernest H. Wilson claims ten, G. Koizumi eleven,[21] and the U.S. National Arboretum eight),[22] and China, which Wilson appropriately calls the "mother of all gardens," is home to twenty-three species—almost as many as all the others combined.[23] Regarding this disparity, Wilson postulates that because the more recent glaciations were not as severe in China as in Europe or North America, China's flora suffered considerably less. To Americans—linguistically, culturally, and historically allied with Europe—he also explains that the eastern United States' closest botanical affinity is with China: "There are many instances in which only two species of a genus are known—one in the eastern United States and the other in China. Noteworthy examples are the Tulip tree, Kentucky Coffee tree, the Sassafras, and the Lotus Lily." [24]

In the period (about 10,600 years ago) that marks the origins of horticulture, the culture of the garden or spaces closest to home, our remote ancestors selected some of these *Prunus* varieties for their wholesome qualities and brought them into cultivation—"in the West mainly for the sake of their fruit, in the East chiefly for the beauty of their flowers." Archaeological evidence indicates, for example, that cherries were part of the diet of prehistoric Swiss lake-dwellers. [25]

Botanists feel confident in claiming *Prunus avium* and *P. cerasus* as the botanical parents of our contemporary pomological cultivars, but there is no clear agreement on the precise lineage of the flowering cherries—in part because ornamental trees lack the economic value of their fruitful cousins, they are not studied as extensively. However, after investigating the flora of China and subsequently that of Japan, Wilson concluded in 1916 that "nearly all the double-flowering Cherries of Japanese gardens are derived from *Prunus serrulata* . . . and *Prunus Lannesiana.*" [26] But many other species, such as *Prunus subhirtella, P. incisa, P. yedoensis,* and *P. sargentii* (named for Wilson's supervisor and the Arnold Arboretum's first director, the previously mentioned Charles Sprague Sargent) have also made significant contributions to the genetic pool. "Some of these species and others introduced from various parts of the Orient hybridized naturally during the early horticultural development of Japan and produced many of the cherry cultivars in cultivation today." [27]

Yoshino and Kwanzan are two examples. These are the two most commonly grown Japanese flowering cherry cultivars in the United States. The National Park Service calls Yoshino "Japan's favorite cultivated cherry tree" and describes it as a cultivar of *Prunus yedoensis* and Kwanzan as a double-flowering cultivar of *Prunus serrulata.* [28]

But the naming and claiming are not, apparently, over. Flowering cherry names, it turns out, are as confusing to specialists as they are to

16. Prunus serrulata f. purpurascens *from M. Miyoshi,* Journal of the College of Science Imperial University of Tokyo, *1916, now generally known as* Prunus serrulata Kwanzan. *(From the collections of the Missouri Botanical Garden Library)*

amateurs. Instead of elucidating the details of plant lineage—one of the principal purposes of botanical nomenclature—they confuse and obscure it by, for example, assigning "Latin names that should only be used for wild cherries to cultivated selections." [29] So, in 1984 two Americans, botanist Roland M. Jefferson and research assistant Kay Kazue Wain, decided to untangle the thicket by dividing the flowering cherries into two groups: Yama-zakura, or mountain cherries for the wild species, and Sato-zakura, or village cherries for the cultivated plants (a system with precedents in Japan and Europe). They placed all of the cultivated cherries of uncertain parentage in the second category and reestablished romanized Japanese names (instead of Latin names) with the result that Kwanzan, for example (called *Prunus serrulata* f. *purpurascens* by Miyoshi, as in the botanical illustration in figure 16), is called Sekiyama and its parentage is confused (although this is botanically correct, Jefferson indicates that nurserymen will probably continue to use the name Kwanzan, since it is so well known).

But that is not all. Claims by Korea during World War II—while that nation was suffering under Japanese occupation—challenged the very origins of the trees, suggesting Korean, not Japanese, ancestry. The April 5, 1942, *Washington Herald* carried the following anonymous report:

> In what veteran diplomats here described as one of the most strongly worded documents in international history, the Korean-American Council telegraphed Secretary of the Interior Ickes: "In common with the other loot stolen from the Korean and Chinese peoples by the rapacious Japanese, the so-called and erroneously termed Japanese cherry tree first was developed in Korea and therefore should be rightly known as the Korean cherry tree."

But, perhaps alluding to that earlier tale about Washington chopping down the cherry tree, USDA botanist Paul Russell responded: "Facts are terrible things, but the double-blossom cherry trees really were developed in Japan. A shame, but that's the way it is—we must tell the truth." He did say, however, that the trees could be called Oriental, instead of Japanese, cherries.[30]

Regardless of their names, their numbers are impressive. Several decades before Wilson arrived in Japan, the centuries of natural and artificial selection had produced "more than 130 recognized cultivated selections."[31] By 1984, Jefferson and Wain's *Nomenclature of Cultivated Japanese Flowering Cherries* listed well over 200 cultivars. The cultivation equally extends to literature, as myths, legends, poetry, and history have also flowered, each expressing the importance of this national tree in Japanese culture.

Around the time the Romans were withdrawing their legions from Britain to protect Italy, the Japanese Emperor Richü was admiring the blossoms of a winter-flowering cherry (*Prunus subhirtella* var. *autumnalis*) from a pleasure boat at his "'Palace of the Young Cherry Trees' near Nara," when some of the petals fluttered into his upheld sake cup, "crowning his cup as the Romans crowned their goblets with roses."[32] From this event is said to date the enduring practice of combining sake and sakura (Japanese for "flowering cherry") viewing. When the Japanese came to write their *Kijoki,* or *Record of Ancient Matters,* in 712, they included the oral legend of

Ko-no-pana-no-saku-ya-bime, the maiden who causes the trees to bloom by "awakening the dormant trees to life with her delicate breath," [33] thus explaining the mortality of the emperors and, in another account, the brevity of all human life. [34] Although of heavenly ancestry, the emperors were born of Ko-no-pana-no-saku-ya-bime, whose father cursed her progeny with a life that "shall continue only for the interval of the blossoming of the trees." [35] Another tree bound up in explaining human mortality.

First admired and grown by the court and the nobility—as were prized plants in early European gardens—choice cherry specimens were planted in the palace and mansions of the then capital city of Kyoto as early as 794, according to early records. After the court was replaced by the military shogunate, which ruled in the emperor's name from the twelfth through the nineteenth centuries, Japan's leaders demonstrated an eagerness to appropriate and display symbols of imperial continuity and culture, including cherry trees. Named varieties, such as Fugenzo, were recorded as early as 1555 and extensive plantings, such as the avenue of 1,500 trees stretching three to four miles at Koganie, a village near Tokyo, were established between 1736 and 1740. Also, "the wood of the Sakura is of excellent quality and is used for building, carving, and block printing." [36]

"Except Fuji-yama and the moon, no other object has been theme and inspiration of so many millions of Japanese poems," the journalist and first female member of the National Geographic Society's Board of Managers, Eliza Ruhamah Scidmore, wrote in 1910, adding that "forty cherry-blossom crests are found in books of heraldry . . . the young peers at the Nobles' School wear a metal cherry-blossom on their caps and collars, and in April all the sweets and cakes, and half the pretty things one eats, are in the shape of the five-petaled flower, or at least are ornamented with it." [37] Contemporary Japanese interest is no less effusive or extensive.

> Japan's TV stations, radio stations, and newspapers report regularly on the anticipated date for Sakura to bloom. The news media treats and follows blooming forecasts of Sakura blossoms from Okinawa to Hokkaido, as they would cover a powerful typhoon. At the end of February, the so called Sakura Front is formed in the south and is tracked thereafter as it advances northward. [38]

"My feeling for trees probably began with my ancestors," George Nakashima has said. [39]

A similar response can be found in Korea, where in a single day 96,000 visitors have been recorded visiting Shotokeun Park, in Seoul, to view the masses of Korean Hill Cherries (*Prunus serrulata* var. *pubescens*) in bloom.[40]

In a sense, however, the story of Washington's cherry blossoms begins where much of the rest of our relationship with Japan began—with Commodore Matthew Calbraith Perry. When Perry entered Japan in 1853 and 1854, one of the plants he collected was the flowering cherry. Learning at that time that the port city of Shimoda had been opened to foreigners, the Japanese poet Gessho expressed the tree's symbolic and imaginative importance to Japan:

> Only the cherry blossoms take not on the rank barbarian stench,
> But breathe to the morning sun the fragrance of a nation's soul.[41]

Unfortunately, Perry's arrival, and the subsequent political upheaval, caused a decline in all of the arts, including horticulture, and many cherry gardens were devastated. Recognizing the significance of this loss, a number of individuals worked to preserve the trees, but in the case of one particular person, the gardener Magoemon Tagaki, the commitment was extraordinary, extending to three generations and at least seventy-eight different varieties. It was those cherries, grown by the Tagaki family, that were planted in 1886 along the banks of the Arakawa River, near Tokyo, and it was subsequently grafts of those same trees that were presented to the United States in 1912.[42] A simple shovel, it seems, could sever culture from horticulture and send the "soul" of one nation off to be the ornament of another. Or could it?

In 1909, although there was a new administration in Washington—that of William Howard Taft—the same party was still in power and many of the same faces, like that of Secretary of Agriculture James Wilson, were still around. During the previous administration, Wilson had espoused a goal of American agricultural self-sufficiency and a strategy of exploration, discovery, and introduction of non-native plants, which the historian Philip J. Pauly has called "bring[ing] home the fruits of empire."[43] He had also established a new bureau, the Section for Foreign Seed and Plant Introduction, and hired plant explorer David Fairchild as its head (Fairchild's story of these explorations, *The World Was My Garden*, became a nonfiction

best-seller in 1938). Simultaneously, another of Wilson's divisions, the
Bureaus of Plant Industry and Entomology, had begun to develop proce-
dural and legislative safeguards against the introduction of foreign diseases
and insects. And, on her arrival in the capital in 1909, the new First Lady,
Helen Herron Taft, undertook the beautification of Washington's Potomac
Park, the recently reclaimed former swamp. (Between 1870 and 1907 the
U.S. Army Corps of Engineers had worked to make the Potomac more
navigable by first building a retaining wall along its banks and then dredg-
ing the river silt and depositing it on what has since become the grounds
of the Lincoln Memorial and East and West Potomac Park.[44]) Each of these
goals—beautification, agricultural protection, and agricultural expansion—would collide over the planting of the Japanese flowering cherry
trees.

Significantly, all of the principal players had firsthand knowledge of Japan. Before coming to Washington as Teddy Roosevelt's secretary of war,
Taft had been the first American governor-general of the Philippines, serving from 1900 to 1905. While there he had openly supported the Japanese
before and during the Russo-Japanese War, a position that made him quite
popular in Japan.[45] Stopping there when he was recalled to Washington as
secretary of state, Taft received a hero's welcome that included a daytime
fireworks display in Yokohama harbor (where Perry and Japanese officials
had signed the treaty opening two Japanese ports to Americans), crowds
of cheering people, a welcome by Tokyo's Mayor Ozaki, and dinner with
the emperor and empress of Japan. Ozaki later wrote in his autobiography,
"I always wanted to show, in some way, appreciation to the government
of the United States for their kindness shown to Japan during the Russo-
Japanese War. When I heard that Mrs. Taft was interested in planting Japanese flowering trees in Washington, I took the liberty to send the trees as
a gift from the city of Tokyo."[46]

While Taft was serving in the Philippines, Charles E. Marlatt, Bureau of
Entomology assistant chief, was traveling in China and Japan. The occasion
was his honeymoon (1901–1902), which he used as an opportunity "to
inspect Japan and eastern China for scale insect species that might endan-
ger American fruit trees." While abroad, his bride, Frances Brown Marlatt,
contracted an infectious illness, which resulted in her slow death on their
return to the United States. "He was thus deeply concerned about the
dangers that foreign organisms posed to Americans. No one would stand
in his way."[47]

David Fairchild had also traveled in Asia, first as a young man and again in 1902, when he visited Japan and, after admiring "the picturesque beauty of the cherry trees lining the country's streets and waterways," determined to plant them on his own property. By 1906 he and his wife, Marian, had imported 100 cherry trees (and a Japanese gardener named Mari) to adorn their Chevy Chase estate, In the Woods. The following year they began promoting the trees as ideal street trees for the Washington area.[48] Recognizing that the recently established Arbor Day would be an ideal publicity vehicle, Fairchild contacted the Washington public schools and offered to provide a tree to each school in the district, to be planted in its schoolyard in celebration of Arbor Day, March 27, 1908. The offer was accepted, the trees were planted, and Fairchild spoke at the Franklin School (where because of the lack of a schoolyard the tree was planted across the street in Franklin Park), publicly promoting the idea of a "field of cherries"[49] in Potomac Park. His distinguished guest Eliza Ruhamah Scidmore, who had first proposed this idea while visiting the Fairchilds at their home,[50] then took the suggestion to Mrs. Taft.[51] The *Washington Star* covered the event, writing that Fairchild had "aroused the enthusiasm of his audience by telling them that Washington would one day be famous for its flowering cherry trees."[52]

Although certainly not the cruelest month for the cherries, April 1909 marked an acceleration of activity toward an unhappy denouement. Fairchild offered to donate fifty Japanese flowering trees for planting in Potomac Park. The offer was "indorsed" by both the landscape gardener and the superintendent of Public Buildings and Grounds with the latter noting that "Mrs. Taft has expressed a desire to have magnolia and cherry trees, and other similar early blooming trees, planted in Potomac Park"[53]—replacing the recently planted American elms.[54] The superintendent also ordered an additional ninety Japanese double flowering cherry trees from Hoopes Bros. & Thomas Company of West Chester, Pennsylvania[55] (some varieties of Japanese flowering cherry trees have been available in the United States since 1846).[56] And, in 1909, Charles Marlatt took over the USDA's efforts to control the importation of plants.

In July the secretary of state met with the Japanese ambassador to apprise him of the project. On August 30 the Department of State was notified by the Japanese Embassy, "the news that planting of Japanese cherry trees along the Potomac Drive of the City of Washington is contemplated having reached Japan, the City of Tokyo, prompted by a desire to show its friendly sentiments towards its sister Capital City . . . has decided to offer as a gift two thousand young trees raised in Japan."[57] In December the trees arrived in Seattle where, following their first inspection, they were placed in temperature-controlled railroad cars bound for the nation's capital. They reached their destination on January 6, 1910. On January 28, 1910, following an extensive inspection by experts in Marlatt's Bureau of Entomology, which revealed the trees were infested with two kinds of scale—a wood-boring larva, and root gall worm—all of the trees were destroyed, reduced to ashes near the Agriculture Department's greenhouses on the grounds of the Washington Monument.[58]

Although the arboreal *auto-da-fé* was embarrassing to both governments, as anyone who has visited Washington knows, there *are* flowering cherry trees growing in Potomac Park. Still eager to root their national symbol in the landscape of official Washington, the Japanese government immediately decided to replace the trees with 3,020 new ones and, to avoid a second embarrassment, enlisted experts from the Imperial Horticultural Station, the Imperial University of Tokyo, and the Imperial Quarantine Service to assure the health of the new shipment.

At the same time, Marlatt's actions had helped orchestrate an important shift in political power enabling his fellow protectionists to gain passage of the Plant Quarantine Act of 1912, which created the Federal Horticultural Board. The Board, which was empowered to "regulate plant imports," was controlled by Marlatt for almost two decades. It effectively ended the "biotic laissez-faire" that had characterized American policy from colonial days onward—allowing individuals, for example, to import the original fruit cherries—and instead fostered "ideals of autonomy and isolation" that ultimately found expression in policies, such as the Immigration Act of 1924, which sought to manage human aliens in much the same way as plant aliens. Regarding the flowering cherries, however, although Marlatt's Bureau had raised no objections to the second shipment of trees, he complained several years later that it had introduced "the oriental fruit worm, which is now widespread in the eastern half of the United States, and is occasioning losses estimated well into the millions."[59] Even the most carefully crafted *Titanic* meets an iceberg.

Thus as Mrs. Taft and the Viscountess Chinda, wife of the Japanese ambassador, planted the first two Japanese flowering cherry trees (grown from scions of twelve different varieties selected from the planting along the Arakawa River) in Potomac Park on March 26, 1912, forces were lining up against similar plant exchanges in the future. However, oblivious to the controversy, the trees themselves grew more beautiful each year. A seemingly prescient fourteenth-century Japanese poet wrote:

> The cherry blossoms
> Unmindful of the sad world,
> Have burst into bloom.
> And in the capital too
> Now must be their glory.[60]

As early as 1925, the mayor of Columbus, Ohio, petitioned the State Department to solicit similar trees on that city's behalf (the request was denied),[61] and in 1927 the first "Cherry Blossom Fete" was organized. The event, which attracted 10,000 visitors, included "little actors and actresses from both the public and private schools of the city"[62] as well as the children and adults of Washington's diplomatic community. In 1938, a group

17. The boulder marks the location of the first ceremonial planting of Japanese flowering cherry trees by Mrs. Taft and Viscountess Chinda on March 26, 1912. (Photo: Gayle B. Samuels)

of Washington garden-club members, led by Eleanor Patterson, chained themselves to some trees (in a forerunner to contemporary environmental protests) to protest their removal to make way for the Jefferson Memorial (they and the trees were removed and eighty-three of the transplanted trees died). During the Second World War (when the American-born George Nakashima and his family were interred at the Camp Minidoka Relocation Center in Hunt, Idaho) four trees were cut down because of "bitter feelings" toward the Japanese.[63] In 1949 the Cherry Blossom Festival added the selection of "princesses" from every state and territory to the annual festivities, and in 1957 the Mikimoto Pearl Crown was donated to crown the festival queen. However, when the Japanese made an additional offer of cherry trees during the Johnson administration, the full force of the USDA, plus nurserymen and fruit growers nationwide, lined up against allowing the additional trees to be imported. Citing the 1948 enactment of Nursery Stock, Plant and Seed Quarantine No. 37 and its specific prohibition against "plants of all species and varieties of the genus *Prunus* . . . from Europe, Asia, Africa, and Oceania, including Australia and New Zealand, because of the presence in those areas of a diversity of plant diseases not known to occur in the United States," as well as the fact that "it is generally believed that a shipment in March of 1912 . . . was responsible for the introduction into the United States of the oriental fruit moth,"[64] the USDA suggested the compromise eventually adopted, that the new plantings be done with trees grown in the United States. These trees, also the gift of the Japanese government, were planted on the grounds of the Washington Monument, near the site of that earlier ignominy, with Mrs. Lyndon B. Johnson and Mrs. Ryuji Takeuchi, the wife of the Japanese ambassador, participating in the planting.[65]

At the same time, beginning in 1951, the trees were traveling again— this time back to their original roots. In that year the Japanese asked if cuttings could be taken from the Washington Cherry Trees and repatriated to Japan to restore the collection of trees on the Arakawa River, which had declined during the war years. National Capital Parks officials were happy to oblige and in 1952 "55 scions from 11 of the original Potomac Park Yoshino cherries" were sent back to Japan.[66] "What is good," Lewis Hyde has written in *The Gift*, "is given back."[67] Again, in 1980, a similar request was received owing to losses sustained from changing the course of the Arakawa River and, in 1981, 2,000 scions were provided. Cuttings were

18. *The Jefferson Memorial, site of a 1938 protest over the removal of cherry trees to make way for the monument, seen through the branches of a flowering cherry in March 1997. (Photo: Gayle B. Samuels)*

again taken from the Yoshino cherries (*Prunus yedoensis*), "one of the last survivors" of the original twelve varieties in Potomac Park.[68] Through the efforts of U.S. National Arboretum research botanist Roland M. Jefferson, seven other original varieties were located elsewhere in the United States, and cuttings of those trees were also sent to Japan.[69] At a White House ceremony in February 1981 marking the repatriation, First Lady Nancy Reagan presented Japanese Ambassador Yoshio Ogawara with a three-foot-high tree grown from a cutting taken from the Yoshino cherry planted by Helen Taft in 1912. The tree, called the President Reagan Cherry Tree, was subsequently planted in a park near the Arakawa River and marked with a plaque.[70] Then in 1982, the exchange expanded.

In that year Roland M. Jefferson was sent to Japan by Friends of the National Arboretum to collect flowering cherry tree seeds with "direct friendship ties to the Japanese people."[71] The National Arboretum had recognized that America's loss of many ornamental cherry cultivars, coupled with an inability to import new varieties because of restrictions imposed by our plant quarantine laws, had resulted in a declining genetic pool of cherry cultivars. American scientists eager to develop improved flowering cherry varieties—pest-resistant and cold-hardy, for example—needed a more diverse gene pool to draw upon. The solution was to send a botanist to Japan to evaluate and collect seeds from superior trees. National Arboretum botanist Roland M. Jefferson was chosen and he began collecting on

19. Roland W. Jefferson (center) surrounded by Japanese schoolchildren, parents, and teachers at a shrine in the northern part of the island of Honshu, Japan, taken in 1982 the day before collecting wild cherry seeds as part of the Friendship in Flowers exchange. (Courtesy of Roland W. Jefferson)

Japan's southern island of Kyushu in March 1982. However, he soon became concerned that the birds would eat the seed-containing fruits faster than he could collect them, so he approached Japanese schoolchildren, "with the aid of the Flower Association of Japan," and asked for their help. Thus was born Friendship in Flowers.[72]

Jointly sponsored by the Flower Association of Japan and the U.S. National Arboretum, the project enlisted schoolchildren in both countries to collect seeds of their native trees, which would then be exchanged with each other. The Japanese schoolchildren collected cherry fruits, then removed, cleaned, labeled, and dried the seeds to send to America, while American schoolchildren, contacted through schools and arboreta nationwide, did the same with our native dogwood (*Cornus florida*). Beloved by Presidents Jefferson and Washington (who planted "a circle of Dogwood with a red bud in the Middle, close to the old Cherry near the South Garden House" at his Mount Vernon home on his birthday in 1785),[73] this exquisite native tree apparently gets its ungainly name from the fact that its bark was once used as a remedy for dog mange. More than 2 million seeds were collected, cleaned, labeled, and exchanged. Gifts now grown old were revitalized in both countries, for after we had received our original gift of cherries in 1912 we had sent our dogwoods to Japan. Some were planted in one of Tokyo's parks, two were planted in the garden of the American embassy (these died and were replaced by three dogwoods in 1961, to the gratitude of Douglas MacArthur II), and "thousands of seedling American dogwoods were later sent out to the schools of Japan."[74] Plant a tree and you can, to mix a metaphor, eat your cake and have it too.

Or, to put it another way, plant a tree and you can be an Indian giver. "An Indian gift," Thomas Hutchinson explained to his readers in 1764, "is a proverbial expression signifying a present for which an equivalent return is expected."[75] Hutchinson makes it all sound a bit unseemly, that word "expected" is so pejorative. But not Walt Whitman:

> The gift is to the giver, and comes back
> most to him—it cannot fail . . . [76]

And not all of the fairy tales we read when we were young that included the appearance of a beggar who, if he were well treated, or given of the main character's substance, returned the gift manyfold, but if he were turned away, left whomever with everlasting curses. What would the beggar say, I wonder, to 2 million seeds?

Anticipating my trip to Washington to see the cherry blossoms, I hoped for an experience like that described by Lafcadio Hearn in his essay "My First Day in the Orient." "I see before me," he wrote around 1890, "a grove of cherry-trees covered with something unutterably beautiful,—a dazzling mist of snowy blossoms clinging like summer cloud-fleece about every branch and twig; and the ground beneath them, and the path before me, is white with the soft, thick, odorous snow of fallen petals." [77] But, of course, none of us experiences any aspect of nature in quite the same way as another. That is one of its most fundamental attractions; unlike art, nature is always new, always being created before our eyes—just for us, so to speak.

What was created for me was exceptional—and I use the word in its original meaning. I arrived in Washington on March 31, 1997. Winds were gusting to 50 mph and the temperature was hovering at a chilly 40. The Washington weather forecast was describing the storm I was experiencing, which would dump a record 25-inch snowfall on Boston and paralyze the entire Northeast, as a "coastal bomb." But, I had come to see the cherries, fully in blossom as of March 24, according to the Washington Post "Blossom Watch column," and off I went, nylon coat flapping like an untethered sail behind me. What I saw was a blizzard, of cherry petals—like horizontal snow being whipped off the trees—whitecaps on the Tidal Basin, and, considering the weather, a surprising number of other visitors who couldn't resist seeing the trees.

Today's trees comprise eleven ornamental cherry selections (only three of which were part of the 1912 gift) and are mostly Yoshinos (2,763), with smaller numbers of Kwanzan (481), Akebono (112), Takesimensis (190), Weeping Japanese Cherry (94), Sargent (21), Autumn Flowering (21), Fugenzo (14), Afterglow (2), Shiroflugen (1), and Okame (1). The National Park Service descriptive sign in West Potomac Park tells visitors that "individual blossoms last only three days but with good weather the overall display can last up to two weeks. An old Japanese proverb says 'Life is short, like the three days' glory of the cherry blossoms.'" [78]

I stayed for four glorious days and spoke to tree-gazers from Alabama,

20. Cherry trees in flower along the Tidal Basin in March 1997. (Photo: Gayle B. Samuels)

England, Korea, Pennsylvania, Michigan, Sweden, Germany, Wisconsin, Hong Kong, California, and Iran. We were some of that year's more than 600,000 visitors estimated by the National Cherry Blossom organization to visit the trees each spring.[79] The Iranians, two brothers and their families, are now living in the United States, one in New Jersey, the other in Louisiana. They had decided to meet in Washington to celebrate the Persian New Year and, although one brother said that "monoculture is not good for the urban forest," he added, "it might be justified" here because it attracts so many visitors to the park. They were aware that the trees were a gift of friendship from Japan to the United States, but they had come to see them because they represent both the beginning of their New Year and a symbol of spring. That sentiment, of the cherry trees as a symbol of spring, was echoed by almost all of the people I spoke with. Few thought about the tree's association with Japan, which two, the woman from London and the couple from Alabama, had not known about until shortly before arriving at the scene. A man from Michigan said that "when I think of Washington, I think of the cherry blossoms"; and so, it seems, do most of us.

We call them the Washington Cherry Blossoms, because that is what they have become—Americanized, both imaginatively and botanically. Mirrored, as they are, in the Tidal Basin, they are a reflection of America. They, like all of us hyphenated Americans and the introduced bounty of our land—from our apples and cherries, to our amber waves of grain, our oranges (thought to have been introduced in Florida in 1518 from seeds planted on Haiti by Columbus), and our avocados and mangoes introduced by David Fairchild's Bureau—have become a part of the land and people we call America. Where I live, for example, in the Northeast, each fall brings another opportunity to see how many botanical immigrants have found a place among our natives. As the botanist Edgar Anderson explains:

> Take the autumnal aspect of the central and eastern United States, roughly the region from Boston and Philadelphia to Minneapolis and Kansas City. In all that area, green in the landscape is a measure of European influence. The green grasses of pasture and roadside, the green trees of orchards and parks, are greens which have come with us from Europe. Our own native flora is bred for our violent American climate. It goes into the winter condition with a bang.[80]

Unlike Kublai Khan who, according to Eleanor Perényi, created the first Chinese arboretum from trees "brought from every part of his empire," we have distributed our assembled wealth across our entire continent. "Alien vegetation," Perényi continues, "is one of the signs of advancing culture, and progress can be measured by the acquisition of plants that produce food, medicine and new materials . . . [b]ut the ultimate luxury is the plant imported for its beauty alone."[81]

Nonetheless, prudent safeguards are essential. We need to select carefully, to weed out the botanical Boston stranglers and make every effort to protect our "biotic borders" [82] in the same way we protect our physical borders. However, we also need to recognize that growing human populations and the consequent reduction of native habitat also threaten our native plant life and, had Mrs. Taft not removed the American elms to make way for the Japanese flowering cherries, the elms would probably have died anyway, victims of an introduced fungus called Dutch Elm disease. First discovered in the United States in Ohio in 1930, after the Plant Quarantine Act had been in effect sixteen years, Dutch Elm disease has ravaged our native elm population. Try as we might to "protect our own," as David Fairchild recognized in 1917, "the whole trend of the world is toward greater intercourse." [83] The flowering cherries, on the other hand, have continued to grow in beauty. Approximately 90 percent of the 3,700 trees growing around the Tidal Basin and on the grounds of the Washington Monument are now American grown, propagated from stock introduced at the beginning of this century. The trees, says National Park Service Chief Horticulturalist Robert De Feo, have found a "balance of existence," they have adapted to the urban environment and the regional temperatures, soil conditions, and rainfall. [84] But while the trees have retained much of their genetic substance, they have also been imbued with a new spirit. Here in America, the flowering cherries have come to symbolize not the brevity of human life expressed by the Japanese proverb, but rather the eternal renewal of spring.

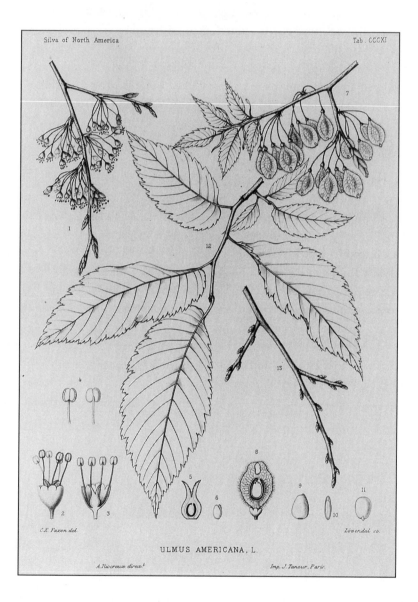

C.E. Faxon del.   Lövendal sc.

ULMUS AMERICANA, L.

A. Riocreux direx.t   Imp. J. Taneur, Paris.

CHAPTER FIVE

RETURNING NATIVES

LEAF: THE MAIN PHOTOSYNTHETIC ORGAN OF MOST GREEN PLANTS. . . .
THERE ARE USUALLY A GREAT NUMBER OF LEAVES ON ANY ONE PLANT,
ALTHOUGH THESE MAY BE LOST IN THE COLDER OR DRIER MONTHS IN
DECIDUOUS PLANTS.

STEPHEN BLACKMORE, *The Facts on File Dictionary of Botany*

M

y sister is telling me a story. It is about a woman who moved east from the prairie, following the prevailing winds. The woman, my sister says, felt confined. She could never get used to our eastern hills. She is telling me this story because I have just made the woman's journey in reverse, traveling against the wind, but with the flow of American history. Though mine was only a short stay, I tell my sister that it is impossible to be on the prairie for any time at all without understanding what the woman means.

Some have compared the prairie to the ocean: a long unbroken vista with the gentle wavelike motion of the tall grass moving in the wind. Others, and I am among them, find that "it is hard for the eye to wander from sky line to sky line, year in and year out, without finding a resting place!" [1] And, perhaps most famously, when Major Stephen H. Long was sent in 1820 to present-day Colorado on an unsuccessful search for the source of the Platte River, he designated Colorado's eastern plains the "Great American Desert" on his maps—maps that were then incorporated in school texts so that generations of Americans "grew up believing the high plains did indeed resemble the sandy Sahara" [2]—and he deemed the region "uninhabitable by a people depending upon agriculture for their subsistence." [3]

Long's reports were echoed. The explorer John Charles Frémont called Colorado's plains a "parched country," and the Vermont lawyer Thomas Farnham described the region as a "scene of desolation scarcely equaled on the continent." [4] The particular eastern Colorado grasslands that the three men and Long's botanist, Edwin James, found so "tiresome to the eye and fatiguing to the spirit" [5] are what we now call shortgrass prairie. The shortgrass is one—along with tall-grass, mixed-grass, California grassland, Palouse, and desert—of a vast network of grasslands that originally covered almost 40 percent of the United States. They are our largest

21. *Charles Sprague Sargent,* The Silva of North America, *vol. 7. (The McLean Library, Pennsylvania Horticultural Society, Philadelphia)*

biome—a term used by ecologists to describe a habitat created by shared vegetation and climate—and one of our most endangered: "an estimated 99 percent of the tallgrass prairie east of the Missouri River has been destroyed." [6]

Of the four major biomes covering the earth's surface—grassland, desert, forest, and tundra—grasslands are the largest. When the acreage of the North American prairies is combined with other corresponding patches of grassland—the Russian steppe, South American pampas, Hungarian puszta, and the South African veld—grasslands account for 24 percent of the earth's vegetation and include the plants "which have contributed the germ plasm [or DNA] for the principal human food crops." [7] Among these are wheat, barley, oats, and rice (the first two were domesticated about 10,600 years ago in the Middle East).

So it is not that the prairie is, or was, unproductive. The American prairie, for example, once provided forage for a herd of bison estimated to number around 50 million (compared with today's "45.5 million head of cattle in the ten states that were the main area of the original bison range"). [8] "Most of the productive, arable lands in North America," according to botanist Phillip L. Sims, "were once grasslands." [9] As Long told his men when they joined in an Independence Day toast on July 4, 1820, they were camping where "imagination only" had "traveled before." [10] And their imagination—and mine—was shaped, or some might say limited, by the eastern forested landscape.

The great divide that separates the prairie from the forest is water. Although the staggering diversity and adaptability of plants means that there will always be exceptions to any rule, tree growth is generally limited by two conditions—cold and moisture. Trees need 15 to 20 inches of annual precipitation and a frost-free period of around fourteen consecutive weeks. The American prairies were once covered by an inland sea, but the sea started to retreat about 75 million years ago as the Rocky Mountains began to rise, and the plains are now a mostly dry region. Average annual precipitation varies enormously from east to west—from almost 42 inches in some parts of the eastern tall-grass prairie to just about 8 inches in the southwestern desert grasslands—but, except for the tall-grass region, evaporation exceeds precipitation.[11] "Native tree growth," botanist Paul E. Collins explains, "is limited to stream courses, lake shores, hillside breaks and mountainous areas where soil-moisture relationships are favorable."[12]

But lack of moisture is only one of the two principal factors responsible for the creation and maintenance of the treeless prairie: the second is fire. First caused by Native Americans and lightning and later by steam engines and cowboys, fire "has been almost a constant event at one place or another in the grasslands, and some of these fires have been severe and enormous in size." Though it would seem that periods of high precipitation would eliminate fires, that is not the case. Both drought and high precipitation have stoked these fires, the latter by producing an abundance of fuel and the former by providing the tinderbox ready for any match.[13]

The results are the same in both cases: lack of trees. The combination of low moisture and frequent fire is more disastrous to trees than to grass. Because many grasses either have below-ground rhizomes or crowns which can survive fires and resprout quickly or produce seeds that can germinate under relatively dry conditions but stay dormant if those minimal conditions are not met, grasses can rush in where trees take longer to root.[14] Thus that vast horizontal landscape, unbroken by the vertical presence of trees. On a clear day, without hills or other obstructions, I am told you can see thirty miles to the horizon. Every one of my days on the High Plains or Colorado prairie was clear, and thirty miles is a long way to see.

From the air, of course, you can see even farther, back to the United States Geological Survey (USGS) lines. Everyone who flies across this continent remarks on our survey grid, our giant patchwork quilt created from bits of land taken from some, bought from others, and won from still others and then pieced together into a new American whole. The quilt now sports circles, appliqued on the earlier squares by pivot irrigation, but the squares that gave rise to the term "square deal" still remain, as does the landscape they created.

On May 20, 1785, when Congress passed the legislation authorizing the survey that would eventually cover two-thirds of the continental United States with a grid of six-mile-square townships, they were meeting in New York. "Each township, Congress directed, would be bounded by lines running due north-south and east-west; other parallel lines would divide each township into thirty-six square sections of 640 acres each."[15] Had they been meeting in Philadelphia, as they did earlier and later, they could have seen William Penn's grid in operation. Unlike the static circles of walled European towns, planned with a single town center in mind, the grid was a dynamic urban form that could be modified and extended in any direction without deviating from its original structure. It was also easily understood and easily replicated.

The particular dimensions chosen for the national grid by Congress reflected both technological advances and New England ideals. Edmund Gunter's early-seventeenth-century invention of "Gunter's Chain," a 22-yard chain of 100 links, eliminated the need for the mathematical skills formerly required for surveying. One acre, in Gunter's system, equals ten square chains and "640 acres fit precisely in a square mile of ground." Thus even in a new country where skilled surveyors were hard to come by, a 640-acre square was easily measured and just as easily divided into the 160-acre quarter sections Congress had decided upon as being the appropriate amount of land for America's yeoman farmers: Congressmen believed too much would make barons and too little would create paupers. The combining of 640-acre square parcels into six-mile-square townships—a size considered ideal for a New England–style settlement clustered around a central meetinghouse—reflected the New England settlement ideals first voiced in the anonymous 1638 document, "The Ordering of Towns." As with many ideals, this too hardly reflected reality, however, since New England towns were almost never square.[16]

The national survey began west of Pennsylvania and reached Colorado's High Plains between 1867 and 1872, planting the urban grid foursquare on the rural prairie. "Curved lines, you know," remarked Daniel Drake [in 1794], "symbolize the country, straight lines the city." Nonetheless, according to the historian John R. Stilgoe, "Americans accepted the grid . . . not only because it was a useful invention tempered with such traditional attributes as the statute mile and the 640-acre allotment but because it directly encouraged common enterprise. Philadelphia proved that an urban grid allowed every sort of adaptation, and the ordering of Ohio proved that within a gridded wilderness industrious settlers could shape the land according to whatever techniques suited them best."[17]

The techniques that suited the moist eastern woodlands of Ohio, however, would not be those that suited the dry prairies of Colorado, but the
survey made no distinctions. It ignored geography and local knowledge of
place in favor of a geometric ideal of land distribution. By being even-
handed it was not always realistic or fair: "160-acre tracts . . . were suffi-
ciently large in humid regions but far too small on the arid plains. Even
when the unit was increased to 320 acres in 1909, and to 640 acres in 1916,
it was still too small. In one-crop dry farming, half the land often has to be
allowed to lie fallow each year to accumulate moisture and furrows must
be plowed farther apart than ordinary."[18] But it was the Dust Bowl that
finally proved that the Plains could not be farmed in the same ways as
the more humid regions of the country: "the chief measure of the non-
adaptability of the humid-area culture to Plains conditions is the movement of dust. Dust indicates an over-extension of farming into areas best
used for other purposes."[19]

And, as the historian Patricia Nelson Limerick has remarked, "Only in
the imagination could virgin lands move smoothly into the hands of new
owners, transforming wilderness into farmland, idle men into productive
citizens. The 'virgin lands' were not vacant, but occupied. Redistributing
those lands to the benefit of white farmers required the removal of Indian
territorial claims and of the Indians themselves."[20] It was in 1867 that Colorado's Plains tribes, the Cheyenne and Arapahoe, were moved to reservations in Oklahoma—by about 1871 "removal of the Indians from eastern
Colorado" was complete[21] —it was also the year surveying began and the
year the railroad reached the Colorado border (two years before the trans-
continental linkage of the Union Pacific and Central Pacific in Utah). The
railroads made all sorts of transport faster and less expensive, including
transport of the heavy buffalo hides. The result was that the decade which
saw the removal of the Indians also saw the rapid dwindling of the once-
vast bison herds.[22] Then the farmers came—immigrants lured by cheap
land sold by the railroads and Americans eager to claim the 160 acres prom-
ised by the Homestead Act—and plowed the virgin prairie. Thus, as in the
drama that had been played out on the East Coast more than two hundred
years earlier—the age-old battle between Cain and Abel, between the
needs of a land-owning sedentary population and a land-using migratory
culture—ownership would change the face of the land.

• • •

"Of all the bewildering things about a new country," Willa Cather wrote in *O Pioneers!,* "the absence of human landmarks is one of the most depressing and disheartening." On the mostly featureless prairie, that feeling was intensified by the additional absence of natural landmarks, such as trees. The pioneers, wrote O. E. Rölvaag in *Giants in the Earth,* found that "nothing but an eternal, unbroken wilderness encompassed them round about, extending boundlessly in every direction." [23] A historic trail map that traces the route of the Overland Trail through the 7,230 square miles in the northeast corner of Colorado makes note of four trees, one with a question mark. In his 1888 work, *Trees and Tree-Planting,* General James S. Brisbin relates the effect of this treelessness:

> For four years I had lived on the plains surrounded by sage-brush and sand . . . then I was ordered east with troops, to Kentucky. We had been running very fast all night in the cars, and in the morning, just as I was washing in the sleeping-car, I heard the soldiers in the forward coaches cheering. I asked the conductor what was the matter, and he replied, "The soldiers are cheering the trees." We all hastened to the doors and windows, and there, sure enough, found we were running through a grand old Kentucky forest. . . . It was beautiful beyond description. [24]

The settlers who established the prairie's towns, farms, and ranches also felt this lack and made tree-planting a priority. During the first year of establishing the utopian agricultural community of Greeley, in 1870, on Colorado's eastern plains at the confluence of the South Platte and Cache la Poudre rivers, for example, the group of Union Colonists led by Nathan Meeker, agricultural editor of Horace Greeley's *New York Tribune* ("the most widely read periodical in nineteenth-century America"),[25] "surveyed the plot and laid out the streets of their town [naming the streets for trees and the avenues for famous Americans]; they planted trees; [and] they opened a school for their children." [26] They also built their first irrigation ditch, which, with the second and longer ditch built the following year, demonstrated the "potential of irrigated agriculture" [27] and inspired others to follow in their footsteps.

The first trees were less successful. They were brought from Bloomington [Illinois] Nurseries at a total cost of $1,490.90 and arrived "long before

water was in the ditch . . . [and although] most of them made a start . . . the great bulk of them died the following winter. The maples along Main street ditch, and the few elms in the park, are the relics of this early shade tree planting." [28] As Meeker observed in 1877, "when we located in this valley of Colorado, we had no kind of idea of the difficulties attending the culture of many kinds of vegetation. The great variety of forest trees which grow in the states without any trouble, many of them as spontaneously as weeds, can here scarcely be made to live when brought hither with the greatest care and cultivated with the utmost attention. . . . Our experience seems to be, that what we can save from the winter, and we can do a good deal in this way, the grasshoppers seize: they eat out buds and blossoms, cut off leaves, even gnaw bark, and do disgusting work." [29]

The town of Holyoke, due east of Greeley near the Kansas border, likewise set out trees and likewise learned the difficulties of prairie cultivation. Incorporated in 1888 and named "after a man by that name and said to have been from Holyoke, Mass.," the town experienced drought and hail in 1890, prairie fires in 1891, a winter that was so bad that "there was no seed in the community for spring planting," and yet "was beautified with 1500 new shade trees" in 1892. In 1894 there was another drought, this one so bad that "the grass didn't even green up all spring and summer" [30] and by 1896 records indicate that 75 percent of the original homesteaders had left, leaving their lands to be homesteaded again.

These difficulties were the norm, not the exception: regardless of when they came, whether it was first or second, earlier or later, everyone who has tried to cultivate the prairie has experienced the same cycles of weather, fire, and insects that had beset Colorado's first farmers, the "Fremont" peoples of western Colorado and then the Anasazi who inhabited the Four Corners region until around 1300. [31] "In the last quarter of the thirteenth century, the Anasazi abandoned most of their lands . . . [leaving presumably because of] a combination of soil exhaustion and drought seasons with summer flooding and gullying." More contemporary records indicate that "the years from 1865 to 1872 were dry, those from 1873 to 1885 were wet. Since then, droughts have come in cycles of twenty-one

22, 23, 24. The greening of Greeley, top to bottom, 1870 photo showing irrigation ditch; 8th Avenue c. 1887; 8th Street c. 1911. (City of Greeley Museums: Permanent Collection)

years, with the driest years occurring in 1892, 1912, 1934, and 1953. Total rainfall in the bad years drops 15 to 25 percent below normal, with most of the reduction during the July to August growing season." [32]

When Lucy Price's in-laws homesteaded their land near Julesburg, up by the Nebraska border, it was during the second decade of this century so they were among those lucky enough not to be immediately confronted by a severe drought. Nonetheless, what Lucy Price still talks about most when asked about the early years on the family ranch is how the trees were watered. Everyone, Lucy says, wanted trees: trees protected wildlife, provided shade, and served as a windbreak against the prairie winds that would later, during the Dust Bowl years of the 1930s, blow across this same region that Stephen Long had called the Great American Desert,[33] sending a message "east via dust." [34]

Trees also, as Jonathan Raban points out in *Bad Land,* "announced that their owners had water, agricultural know-how, and long occupancy of the

25. Colorado homestead surrounded by trees, 1997. (Photo: Stuart A. Samuels)

land. You could arrive at an accurate estimate of a given family's income, character, and standing in Montana just by looking at their shelter belt." [35]

Water, however, was scarce. To do laundry, for example, the Price family hauled barrels of water from the South Platte River, about ten miles away. When the laundry was done, the children were given their task: they carried the used wash water in buckets out to water the trees. [36]

The Price children were not alone. By the time they were watering their trees, another prairie resident had already enlisted schoolchildren across the country in a national crusade against treelessness. *Nebraska City News* editor J. Sterling Morton, who established "Plant Trees" as his family motto and Arbor Lodge as the family home in Nebraska City, had moved in 1854 to Nebraska, where he and his wife promptly transformed the treeless landscape with flowers, shrubs, and trees. In 1872 he suggested planting on a larger scale: he proposed that a tree-planting holiday be established, called Arbor Day, and that prizes be offered to individuals and counties that planted the greatest number of trees. His proposal was adopted and Nebraskans, according to the Nebraska City–based Arbor Day Foundation, planted more than one million trees that first year. Within two decades the popular idea had been adopted by states and schools nationwide. In his 1907 Arbor Day Proclamation addressed "To the School Children of the United States," President Theodore Roosevelt drew attention to the link between children and trees: "A people without children would face a hopeless future; a country without trees is almost as hopeless." [37]

Of course the future was only part of the equation. J. Sterling Morton and others recognized the very pragmatic and present-day need for trees as well. Trees were needed for building materials, fuel, and soil conservation. They were needed for windbreaks: as Sedgwick County (Colorado) extension agent Gary Lancaster explains, livestock fattens faster and crops grow better when they are protected from the wind. [38] They were needed for shade and they were needed for food. These were utilitarian trees, planted by the yeoman farmers to supply real and present needs.

Most of the first trees planted by the early settlers were what they could find close by: "at first wildings were dug from native stands and transplanted to home sites." [39] The Plains cottonwood (*Populus deltoides occiden-talis*)—the state tree of Nebraska and Kansas—the tree westward-moving settlers eagerly looked for as a marker of nearby water and a provider of cooking fuel, for example, was "prized for transplanting to offer at least token shade and surcease from constant winter winds." [40]

Native trees were, however, soon supplemented, and sometimes re-placed, by the non-native exotics available to municipalities and landowners through nurseries and the various farm- and forest-related programs of the United States Department of Agriculture (USDA). Writing in 1948, U.S. For-est Service landscape engineer Walter E. Webb notes the widespread nature of this practice: "during the past thirty years," *Ulmus pumila*, variously called the Chinese or Siberian elm, "was the main windbreak tree in the shelter-belts planted by the U.S. Forest Service. It comprises the largest proportion of the farmstead windbreaks and protection plantings made during the last two decades by farmers in that region [the Great Plains]. And observation will show that 75 percent or more of all new street, shade, and park trees planted within this area in the last few years are 'Chinese elms.'" [41]

In 1971 Collins noted the continuation of this practice: "since the choice of native species is relatively limited, plant introductions from other areas of the United States and from other continents have become an important part of Plains windbreak plantings. Some of the better introductions have come from Russia, Siberia, and Northern China where the trees have de-veloped under environmental conditions similar to the Great Plains." [42]

Because of its widespread use by the Forest Service, its highly favorable description in two USDA publications—the 1923 catalog of *Plant Introduc-tion* and the 1926 *Yearbook of Agriculture*—and the very complimentary "let-ters of those who had received some of the first trees sent out for trial," which were subsequently reprinted by nurserymen, the Siberian elm was among the most widely, if not the most widely, planted of all the intro-duced species. The catalog of *Plant Introduction,* for example, extolled the tree as "remarkably resistant to drought, alkali, and severe extremes of temperature . . . exceptionally valuable as a shade tree in the semi-arid regions . . . where it has made phenomenal growth. It also seems well adapted to the cold northern plains. . . . A remarkable tree which is rec-ommended highly especially for regions unsuited to most of the common shade trees." According to Webb, "the sales and planting of these trees probably surpassed those of any other single species in the history of this country."[43]

And while it is generally accepted, as Webb states, that "credit for the introduction of *Ulmus pumila* into the United States has been given to the noted plant explorer Frank N. Meyer" (hired by David Fairchild),[44] with the date of introduction most frequently cited as 1908, both of these facts have been disputed. A date of 1905 is suggested by Collins, and Donald J. Leopold, writing in the *Journal of Arboriculture*, supports that date and claims that the credit for introduction goes to "Professor J. G. Jack of the Arnold Arboretum when he sent plants of this species to Boston in 1905." But Leopold also notes, "that same year Frank N. Meyer, an Agricultural Explorer for the Department of Agriculture, and Charles S. Sargent of the Arnold Arboretum separately collected seeds of the Siberian elm in Peking."[45]

It seems clear, however, that it was Meyer's seeds, sent to the USDA and subsequently distributed by that agency to various cooperating field stations and individuals for testing, that ignited public interest, and subsequent demand, for the Siberian elm. Meyer biographer Isabel Shipley Cunningham places the Siberian elm in the first rank of Meyer's "2,500 plant introductions . . . from the Dakotas to Texas his elms serve as windbreaks on formerly treeless prairies."[46] A remarkable accomplishment in the context of Meyer's brief (1875–1918) but highly productive life, which included the introductions of such well-known plants as the dwarf lilac (*Syringa meyeri*), the eponymous Meyer spruce, the hybrid Korean flowering cherry (*Prunus x meyeri*), the Chinese hickory (*Carya cathayensis*), the Russian olive (*Eleagnus angustifolia*), the honey locust (*Gleditsia heterophylla*), two privets (*Ligustrum pisiformis* and *Ligustrum quihoui*), the bamboo (*Phyllostachys heterocycla*) that "became fodder for the famous pandas . . . at the National Zoo,"[47] and the first discovery in the wild of the Ginkgo tree. Cunningham treats the Siberian elm first in describing "the significance of his work":

People who lived on the arid plains and the windswept prairies of the United States during the early years of the twentieth century were pathetically eager to find any shade tree that would grow there. The most widely used of all Meyer's drought-resistant trees have been the Siberian elm (*Ulmus pumila*). This dry-land elm now thrives from Canada to Texas, breaking the searing winds on vast prairies. In the late 1930s a doctor from North Dakota told [David] Fairchild that he had gone as a boy to the USDA experiment station at Mandan and begged a handful of elm seedlings. The tiny plants were no larger than knitting needles, but they became magnificent trees before many years had passed. Multiplying this experience by thousands offers some conception of the extent of Meyer's contribution to life in America through a single introduction. When prolonged drought threatened to turn the prairie states into a permanent dust bowl, Meyer's elm helped to form the shelterbelt, a system of 17,000 miles of windbreaks planted between 1935 and 1942 by the Prairie State Forestry Project in order to reduce wind erosion and to conserve soil moisture.[48]

More poignantly, Donald Culross Peattie remembers opening a letter from a ranch woman in eastern Montana during his days at the Office of Foreign Seed and Plant Introduction. It read: "We got no trees hear. They all blowed down or dide. For God's sake send us shade." Peattie replied: "I sent her Meyer's Mongolian elm. It withstands drought, flood, alkali, insects, fungus diseases, searing heat and killing cold."[49]

Opinion, however, was not universally positive when it came to the Siberian elm. Even as the Prairie State Forestry Project was continuing to plant the trees to combat erosion, two Project foresters, Harold E. Engstrom and Lewis S. Matthew, were suggesting that "native species should constitute the mainstay of any Plains tree-planting program, and that the less hardy exotic species such as the Siberian elm should be included only to the extent necessitated by their important temporary benefits."[50] The catalyst for Engstrom and Matthew's suggestion was their review of the effects of the highly destructive Armistice Day freeze of 1940 on various Plains trees.

In 1938 and again in 1940, a severe freeze hit the Plains on Armistice Day. The effect on trees was: "Armistice Day, 1940, will go down in the annals of Plains history as the starting date of a disastrous blizzard and cold wave which swept through almost the entire Plains country, killing or severely injuring millions of trees." Lessons had been drawn from both experiences. Looking at the 1938 event, Webb had concluded that the trees grown from Siberian elm seed that had been collected from more southerly Chinese sites, such as Nanking, experienced the greatest losses, and he recommended collecting new seed from the Plains survivors to ensure the hardiness of future stock. After studying the 1940 freeze, however, Engstrom and Matthew concluded that "the outstanding lesson to be learned from the Armistice Day freeze is that native species came through without noticeable damage whereas many exotics or species planted outside their native range suffered more or less heavily."[51] The specific native species cited were "green ash (*Fraxinus pennsylvanica* var. *lanceolata*), American elm (*Ulmus americana*), bur oak (*Quercus macrocarpa*), and black walnut (*Juglans nigra*).[52] C. G. Bates, who commented on Engstrom and Matthew's article, was even more forceful: "In my opinion . . . the case against the Chinese or Siberian elm in the Plains region is so incriminating that I cannot see any possible excuse for continuing the expenditure of public funds for planting it in shelterbelts or anywhere else."[53]

This advice, however, went unheeded. World War II interrupted many of the government-sponsored planting programs, but Siberian elms continued to be planted as a landscape tree by the returning GIs who, on the Plains as elsewhere, were buying new homes in record numbers. "Quick shade boiled down to two species," as Morton Arboretum Research Associate George H. Ware points out, "Siberian elm and silver maple."[54] Thus a new stock of elms was added to those already planted.

Other years would see other fall freezes and two new adversaries would also beset the painstakingly cultivated Plains trees, native and exotic alike—an introduced fungus and tree-banning legislation. The 1969 freeze, for example, preceded Colorado's "decade-long 1970s battle to save its American elms from DED."[55] (Dutch elm disease, *Graphium ulmi,* reached the United States in 1930[56] and has resulted in the deaths of "as many as 95% of American elms."[57]) And during that decade and the next, a Plains native, the hardy Plains cottonwood, became the subject of legislation in two Colorado communities. As early as 1941, the WPA guide to Colorado had noted that the Plains cottonwood had fallen from favor: "native cottonwoods, esteemed by early settlers on the hot plains, have been largely replaced in the more populous areas with more desirable poplars, elms, maples, birches, and locusts."[58] In 1976 it fell even further: an anonymous article in the *Greeley Tribune* reported that "Greeley Mayor George Hall doesn't like trees that bear cotton-like seed pods and thinks the city should begin a program of removing them from public right-of-way." [59]

What came to be called "Greeley's Great Cottonwood Controversy" [60] sprung from a petition signed by ten Greeley residents who, with four cottonwoods close by, claimed "'cotton' from the trees poses a health problem . . . it's difficult to keep the 'cotton' out of houses, even when windows are screened." Although Greeley Councilwoman Irma Princic objected, stating "I have a problem with taking down trees that are healthy. . . . It takes so long to grow a tree in this climate," another group of residents supported the first petitioners at a subsequent Council meeting and, in March of 1977, Greeley adopted a new ordinance banning "planting along [city] parkways . . . any trees of the poplar-cottonwood 'populus' species as well as the willow (Salix) species, box elders, Siberian Elms, weeping or pendulous trees such as the weeping birch, any with a bushy multiple growth of more than one leader or trunk, Russian Olives, honey locusts, conifers that could disrupt a sidewalk or any potentially disruptive shrub or hedge." [61] In 1988, the city of Sterling also banned cottonwoods, making it "unlawful to sell or import into the city or to plant or cause to be planted within the city limits any seed-bearing cottonwood tree (Genus populus) or any other specifically designated tree." [62]

Just south of Greeley, however, in rural La Salle, farmer Ken Krause objected loud and long, contacting, in addition to the county officials, the Army Corps of Engineers and the U.S. Soil Conservation Service, when county road crews chopped down three trees of the offending varieties—one willow and two Russian olives—along a county right-of-way. Krause, whose 240-acre farm was homesteaded by his "Russian immigrant-grandfather . . . in the early 1900s" and "nearly blew away . . . during the height of the 1930s Dust Bowl," says of the trees that "it's really hard to get them started . . . but trees do so many things. Once you get them in there, your banks won't erode." [63]

In one sense, contemporary Plains residents had done what their tree-hungry ancestors, like Ken Krause's grandfather, would have found unimaginable: they had cut down healthy trees and legislated against planting species native to the region. Greeley and Sterling, of course, no longer look like their former selves. They both now boast streets and parks lined and planted with trees that are fully mature. These legislators were not the same people who were confronted by the "Great American Desert," but rather people faced with the choices presented by life in contemporary America. And their choice, which continues to be our choice in most places, is to shape the natural world to satisfy human preference. It is the same choice that residents of Albuquerque, New Mexico, made when they decided to ban pollen-producing trees in an effort to reduce the pollen counts "that torture allergy sufferers" like me.[64] It is the same desire that propels us to create fragile gardens out of sturdy wildernesses and plant lawns where climates militate against grass. Or, to put it another way, it is a part of the same desire that led to planting trees on the prairie in the first place. Every so often, however, we are reminded of our limitations; we see these choices—to plant trees in the grassland and grass in the woodlands— in context.

Such a reminder came from October 27 through November 4, 1991, the period that has come to be called the Halloween freeze. On October 27, "a deadly mass of arctic air began to descend from Canada onto the high plains. Record cold temperatures were felt for days: the effects will be felt for decades."[65] Temperatures in Denver, for example, that had reached 89 degrees on October 17, in what had been an unusually mild fall on the Plains, fell to 7 on October 29.[66] And Denver was not unique: Greeley dropped from 91 degrees on the 17th to 8 on the 29th—temperatures at the Greeley high school football game were 10 to 15 degrees at kickoff on November 1 and the 10- to 15-mph winds drove "wind-chill factors to 10 to 15 degrees below zero."[67] "High temperatures [in Greeley] stayed below the freezing mark from Oct. 28 through Nov. 4."[68] "In Lamar, Colorado, 170 miles southeast of Denver, the temperature on the night of November 2 fell from the day's high of 28 degrees F. to −16F., well below the all-time low for that date."[69]

Colorado was one of five states to be affected. The "severe and devastating freeze . . . encompass[ed] the Dakotas, Western Nebraska, Eastern Colorado and Western Kansas."[70] Estimates of tree loss for the region vary considerably from the 401,600 "street and park trees and other public trees"[71] estimated by the Council of Western State Foresters, to figures of "400,000 dead trees in the Denver area" and a total of 850,000 in Colorado alone.[72] The larger estimates try to incorporate losses sustained on private property along with those lost on public land, but, of course, no one knows exactly how many trees have been, and continue to be, lost as a result of the freeze. Placing a dollar value on the dead trees—an estimate of removal and replacement costs—the November 17, 1992, *Rocky Mountain News* put the cost of the freeze at $425 million, making it "more costly than any tornado or snowstorm in Colorado history."[73]

Many trees were unprepared. The warm weather that preceded the freeze caused some tree species to delay dormancy. In *The Growing Tree,* forester Brayton F. Wilson explains the significance of the warm weather:

> Shortening photoperiods cue the tree to develop dormant buds and lose their leaves, but it is the first cold days of autumn that are the environmental cue for trees to develop resistance to below-freezing temperatures. When trees are growing, the cells cannot stand below-freezing temperatures because ice crystals forming inside the cells tear membranes and kill the cells.[74]

So it is the combination of temperature, day length, and the availability of water and nutrients—typically less in the winter than in the other seasons—that are the principal factors influencing dormancy, a process that includes both the familiar shedding of leaves and the invisible hormonal changes that create "'antifreeze' that is reproduced chemically by sap changing from sugars to starches and fats."[75] The Plains trees had also been weakened, according to Plant Pathologist and Consulting Arborist Steve Day, by a freeze in the winter of 1988–89, which "likely resulted in freeze damage, tissue death, and cavitation of xylem vessels (the water conducting system) from which it appears that many trees did not fully recover."[76]

Although there were some immediate signs of trouble, for the most part the loss did not begin to become apparent until the following spring when trees failed to leaf out. The lack of leaves—or, as Emily Dickinson calls them, "ribbons of the year"[77]—meant that the trees would be unable to produce enough carbohydrates, or energy, since the leaves are the principal site of photosynthesis, the chemical process that converts sunlight, water, and carbon dioxide into carbohydrates. It is photosynthesis that makes life on earth possible: first, by creating the food that we and all other animals eat at some point in the food chain, and second, by releasing oxygen as a waste product.

All leaves accomplish this miraculous transformation of nonliving elements into living tissue, but their individual forms, fragrances, and hues are enormously—possibly infinitely—variable. Witness the needlelike leaves of pine trees, the fragrant leaves of the eucalyptus, or the bronze foliage of the European beech (*Fagus sylvatica atropunicea*). Of the 341 specific terms for leaves listed in James G. and Melinda Woolf Harris's *Plant Identification Terminology*, elm leaves can generally be described as simple (meaning undivided, not separated into leaflets), toothed (this refers to the leaf margins; Siberian elms are single-toothed whereas American elms are double-toothed), alternate (as opposed to opposite; a description of its placement on the branch), with its surfaces either glabrous (smooth), scabrous (rough), or pubescent (with soft hairs), generally oblong-ovate in shape, short-stemmed, straight-veined, and unsymmetrical at the base.

It was the leaves that caught the attention of Colorado's assistant state climatologist, Nolan Doesken. He remembers noticing "the different sound of the winter wind"[78] that year. Many of the last trees to go dormant, those that hold onto their leaves late into the fall, such as the Siberian elm, had failed to produce "the abscission layer of cells . . . [that] caus[es] the stem of the leaf to break off"[79] and thus had not shed their leaves before the killing freeze. So winter 1991 had a different sound.

Spring and summer 1992 brought a different look. An anonymous article in the May 1992 *Holyoke Enterprise* reported, under a headline proclaiming "Tree Damage Drastic This Year," that a "casual drive around almost any neighborhood will reveal scattered examples of the freeze injury."[80] The City of Sterling Ten-Year Urban Forestry Management Plan noted that "due to the severe and sudden freeze in 1991, the urban forest in Sterling has suffered almost a complete kill of the Siberian elm trees. The extent of the damage was not determined until the spring and summer of 1992, but even then there were many trees, which looked as if they had survived. As the summer heat approached these trees which appeared to have survived began to completely die."[81] John Laut of the Colorado Forest Service said that "cities lost between 20% and 60% of their tree cover" compared with normal annual die-offs of between 3 and 4 percent.[82] In Kansas, "a loss of 51% of the streetside Siberian Elm occurred in the Northwest's 69 communities and 44% in the Southwest's

55 communities. . . . This represents . . . a combined loss to Western Kansas of 29% of the total streetside population."[83]

In Greeley, which probably lost "10 to 15 percent of its trees" as a result of the freeze, City Forester Joe Lohnes noticed that the original native cottonwoods had survived unscathed. He has also noticed a historical shift in thinking that has affected attitudes toward planting and maintaining trees, as it has toward other aspects of what we call community: Greeley's original settlers "had to buy into community standards" and work to establish "an oasis on the prairie," but "people changed around the thirties . . . they started looking for the government to take care of things." Now, according to Lohnes, many residents "perceive the trees as a liability" because of the care and expense they require. The city that had originally named its streets for trees abandoned those names less than two decades later in favor of numbers (today numbered streets go east and west and numbered avenues run north and south), because "it was less provincial, more efficient and like a big city." The native cottonwood was also replaced and modernized: in the 1960s and 1970s a cottonless cottonwood hybrid gained popularity. But Lohnes believes that "the [cottonwood] hybrids won't be here in the long haul." There is a move afoot, he explains, to use the male native cottonwood again; it generally lives to the century mark whereas the hybrids begin to develop problems at around thirty to thirty-five years old. Today Greeley is "broadening its tree base," adding bur oaks, ash, black walnut (three of the native species recommended by Engstrom and Matthew), and male native cottonwoods, planting far fewer soft maples and using honey locust to a controlled extent.[84]

Sterling's response has been similar—diversification. "To reduce the possibility of having a major kill of the urban forest," Sterling's Ten-Year Urban Forestry Plan suggests, "the replanting effort will need to be towards a diversity of species which are proven to grow well in this region of Colorado."[85] "The seven species selected for addition to the urban forest . . . which includes Honey Locust, Juniper, Pine, Catalpa, Redcedar, and American Elm . . . are: Oak, Hackberry, Green Ash, Blue Spruce, Linden, Pinyon, and Maple." And, as in Greeley, Sterling's director of Parks, Library and Recreation, Mike Jackson, says that 50 percent of homeowners "would rather not have these large trees" because of associated work and expense. "But," Jackson also supports Lohnes's views about the role of government in this regard, "if their neighbors didn't have trees and the town didn't plant trees, I think they'd be planting." [86]

In much smaller Holyoke, which lost about 25 percent of its trees, "everyone," according to City Superintendent Mark Brown, "was pretty sad." Many of the trees had been planted seventy-five years ago when "there was a push out of Nebraska to plant elms." Brown was personally saddened by the sight of the cemetery where his parents are buried. It lost about eighty trees, almost all Siberian elms. "It's heartbreaking to see such a beautiful place turned into nothing but a grass field," he said. "The older generation was heartbroken." "They planted these trees when they were young kids and now they just died." In addition to the generational differences in response to the tree loss, Brown noted differences between farmers and townies. To the farmers "trees served a function, they were not a thing of beauty." [87]

I found the distinction less clear cut: for me and for the ranchers and farmers I spoke with, function and feeling seemed to merge. However the calculations are made, private losses were as high as those sustained by cities and towns. Colorado Acting District Forester Damon Lange estimates that 85 percent of the trees planted around prairie homes were the vulnerable Siberian elms. "Farmers and ranchers lost entire windbreaks planted by their parents and grandparents." [88] Like Ken Krause, Julesburg wheat farmer Leroy "Butch" Blockowitz lost trees that were planted by his parents during the Dust Bowl years. "You want to cry, but you're too damn big," Blockowitz said at first, but later remarked that "anything that's got a pulse or a leaf on, it's going to leave you someday" and "whoever plants a good tree never lives to enjoy it." [89]

Lucy Price said it is "like losing a kid." "Then you have to start over again." And Gary Lancaster, who farms part-time, said, "it's like losing an old friend" and "it's hard to explain the difference—it makes you double tired to work in the wind." Another part-time wheat farmer who, with her husband, has lost half of their trees due to the freeze and subsequent early frosts, says, "we hold our breath every time a storm comes," but also points out that they needed to remove a number of trees when they first bought their farm, because they were planted randomly, not "in rows or anything." [90] Straight lines—of crops, trees, and surveys—allow us to suppress randomness, to feel in control.

Is it harder to lose the landscape we construct than the natural landscape we inherit? Planting a tree on the prairie meant you had decided to stay. It meant putting down roots. Trees shaded homes and graves, protected live-stock and crops, marked the changing seasons and the passing years, and conveyed a certain sense of community with the unspoken knowledge that someone, sometime had planted this tree. Gary Lancaster did not plant his trees and, since he bought his farm, his trees were not reminders of parents or grandparents, but, nonetheless, his trees were "old friends." The con-structed landscape is almost always the landscape we live closest to, the landscape we care for, and the landscape that is a part of our daily lives.

But our daily, and more long-term, experience of life is always a matter of trial and error, an experiment of sorts. "Experience" and "experiment," as it happens, come from the same root word, which means, according to the *Oxford English Dictionary,* "to try, to put to the test." [91] We are always trying to sort out the successes from the failures. In our haste to find so-lutions we sometimes take the quick fix. We think we can let someone else do the planting, as long as there are still trees around. Or we plant today's or yesterday's miracle tree and see that when it is put to the test, as hap-pened with the Siberian elm, it is tomorrow's disaster.

It "turned out that the American elm wasn't fazed," as George Ware said. It turned out that native species were hardier than exotics, that on the Plains, at least, Alexander Pope's famous advice to Lord Burlington to "let *Nature* never be forgot. Consult the *Genius* of the *Place* in all," [92] is worth considering. And, as a result of another experiment of sixty years (an-nounced synchronously as front-page news in *USA Today* during my visit to the devastated Colorado prairie) spanning "three generations of scien-tists and tests on 60,000 elm trees" [93]—the beloved American elm is poised for a comeback. Long favored as a council and treaty tree of Native Ameri-cans (hence the choice of the American elm at Shackamaxon, where Wil-liam Penn and Tamend negotiated "what was probably the only absolutely upright treaty offered the red man"), [94] American elms served as meeting place of all Americans (thus it was under the shade of an American elm that the first local government in what is now Kentucky was convened in 1775). Likewise, on the University of Chicago campus a "Council Elm" was the April 1942 site where "the world's leading atomic scientists held a highly secret discussion—outdoors, for fear of being bugged—in their quest for the first self-sustained nuclear chain reaction."[95] And because the quality of the shade produced by the million plus leaves of a large elm is unique—"an exquisite dapple of airy light and shifting shadow . . . [that] may cast its shade over nearly half an acre"[96]—perhaps we will again come together under its branches.

The new tree, which, like some other American elms introduced during the last decade, has been bred by selecting trees with "anti-Dutch elm disease qualities" has been named Valley Forge by government researcher Denny Townsend "in honor of George Washington's troops, who overcame almost insurmountable odds to survive the winter of 1777–78 at

26. *The Oklahoma City Survivor Tree. The tree, which survived the 1995 blast that killed 168 people and destroyed the Alfred P. Murrah Federal Building that formerly stood behind the tree and in front of the church, will be surrounded by a low circular wall in the bombing memorial. (Courtesy of Mark Bays)*

Valley Forge, Pa."⁹⁷ It is a name that celebrates human triumph over natural adversity. There is another case, however, where another American elm stands for the reverse, a natural triumph over human adversity: the Oklahoma City "Survivor Tree." Victims, survivors, and family members have gathered around that tree to "pour water on the trunk signifying the tears they have shed since the [April 19, 1995] explosion" that killed 168 women, men, and children. The tree is featured prominently in the design for the bombing memorial.⁹⁸

The Survivor Tree, as Oklahoma urban forestry coordinator Mark Bays explains, "really is a true survivor." Because of its setting in the middle of a concrete and asphalt parking lot, "it was already up against odds" before the heat and force of the explosion propelled the hood of a car into its canopy. "It is amazing to see a tree able to grow to that size in that setting." And while the approximately ninety-year-old tree is currently in good health, Oklahoma's Forestry Services are coordinating an entirely volunteer effort by Oklahoma's nursery association, tree-care industry, city employees, foresters, and universities to care for the tree. They are also taking cuttings of the tree for clonal reproduction, Bays explains, assuring that whenever the tree does die, an exact clone will be available to replace it.

The tree, meanwhile, is reproducing itself by forming seeds. The seeds are being collected and presented to the families of survivors and victims to be planted in places of their own choosing to help with the "healing process." Thus we join the birds and other mammals as the agents of seed dispersal. It is, as the seed-distribution process always is, a synergy of species. And in this case, unlike the Siberian elm seeds collected by Frank Meyer and subsequently dispersed across America, we have a better idea that what we are doing will work. It seems that this tree, as Bays tells me, has been "able to adapt to whatever was thrown at it." It seems on any given day at any place on the planet we need that.

Mark Bays doesn't know when seeds of the Survivor Tree might be available for wider distribution, and Valley Forge will not be available to the public for several years. But the Plains cottonwoods and American elms that survived the freeze of 1991 will nonetheless be having company. Called Liberty elms, after Boston's Liberty [elm] Tree which, because it served as a rallying point for the Sons of Liberty before and during the American Revolution, was cut down and burned by British soldiers in

1776, these are among the first of the American elms to be introduced as a result of the decades-long selection process.[99] Which of the American elms will prove hardiest is still unclear, but what is clear is what Joe Lohnes tells me: this spring, the spring of 1998, Greeley will be planting an American native called Liberty.

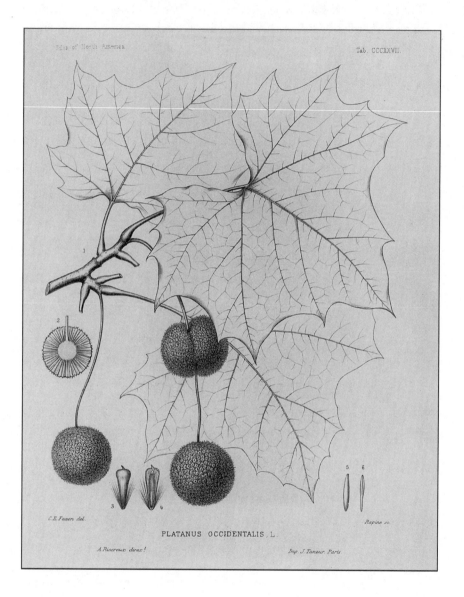

C.E.Faxon del.

Rapine so.

PLATANUS OCCIDENTALIS, L.

A.Riocreux direx.t

Imp. J.Taneur, Paris.

THE TREE
THAT OWNED
ITSELF

BARK: THE OUTERMOST LAYERS OF A WOODY STEM INCLUDING ALL OF
THE LIVING AND NONLIVING TISSUES EXTERNAL TO THE CAMBIUM.

JAMES G. HARRIS AND MELINDA WOOLF HARRIS,
Plant Identification Terminology

AS THE THICKNESS OF THE BARK INCREASES THE OUTER LAYERS MAY
EITHER BECOME FISSURED (E.G. ELM) OR BE SHED AS SCALES (E.G.
PLANE [SYCAMORE]) OR RINGS (E.G. BIRCH).

STEPHEN BLACKMORE, *The Facts on File Dictionary of Botany*

O n August 30, 1918, Curtis Pigmon, acting in his official capacity as clerk of the County Court for Knott County, Kentucky, signed and recorded a deed of conveyance "by and between Alice S. G. Lloyd, Trustee of the Caney Creek Community Center . . . and Mrs. J. W. Elliott of Boston, Trustee for the 'Freed Budd Sycamore Tree', of Caney Creek . . . party of the second part." The deed goes on to say: "that for and in consideration of its shade, coolness and inspiration . . . the party of the first part hereby conveys to the party of the second part, in trust for the use and benefit of the said Sycamore tree, and to itself as absolute owner, together with the terra firma upon which it stands and grows . . . in consideration of the value of itself as a resting place for the weary under the shade of said tree, and the said tree and said terra firma are to belong to themselves absolutely and to each other for all of the purposes for which nature and God intended them, among which is the purpose of the soil to nurture and feed the tree, and that of the tree to shade, grace and beautify the said terra firma." [1]

The history of the two women and the tree reveals that the tree was the only Kentucky native (although we can't be certain about the ephemeral Mrs. Elliott). Alice Spencer Geddes Lloyd moved to Kentucky at the age of thirty-eight and spent the next forty-seven years of her life there, "leaving behind a college, a community center, and a legend." [2] The Massachusetts-born Lloyd, her husband, and her mother settled in Kentucky in 1915, according to Lloyd biographer P. David Searles, as the result of a search for a locale "where they might continue their benevolent work," which had come to an unhappy conclusion in New Hampshire. [3] They moved to eastern Kentucky, in the same remote Pine Mountain region as the Hindman Settlement School, where, on a September evening in 1917, the English ballad collector Cecil Sharp "listened to mountain children sing ballads that, though nearly extinct in England, still thrived in the

27. *Charles Sprague Sargent, The Silva of North America, vol. 7. (The McLean Library, Pennsylvania Horticultural Society, Philadelphia)*

mountains of eastern Kentucky."[4] The area was impoverished as well as remote. "Knott County in 1916 had only one college graduate; few of its citizens could read or write and there was no public high school in an area encompassing parts of four counties. The average annual income was under twenty-five dollars."[5]

Although Lloyd and her husband separated in 1918, Lloyd stayed on and established the Caney Creek community center, seven high schools, the college that still bears her name, and, along the way, changed the name of the community from Caney Creek to Pippa Passes (after the Robert Browning poem of that name, which tells the story of one person's ability to effect a positive change in the lives of those with whom she interacts). From the outset, Lloyd's goal was to train community leaders, and her tuition-free college required that students work at school maintenance during their studies there and sign a pledge to serve the region's people after graduation. During her lifetime—Lloyd died in 1962—"more than 200 graduates went on to universities, all expenses paid, while over 1,200 served as educators in mountain counties."[6] The tuition-free nature of the institution, however, required that Lloyd be a nonstop fund-raiser. This perennial activity was the catalyst for the deed of conveyance.

June Buchanan, who worked closely with Lloyd, recalled the event in a 1975 newspaper interview: "When Alice Lloyd first arrived in Caney, the loggers had already been through the area leaving naked hillsides. Because of this, the few big trees . . . were dearly prized. . . . the Sycamore tree was used by the Indians for a trail blazer. A woman came from Boston and said to Mrs. Lloyd, 'I'll give you two hundred and sixty dollars, if you'll sell me that tree.'"[7] After establishing that the purpose of the purchase was to preserve the tree, Lloyd, who was perennially short of cash, accepted the gift of the woman identified on the deed as Mrs. J. W. Elliott of Boston, and the deed was drawn, manumitting the tree, like a human slave.

The choice of the sycamore—instead of one of the other large trees—is an interesting one considering the species' history. Sycamores are not only native to Kentucky in our time, they have been natives of that place since the evolution of flowering plants almost 130 million years ago. And for the past 130 million years, the preferred habitat of the sycamore has been the same habitat as that of the Caney Creek Freed Budd Sycamore,

28. The Freed Budd Sycamore Tree, probably in the 1920s, standing adjacent to Sycamore Dormitory on the grounds of Alice Lloyd College. (Special Collections, Alice Lloyd College)

29. Middle Eocene (c. 43 million years ago) sycamore fossil leaf (Platanus sp.) (Photo © David Dilcher. Courtesy David Dilcher and Terry Lott, Florida Museum of Natural History)

alongside a stream or riverbank. (Recent Chinese discoveries of the fossil remains of a 142-million-year-old flowering plant, or angiosperm, suggest that paleobotanists will be pushing this date back significantly. Announced jointly by Ge Sun of the Nanjing Institute of Geology and Paleontology and David L. Dilcher of the University of Florida, and reported on November 27, 1998, in both the journal *Science* and the *New York Times,* this discovery supplements earlier, but inconclusive, reports based on less complete fossil evidence.) Nevyle Shackelford, University of Kentucky College of Agriculture public information specialist, writes of the eastern Kentucky habitat of this sycamore: "the area had seen the growth and decay of the giant horsetails of prehistoric times. It had known Indians of the Adena and Hopewell cultures and was a living library of botanical and geologic records dating back to time primordial." [8]

Members of a group of plants called platanoids, which "represents some of the most ancient of the flowering plants," sycamores emerged before the present continents took shape, before the last of the dinosaurs died out, and before the Alps, Andes, and Rockies were formed. During the late Cretaceous period (about 95 million years ago) the platanoids ranged "from Alaska and Greenland to New Mexico, from Portugal and England to Siberia and Japan . . . inhabit[ing] nearly all of the Arctic landmasses and even extend[ing] to within 500 miles of the North Pole." Today *Platanus,* the genus of the sycamore, is the only remaining platanoid and its range has contracted considerably, "due, in part, to the evolution of members of the Willow Family, particularly the willows, poplars, aspens, and cottonwoods which competed with the platanoids for space in the riverside habitat." Eight species remain with the largest contemporary population in North America and smaller populations in Greece, the Himalayas, southern Cambodia, Laos, and Vietnam.

Of these eight, three species are native to the continental United States: the American sycamore (*Platanus occidentalis*), the California sycamore (*P. racemosa*), and the Arizona sycamore (*P. wrightii*), with the largest of these being "the American sycamore [which] is native to the eastern and southern United States . . . and may grow as tall as 170 feet and attain a trunk diameter of fifteen feet." [9]

This most massive of our native deciduous trees was frequently cut into cross-sections and fashioned into cart wheels by the pioneers, according to Donald Culross Peattie. "It is told," the *WPA Guide to Kentucky* notes, "that some of the hollow sycamores were so large that families were known to have camped in them until they could build cabins." [10] Later, we used sycamore for barber poles, lard pails, piano and organ cases, and the "broad panels that could be sawed out of Sycamore recommended it for use in Pullman cars." Because of the difficulty of splitting the wood, today's sycamore, the tree Peattie calls "the outstanding riverbank tree of the primeval forest, unsurpassed in picturesque grandeur and in the cooling depth and mighty spread of its shade," [11] most frequently shows up in butcher blocks or, more ingloriously, as wood pulp. (I, of course read "wood pulp" and think of paper napkins, not the pages of this book. What vanity.)

Commenting on another of the sycamore's characteristics, the well-known English apothecary and plantsman John Parkinson reported as early as 1640 that "they are planted by the waysides and in market places for the shadowes sake onely," [12] drawing attention to the large leaves from which the sycamore derives its genus *Platanus,* from the Latin word for "broad." "The sycamore leaf was well designed for maximum photosynthetic efficiency," according to paleontologist Kirk Johnson. "Sycamores produced immense deciduous leaves that gathered a maximum amount of sunlight with a minimum investment of energy in the production of supportive tissue by the plant." [13]

They are memorable trees in any locale. Herodotus, for example, tells the story of the Persian King Xerxes, who paused on his way to invade Greece because he was so taken by a particularly magnificent sycamore along the banks of the Maeander River near Kallatebos in western Turkey. So taken was he by this tree that he halted his army for days to admire its beauty, festooned it with gold trinkets, and appointed a man to guard the tree forever. [14] In his early and comprehensive study of America's trees, his 1819 *The North American Sylva,* the French botanist François A. Michaux provided firsthand information about the extraordinary size attained by some sycamores:

> [In Ohio] my father measured a Buttonwood [another name for sycamore] which . . . was more than 13 feet in diameter. Twenty years before General Washington had measured the same tree, and found it to be of the same size. . . . [There is also] the famous Plane Tree [yet another name for the sycamore] of Lycia spoken of by Pliny, whose trunk, hollowed by time, afforded a retreat for the night to the Roman Consul Licinius Mutianus, with eighteen persons of his retinue. [15]

And about a hundred years before the Freed Budd Sycamore came to own itself, well after we had decided to sever our political ties to the Old World, our botanical ties were reasserted in the cross of the two sycamore species mentioned by Michaux. This cross of the American sycamore and the Oriental sycamore (*Platanus orientalis*, native to Greece, Turkey, and the Himalayas) produced "perhaps the best of all street trees," [16] and one of the most widely grown on both continents, *Platanus acerifolia*, the tree in front of my grandmother's house.

Regardless of their country of origin, however, all sycamores share the distinguishing characteristic that most of us remember them by, the conspicuous mottled bark and whitewashed branches that make them so beaconlike in the winter landscape. Their look of dappled sunlight discernable even on a cloudy day is a characteristic reminiscent of the "twilight effects" of Kentucky's primeval forests. This is because, as Harriet L. Keeler tells us in *Our Native Trees,* the sycamore "casts its bark as well as its leaves," [17] a process necessitated by the bark's unusual lack of elasticity—like snakes, sycamores need to shed their skin in order to grow, only sycamores do it piecemeal.

The cork cambium produces "most of the hard part of the bark." But, while all trees have cork cambium (the cork in wine bottles, for example, comes from the cork cambium, or bark, of two oak species found in the western Mediterranean, Spain, and Portugal), forester Brayton F. Wilson explains how they differ:

> There is a tremendous variation in the extent and longevity of cork cambia in different tree species. Trees with thin, smooth bark, like beech, have a long-lived cork cambium that forms a sheath around the tree stem . . . and expands as the stem thickens. Trees with rough bark, however, have many cork cambia, each of small area and relatively short-lived. [18]

The youngest bark is the closest to the trunk. So there is something generational going on in sycamores (and in other exfoliating species like eucalyptus), a bite, so to speak, to their bark. What we see is the young casting out the old. As with us, it is the old that wear the somber shades and wrinkles. The lighter, smoother, and tighter is younger. That, then, is the nature of the thing.

But there is something else to be said as well. That is that it requires the relationship of young to old, the proximity of youth and age, to give the

30. *Paul Landacre woodcut of our native sycamore,* Platanus
occidentalis. *(Illustration from* A Natural History of Trees of
Eastern and Central North America *by Donald Culross Peattie.
Copyright © 1948, 1949, 1950 by Donald Culross Peattie. Copyright
© renewed 1978 by Noel R. Peattie and Joseph M. Landacre.
Reprinted by permission of Houghton Mifflin Company. All rights
reserved.)*

sycamore the beautiful body that we remember it by. For sycamores are
beautiful even when unadorned with their characteristically large leaves or
the funny, furry buttonballs that give the tree one of its alternate names
(buttonball-tree, buttonwood).

Standing away from the tree, we can easily see the multilayered irregu-

larly shaped slabs of bark as pieces of a jigsaw puzzle, and we may think of
each piece as a fragment of time or a part of a generation: bits of the past
have been lost, the present is partially obscured, and the future is still in-
complete. "Life must be lived amidst that which was made before," the
geographer Donald Meinig writes. "Every landscape is an accumulation.
The past endures." [19] And it is revealed in the present, written clearly on
the body of the sycamore. But dig as we might, all of this rooting around
only uncovers a portion of "the purposes for which nature and God intended" alluded to in the deed.

God's green purposes were most completely revealed to humankind in
the lushly diverse landscape of Eden. Kentucky apparently once consti-
tuted another kind of paradise—an arboreal paradise. Perhaps that is what
the Methodist preacher had in mind when he told his congregation that
"Heaven is a Kentucky of a place." [20] Sited in the midst of a nine-state region "considered the best hardwood growing area in the northern hemisphere," Kentucky, as Thomas Crittenden Cherry's *Kentucky, the Pioneer
State of the West* informs us, boasted: "Giant forests of oak and tulip, beech
and ash, sycamore and linden, cedar and pine, and many other varieties of
trees grew so close that their leafy branches spread a canopy through
which the rays of the sun could scarcely penetrate, producing twilight effects even at high noon." [21]

The early pioneers, however, doggedly penetrated where even the sun
could scarcely reach and saw in these forests an easily accessible and
seemingly inexhaustible commodity. Settlers moved in steadily, beginning
around 1775 when the first permanent settlements were established. By
1813, as the brothers Grimm were publishing their well-known fables
and fairy tales and their less widely read anthologies of forest legends and
lore—seeking "German authenticity" [22] in the German forest—the saw-
mills were making ever greater inroads into Kentucky, a state whose land
"surface of 25,982,720 acres was once covered by an estimated 24,320,000
acres of virgin forest." [23]

The foundations of one of Kentucky's forest-dependent industries were
laid in 1789 when it was discovered that "storing sour mash whiskey in
charred kegs would remove foreign substances, change the color and improve the taste . . . [and] as early as 1845, white oak from the head of Green
River was exported to France for the manufacture of wine casks." [24] "Even

before Kentucky became a State [1792], tobacco shared with hemp the distinction of being one of the two crops grown commercially. . . . It was believed in the early years that only virgin ground would grow good tobacco. . . . Practically all land used for tobacco was originally covered with hardwood forests; but there was no market at the time for timber cleared to make room for tobacco, and great quantities of walnut, cherry, chestnut, hickory, oak, and poplar timber were cut and burned as waste." [25] At the same time great quantities of timber were being used for fuel, to fashion furniture and carriages, to produce the bridges, crossties, and trestles for the railroads, and to provide the roof props and crossties for the underground coal mines.

As Susan Cooper writes in *Rural Hours,* her 1850 book of natural history observations dedicated to her father, James Fenimore Cooper:

> In these times, the hewers of wood are an unsparing race. The first colonists looked upon a tree as an enemy, and to judge from appearances, one would think that something of the same spirit prevails among their descendants at the present hour. It is not surprising, perhaps, that a man whose chief object in life is to make money, should turn his timber into bank-notes with all possible speed; but it is remarkable that any one at all aware of the value of wood, should act so wastefully as most men do. . . . One would think that by this time, when the forest has fallen in all the valleys—when the hills are becoming more bare every day—when timber and fuel are rising in prices, and new uses are found for even indifferent woods—some forethought and care in this respect would be natural in people laying claim to common sense. [26]

So while a large sycamore is memorable in any location, the Freed Budd Sycamore—not enormous at ten feet in circumference three feet above the ground—was still noteworthy because of its presence on the grounds of Alice Lloyd College (then Caney Creek community center) in the midst of a heavily logged area in eastern Kentucky. Kentucky's statewide lumber production reached a peak in 1907 when 912,908,000 board feet (2.3 percent of total U.S. production) were produced. [27] *Southern Lumberman* magazine acknowledged in 1917 that "wanton waste was general. When ground was cleared, good timber was cut into lengths and burned on the ground." In 1923 the same publication called eastern Kentucky "the El Dorado of many lumbermen and large corporations" and reported that "lumber was cut at the rate of 100,000 to 150,000 feet per day." [28]

Good luck, therefore—an attribute that Aristotle ranks right up there with moral virtue—probably explains the original preservation of the Freed Budd Sycamore. But its continued survival was the result of a rarity, the deeding of a tree to own itself. Other communities have accomplished the same objective, the lifelong protection of specific trees, in less dramatic ways: through community pressure, as in Newburgh, New York; through historic designation (though this case is still undecided, other communities have successfully used this approach) as in Albany, Georgia; through town ordinances, as in Summerville, South Carolina; and through common consent, as in Korea.

The motivation is similar in all times and all places. In New Orleans, for example, residents threatened with a termite infestation that is devastating almost 20 percent of the city's live oaks, crape myrtles, magnolias, and willows say their trees "form the character of New Orleans as much as the architecture"; they are as central to the city's identity "as the crumbling bricks of the Vieux Carre, or the sound of a saxophone flowing from a doorway, or the big brown river itself." [29] In other communities across the nation, highways and other plans that call for the felling of ancient trees— such as the 296-year-old Balmville Tree in Newburgh or the 300-year-old Friendship Oak of Albany—meet with a kind of widespread and sustained protest that is noteworthy in our generally apathetic times.

Knowing the dangers of the word "always," it is still safe to say that it has always been this way. Almost from the moment we flopped out of the sea onto dry land we have been awed by the regenerative and transformative powers of trees, especially deciduous trees. Alchemists *par excellence,* they create wood, leaves, and fruit from sunlight, air, and water. And they do it again and again "in the present, as we experience it"—a characteristic that distinguishes nature from art, as John Fowles points out. [30] In the process, their regular and reliable cycles provide a "consolation for our mortality" [31] and an inspiration for our lives.

Dancing around the Maypole—a symbolic tree—our ancestors engaged in a ritual enactment representing our individual and collective hopes of renewal and continuity; when we rally to save an ancient tree we are expressing something very similar. Newspaper accounts of the ongoing three-year battle to save Albany's Friendship Oak—site of Indian gatherings, a stagecoach stop, and the campground of 3,000 soldiers who served in the Spanish American War[32]—include those of the judge who, while lifting a temporary restraining order protecting the tree, commented: "It is regrettable that the court is not in a position to rule on the emotional feelings of the community. I know what the emotional feelings are. I know what my own feelings are. That tree means I'm home."

A *New York Times* article similarly characterized Newburgh's Balmville Tree—a cottonwood with a history that includes the repeated admiration of Franklin Delano Roosevelt and an association with George Washington, who rode past the tree *en route* to his headquarters in Newburgh—as a "neighborhood's unifying symbol" and the "touchstone" of individual lives. One Newburgh resident said, "I don't understand why we have the frontier mentality of cutting things down and moving on. Community is not something you can create overnight. It's a long-term thing of growing up together and having a symbol you can relate to."[33]

But ours is a nation founded by forbears with a "frontier mentality." Our ancestors came here to claim and tame a "hideous and desolate wilderness,"[34] and it is both the claiming and the taming that we are heir to. Ours is a landscape created by those who were simultaneously, but not equally, planting the future, consuming the present, and leaving behind random remnants of the past—like the Balmville Tree and the Friendship Oak. Their activities grew out of an intellectual framework that was then new on this continent. As William Cronon observes in *Changes in the Land,* "more than anything else, it was the treatment of land and property as commodities that distinguished English conceptions of ownership from Indian ones."[35] To put it another way, everything has a price in a market economy, a value that can be established and agreed upon for purposes of sale. The green of nature, as Susan Cooper explained, is fairly easily transmuted into the green of money.

Today, of course, our market economy is considerably more sophisticated. Raw materials are not the only commodities subject to sale and removal. Now each of the basic elements that once contributed to a distinct sense of place—work, play, and food or, to put it another way, our once home-grown businesses, sports franchises, and even "local" or "regional" cuisines—is as mobile as the logged forest once was. In places like Newburgh, New York, and Albany, Georgia (and what place is not like these?), it sometimes seems that only those random remnants of the earlier landscape are permanent enough to provide the points of cultural unity, or community, we all seek. But this *is* a market economy. So how do we value the Friendship Oak, the Balmville Tree, or, for that matter, our "purple mountains majesty"?

Though still unresolved nationally—as conflicts over logging in the Northwest's national forests make amply clear—this question has been addressed for quite some time locally by communities and individuals who have developed a variety of strategies to preserve both community land-scapes and individual trees from human despoliation by placing them out-side the market economy.

When, for example, the city of Philadelphia (originally designed by its founder, William Penn, to be a "green Countrie town") ordered, in 1782, that all street trees be cut down to facilitate the "operation of the fire en-gineers," it was a signer of the Declaration of Independence who took up the cause of the trees. Francis Hopkinson, who succeeded in his efforts to preserve the trees, stated, "trees, as well as men, are capable of enjoying the rights of citizenship, and therefore, ought to be protected in these rights, that having committed no offense, the arbitrary edict cannot con-stitutionally pass against them." [36]

Elsewhere, it was not long after Ralph Waldo Emerson had prescribed "medicinal" nature for the "body and mind which have been cramped by noxious work or company," [37] that Summerville, South Carolina, recog-nized the relationship between civic health and the town's pine trees. An 1848 ordinance (only modestly changed in the 1995 revision) [38] made it "unlawful for any person . . . to in anywise injure or destroy any living tree or sapling within the corporate limits of the town except through . . . per-mission from the Town Council." [39]

That was sixteen years before Congress, perhaps looking to the health of the nation, acted to preserve Yosemite, our first national park in every-thing but name. It was in the heat of the Civil War, on June 30, 1864, that President Lincoln signed the Yosemite Act into law, providing for the pres-ervation of the Yosemite Valley and its big trees "inalienable for all time" and for "public use, resort and recreation." [40] Initially administered by the state of California, Yosemite became a national park in 1905.

Individual trees have also been preserved. The story of a tree in Athens,

Georgia, thought by some to be the "Son of the Tree That Owned Itself," is the subject of an enduring legend that claims the original tree was deeded the land it stood upon in the 1890s by a University of Georgia professor who had formed a deep emotional attachment to the tree as a child.

And internationally, the Korean War and the consequent impoverishment of that country's population caused deforestation on a scale not unlike that of Kentucky. Nonetheless, as Morris Arboretum Director Paul W. Meyer remembers, each village preserved a "grand old tree, typically a Zelkova (*Zelkova serrata*) or a Ginkgo (*Ginkgo biloba*)." Especially notable in a country where winters are harsh, and war made fuel exceptionally scarce, the trees were preserved for their "religious significance . . . the belief that spirituality can be found in nature." [41]

Religious differences notwithstanding, the American and Korean actions are more alike than different. As Christopher D. Stone points out in his widely read essay credited with influencing the legal/environmental views of U.S. Supreme Court Justices Douglas, Blackmun, and Brennan, "Should Trees Have Standing?" while we westerners may attribute the roots of our current environmental degradation to a Judeo-Christian ethic granting humans dominion over all nonhuman life, Chinese and Indian beliefs "in the unity between man and nature had no greater effect than the contrary beliefs in Europe in producing a balance between man and his environment." [42]

But back to the Freed Budd Sycamore. First, if you remember, the Charter Oak saved our ancestors by protecting their charter. Now we save the Freed Budd Sycamore by giving it its own charter, or deed. Is this merely symmetry? Are we simply playing tit for tat? Stone suggests otherwise:

> For some time now I have been thinking about the interplay between law and the development of social awareness, emphasizing . . . that societies, like human beings, progress through different stages of sensitiveness, and that in our progress through these stages the law—like art—has a role to play, dramatizing and summoning into the open the changes that are taking place within us. [43]

It is true that the residents of Summerville and Albany, like the two women who saved the Freed Budd Sycamore, have invoked the law in their efforts. Withdrawing a valuable commodity from a market economy clearly requires a law, a reason, an ethic, or a set of beliefs—call it spirituality, God, community, or the simple self-interest that recognizes that we need trees—allowing us to see an individual tree as just that, a valued individual. Like human individuals, or pets, the American trees have also been given names (perhaps the Korean trees have as well?); not the unfamiliar Latin, or Linnean, names culled from a long-dead language by botanists needing to develop a universal language suitable for academic and commercial exchange, but local names in everyday languages, used by ordinary people, names rich in symbolism that re-infuse nature with human meaning and differentiate individual trees by acknowledging their role in the life of the community—in the same way that some human surnames, such as Miller, Cooper, and Cohen, once did.

The names, stories, and experiences that transform trees into individuals also allow us to acknowledge the two traditions that have shaped our continental landscape: the Native American and the Euro-American. The landscape the first Europeans encountered was a landscape manipulated by Native Americans through selective and repeated burning to produce both open agricultural areas and to attract game to areas of new, and tender, plant regrowth. Because burning favors certain species, like the thick-barked oaks, Indian techniques affected both the content and the extent of forest growth. The precontact landscape was not, as Robert Frost suggests: "unstoried, artless, unenhanced."[44] It was simply a land embellished by techniques and stories different from the ones the Europeans brought with them. Or was it?

Chief Luther Standing Bear says of the Lakota: "The old people came literally to love the soil and they sat or reclined on the ground with a feeling of being close to a mothering power. . . . That is why the old Indian still sits upon the earth instead of propping himself up and away from its life-giving forces."[45] The colonists would have been familiar with the story of the Greek giant Antaeus, son of Poseidon and Ge, who drew his considerable strength from contact with his mother, the Earth. Hercules could only destroy Antaeus by holding him in the air and squeezing him to death. Today, in our less mythic times, we simply say that someone who has lost "touch," is "out in space," is not "rooted" or "grounded" in reality.

These trees remind us that it is time to abandon another old idea, the jungle metaphor, and replace it with the garden. It is clearly not an untamed jungle out there, it is more like a mostly abandoned garden, the result of longstanding and widespread human intervention gone awry, as Susan Cooper pointed out. Like all good gardeners, including our ancestors in Eden, we need to learn "to till *and* to tend" our places. Chief Luther said, "The man who sat on the ground in his tipi meditating on life and its meaning, accepting the kinship of all creatures and acknowledging unity with the universe of things was infusing into his being the true essence of civilization. And when native man left off this form of development, his humanization was retarded in growth." [46] Now listen to Aldo Leopold tell us how to nurture nature: "We abuse land because we regard it as a commodity belonging to us. When we see land as a community to which we belong, we may begin to use it with love and respect." [47] And John Donne: "No man is an island, entire of itself." [48] But, as Garrett Hardin observes in his foreword to *Should Trees Have Standing?*:

> The poet's rhetoric does not automatically give us answers to the thousand and one practical questions with which we are daily confronted, but it does furnish a framework within which acceptable solutions may be found, namely the ecological framework. The world is a seamless web of interrelationships within which no part can, without danger, claim absolute sovereignty in rights over all other parts. [49]

It is danger, then, that we are trying to avoid. Danger once meant losing a charter. Today, we are told, it means losing a world. These ideas are not new. Donne, after all, lived from 1573 to 1631; Chief Luther was born in 1868, eighteen years after Susan Cooper wrote *Rural Hours;* Aldo Leopold penned his words in 1948; Garrett Hardin in 1973, and Christopher Stone in 1974. A 1997 report, the *Red List of Threatened Plants* issued by the World Conservation Union, indicates that "1 of every 8 plant species in the world—and nearly 1 in 3 in the United States—is under threat of extinction." [50]

In Kentucky, in 1918, two women stood on a denuded hillside and practiced tree triage. I admire them. I admire the way they used the principal tool of the market economy, money, to save one tree. But this is a story, not a strategy, although some suggest otherwise. Writing in *Nature's Ser-*

vices: *Societal Dependence on Natural Ecosystems,* Gretchen C. Daily suggests that we do need to put a price tag on nature if we are to preserve it: "establishing sound ecosystem conservation policies requires determining the costs of destroying the next unit of relatively intact natural habitat."[51]

This, then, is one of the practical questions Hardin alluded to. This *is* a market economy. How *do* we value a tree? The biologist Edward O. Wilson explains the problem:

> Governments everywhere are at a loss regarding the best policy for regulating the dwindling forest reserves of the world. Few ethical guidelines have been established from which agreement might be reached, and those are based on an insufficient knowledge of ecology. Even if adequate scientific knowledge were available, we would have little basis for the long-term valuation of forests. The economics of sustainable yield is still a primitive art, and the psychological benefits of natural ecosystems are almost wholly unexplored.[52]

A market economy, it seems, can only place a value on an item in the marketplace. It cannot value the myriad actions and services that are not transaction-based. Women's work is a traditional example of this failure; the unpaid, but nonetheless enormously valuable, activities centered on child-rearing and homemaking. The larger role of nature is another. That the worldwide economy is "a wholly owned subsidary"[53] of our global natural ecosystems is a fact that seems to have escaped widespread notice.

There is another thing, though, I need to say about those two women in Kentucky. At the same time that I admire their actions, I also admire their words. Placing a dollar value on a tree, a lake, a wetland, or a grassland is necessary, but not sufficient. It might preserve anonymous space, but because that is the way economies work, it will never fully compute the value of meaning-laden place. Who can, after all, place a value on Wordsworth's golden daffodils or Emily Dickinson's prairie? We do not yet know or understand, scientists tell us, "all the purposes for which nature and God intended."

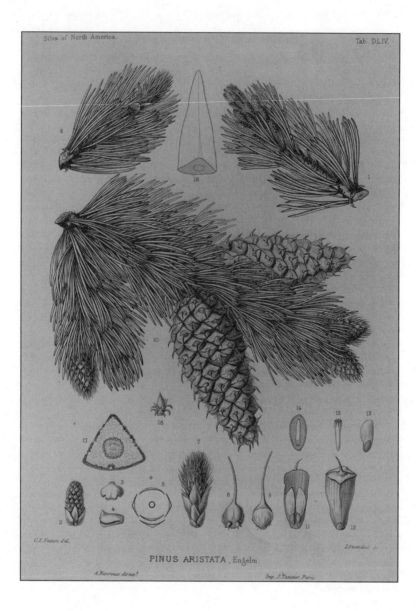

C.E.Faxon del.

Lövendal sc.

PINUS ARISTATA, Engelm.

A.Riocreux direx.￼

Imp. J.Taneur, Paris.

METHUSELAH'S WALK

TRUNK: THE MAIN STEM OF A TREE BELOW THE BRANCHES.

JAMES G. HARRIS AND MELINDA WOOLF HARRIS,
Plant Identification Terminology: An Illustrated Glossary

The sharp, squeaky-clean colors of things were what I noticed first. Against a cloudless lupine-blue sky, living and dead trees, weathered in flowing striations of brown and gray ranging from butterscotch to mahogany and stainless steel to charcoal, stood at all possible—and some impossible—angles. Their bottlebrush-configured needles bristled smartly in shades of deepest green. At their feet, braided rivers of cast-off pinecones wearing their distinctive class colors hugged the dry furrows of the mostly gray-brown hillside with its patches of chalk-white soil. This is what I had come to see.

It was June 28, 1997, and my son and I had reached Inyo National Forest's Schulman Grove, home of the Great Basin bristlecone pine (*Pinus longaeva*) that is the very oldest of the world's trees. We had traveled by plane and by car to the town of Bishop in California's Owens Valley, then left the piercing valley sun and its shadscale scrub behind and met up with sagebrush, climbed through the open woodlands of Utah juniper and piñon that dot the slopes of the White-Inyo Mountains, and were finally at 10,000 feet and Schulman Grove's 4.2-mile Methuselah Walk.

Schulman and Methuselah; scientist and tree, or scholar and ancient text if you will. It is not an exaggeration to say that Edmund Schulman's discovery of Methuselah—the 4,767-year-old Great Basin bristlecone pine that is called the world's oldest living thing—had changed both history and science. But it is also true that neither science nor history had drawn me up this mountain or filled me with the joy I was feeling in the day, the trees, and the world. I had come to see this place in its particularity to learn something of the values that can be extracted from a place. I had "come to the woods to see how the pine lives and grows and spires, lifting its evergreen arms to the light," as Thoreau writes, "to see its perfect success." [1]

I had come as anyone must do who wants to see the bristlecones.

31. *Charles Sprague Sargent,* The Silva of North America, *vol. 11. (The McLean Library, Pennsylvania Horticultural Society, Philadelphia)*

32. Edmund Schulman (right) and White Mountain district ranger Richard Wilson with Pine Alpha in October 1956. (Courtesy Laboratory of Tree-Ring Research, University of Arizona, Tucson)

Bristlecones do not live among us—along city streets or in suburban yards—they are timberline trees, living on the edge of life in an environment so cold and dry it has been called "a place of last resort." [2] I had come to see the prickle-tipped female cones that give the tree its name, the dolomite soil that it favors, and the way its short (1- to 1.5-inch) needles are bound together in their tight little packages of five. Much later, I would come to see that the pieces of this story—of the scientists, the historians, the natural history of the bristlecone in particular and of the pine species in general, of the Forest Service on whose land Methuselah lives, and of the visitors to and admirers of this tree, including myself—were as closely bound as these needles. And later I would read what Nicholas Mirov, the scholar of conifers, writes: that each needle "is the uppermost terminus of a strand of water coming without interruption from the tree's roots,"[3] "that water movement is not straight up the tree but is spiral," that pine species vary in whether the water flows in a left or right-turning pattern, and that *Pinus aristata* (the former designation for all bristlecones) is right-turning."[4]

I had also come to see its companions, among them the curl leaf mountain mahogany (*Cercocarpus ledifolius*) and the so-called Mormon tea (*Ephedra* spp.), once used as a medicinal tea by the early settlers in "a practice undoubtedly copied from the Indians (a recent innovation in health food stores has been the packaging of dried stems of ephedra [used in China to treat asthma and hay fever] under the name squaw tea)."[5] And, when I had made these travel plans, I told myself I would finally see Methuselah.

Located in a segment of the trail called the "Forest of Ancients"[6] that includes many trees more than 3,000 years old and several over 4,000 (including an unnamed tree that has been dated at 4,790+ years) Methuselah has managed to survive the rigors of altitude, wind, fire, lightning, and lack of moisture, but it is not identified, in order to be protected from an even more threatening adversary—us. Although I had been shown several slides to help me find the champion, I doubt that I did. Nor, it turned out, did I care. As I stood surrounded by those tangled and contorted bodies, I felt the youth of my fifty-four years. And, taking the long view, from trees to mountain and mountain to valley, a thousand years plus or minus hardly seemed to matter at all. I was convinced that the bristlecones, like Zeus's oaks at Dodona,[7] had whispered their secrets centuries ago in the sighing of their boughs on windy wintry nights. Or, perhaps it was as Emily Dickinson suggests, not the boughs but the leaves:

> The Leaves like Women interchange
> Exclusive Confidence—
> Somewhat of nods and somewhat
> Portentous inference.[8]

But except for a few hardy souls like John Muir, whom Joseph Wood Krutch calls "our great poet of the awesome aspects of the American scene," it took a very long time for us to notice.[9] Writing about the bristlecones, which he called needle pines (*Pinus aristata*), in his 1894 work, *The Mountains of California,* Muir rhapsodized:

> Some stand firmly erect, feathered with radiant tassels down to the ground. . . . Again, in the same woods you find trees that are made up of several boles united near the ground, spreading at the sides in a plane parallel to the axis of the mountain, with the elegant tassels hung in charming order between them, making a harp held against the main wind lines where they are most effective in playing the grand storm harmonies. . . . But whether young or old, sheltered or exposed to the wildest gales, this tree is ever found irrepressibly and extravagantly picturesque, and offers a richer and more varied series of forms to the artist than any conifer I know of.[10]

Notwithstanding Muir's lush prose, it was science—and more especially one scientist—that finally drew public attention to the bristlecones. Edmund Schulman, a dendrochronologist studying climactic change, decided to detour through Inyo's White-Inyo Mountains in 1953 because he had heard that there were old trees there. He and his colleague Frits W. Went *only* found a 1,500-year-old tree on their first trip, but Schulman recognized the site's potential and continued to return annually for the next several years. His persistence was rewarded extravagantly in 1957. That was when he discovered the tree he first named Great-granddad, and later called Methuselah: "the first of all [the] four-millenium trees which had not eroded past the center," revealing that it "had begun growth more than 4,600 years ago."[11] It was exactly the kind of "unique record of past climatic change" that Schulman had been seeking, but he could not help noting that "potentially of far greater importance is the fact that the capacity of these trees to live so fantastically long may—when we come to understand it fully—perhaps serve as a guidepost on the road to the understanding of longevity in general."[12] Sadly, however, just as the first public report of his discovery—published in the March 1958 issue of *National Geographic*—was going to press, the discoverer of the world's oldest living thing was struck down by a heart attack at the youthful age of forty-nine.

Schulman's interest in the bristlecones grew out of his work in dendrochronology as an assistant to the founder of the field, Andrew E. Douglass. Both men were astronomers and both were interested in the effects that cosmic events, such as sunspots, might have on weather patterns on earth. Douglass had launched his inquiries around the turn of this century at the Lowell Observatory in Flagstaff, Arizona, but found he was hampered by the lack of reliable weather data reaching back far enough to develop a clear picture about what, if any, correlation might exist between the specific events he was studying. So he began to search for an alternative source that would yield the necessary information. He thought about this problem as he traveled around northern Arizona[13] and finally, as for an earlier scientist named Newton, his answer came from a tree.

Although it had long been understood that one could count the number of a tree's rings to reveal its age, careful observers as early as Leonardo da Vinci—the first to write about the subject—had also recognized "the relationship between tree rings and precipitation"[14]—wet years typically produce wide rings while dry years produce narrow ones. Each spring trees add to their girth by producing a ring of new cells. When moisture is plentiful, typically in spring, the cells produced are large, but as moisture decreases and growth slows down with the approach of fall, the cells become smaller and smaller until growth finally stops for the year. It is the contrast between the large and more lightly colored cells of the early spring growth (earlywood) and the small and darker cells produced later in the growing cycle (latewood) that produces tree rings or, as John Hill described them in 1770, the "circles of the seasons."[15]

Incrementally and measurably, as trees build rings and other living things, such as tortoise shells, ibex horns, and mammoth teeth, record their annual growth, scientists first clarified the specific anatomical and physiological processes involved in producing rings and then began to study the relationship between tree rings and weather.[16] Today, scientists Thomas E. Graedel and Paul J. Crutzen explain the continuing validity of this approach in *Atmosphere, Climate, and Change:* trees "are especially rich repositories of atmospheric information for a number of reasons: they interact with the atmosphere (and retain signatures of that interaction); they reflect some of the properties of the climate in which they grow; their age pro-

33. *Andrew E. Douglass shown using a Swedish increment borer to core a Ponderosa pine on Mount Lemmon in the Catalina Mountains north of Tuscon, c. 1946. (Courtesy Laboratory of Tree-Ring Research, University of Arizona, Tucson)*

vides long, continuous records; and tree records can be very accurately dated, generally to within a specific year." [17] But it was Douglass who, early in this century, achieved the undisputed title of "father of dendrochronology" [18] by being the first to recognize the applicability of tree-ring data to such diverse fields as astronomy, archaeology, and climatology.

Douglass's breakthrough came in 1911. When he observed similar ring patterns in trees growing fifty miles apart he understood "the full significance of his observations" [19]—that regional tree-ring chronologies could be

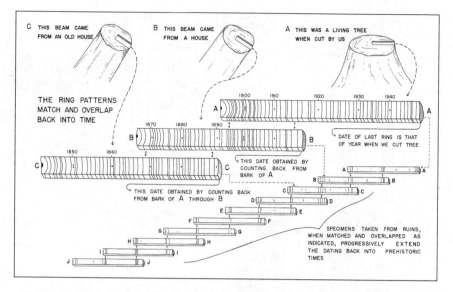

34. Diagram illustrating principle of cross-dating. (Courtesy Laboratory of Tree-Ring Research, University of Arizona, Tucson)

established by cross-dating trees from separate sites. Remarkably, these regional chronologies—called master chronologies—are unique. "Nowhere, throughout time, is precisely the same long-term sequence of wide and narrow rings repeated, because year-to-year variations in climate are never exactly the same."[20] By 1914, now at the University of Arizona at Tucson, Douglass was able to assemble a 500-year chronology using the rings of ponderosa pine (*Pinus ponderosa*). By the end of the decade a relationship had developed between Douglass and Clark Wissler, an archaeologist with the American Museum of Natural History, which would result in a spectacular demonstration of the interdisciplinary uses of dendrochronology—the dating of Pueblo Bonito and other Native American ruins in the Southwest.

The actual discovery of an ancient charred beam that cross-dated with beams collected earlier came in 1929 and provided absolute dates for over forty Native American settlements, demonstrating, according to Douglass, that trees were "unimpeachable witnesses," which recorded certain events "more accurate[ly] than if human hands had written down the major events as they occurred." Writing in his aptly titled *National Geographic* article—"The Secret of the Southwest Solved by Talkative Tree Rings"—

Douglass stated conclusively that "various portions of Pueblo Bonito were under construction at different times—919, 1017, 1033–92, 1102, and 1130" and also that the oldest Mesa Verde ruin, the well-known Cliff Palace, was constructed in 1073.[21]

This dating of sites that could be read out of trees had an additional consequence. As Michael Cohen writes in *A Garden of Bristlecones*: it created one document, so to speak, that "linked the pre-history and modern history of the Southwest [and made] Native American history . . . part of a continuity with European American history."[22]

At the same time the dendrochronological record was also linking environmental and historical events, pointing out possible reasons for both the development and the abandonment of certain sites, by "correl[ating] the increases in rainfall that permitted these villages to expand and the drought years that placed upon them the heavy hand of starvation."[23] The years 840, 1067, 1379, and 1632, for example, were individual years of extreme drought, while the "catastrophically dry"[24] period from 1276 to 1299—called the Great Drought—is presumed responsible for migrations such as that of the Tsengi, who were forced to leave the arid lands of Monument Valley and move south into Hopi territory. "Through long-past ages and with unbroken regularity," Douglass wrote, "trees have jotted down a record at the close of each fading year—a memorandum as to how they passed the time; whether enriched by added rainfall or injured by lightning and fire. By learning how to read these records—specifically those of the pines—we have discovered a magic key to open mysterious books and interpret the meaning of their writing."[25] Dendrochronology had proven itself.

But back to Schulman and the bristlecones. As Douglass's assistant in the 1930s, Schulman had "aided in the development"[26] of dendrochronological methodology—a methodology which needed to make allowances for the factors other than rainfall, such as temperature, slope, wind, soil, sun, and snow accumulation, that could affect ring width. But his chief interest was always dendroclimatology—using the information gathered from tree-rings to understand long-range weather patterns on earth. And while Douglass's work had enlarged the body of relevant data considerably, Schulman still needed far longer retrospective time sequences to test his evolving climatological theories, so he continued searching for trees that would yield longer chronologies. From 1939 through 1953 he searched among coniferous trees at lower elevations—piñon pine, ponderosa pine, and Douglas fir—finding like Douglass "the much longer records of the sequoias not especially useful because of the effects of their semihumid habitat."[27] Then, in 1952, he moved his sights upward.

In that field season Schulman was working above Sun Valley, Idaho, using a Swedish increment borer to sample Douglas firs (a cross-section of rings about 5 mm wide, about the size of a drinking straw, is extracted from the tree's trunk),[28] when a half-dead limber pine was discovered that turned out to be almost 1,650 years old.[29] At around the same time, reports had reached Schulman that an Inyo Forest ranger named Alvin Noren had found extraordinarily large bristlecones in a very remote area of the White-Inyo Mountains then being used by the U.S. Navy for a "missile and cosmic ray research operation."[30] Noren's samples had revealed the tree, which he named the Patriarch, to be 1,500 years old. Schulman was interested.

At the end of that 1953 field season, Schulman and Went made their famous detour through the White-Inyo Mountains, and the rest, as they say, is dendrochronology. Found only in the southwestern United States, the bristlecone range extends across the mountains of six states—California, Nevada, Utah, Colorado, New Mexico, and Arizona. Following the 1953 discovery, Schulman decided to sample a variety of stands to determine which might yield the oldest trees. "By 1956 we knew that we had trees in the 4,000-year-plus-class," Schulman wrote. "We also knew that bristlecone pine trees were able to reach the highest ages at the western limit of their range. Nowhere have trees yet been sampled which approach the top ages of more than 4,500 years found in the White Mountain region of the Inyo National Forest."[31]

After Schulman's death, however, an older tree was found growing in Nevada's Snake Range. During the summer of 1964 a graduate student in geography named Donald Currey was exploring bristlecones on Wheeler Peak, near the Nevada-Utah border. Currey was hoping to find a tree old enough to establish a chronology that would delineate climate changes during the so-called Little Ice Age, roughly 1400 to 1650, when the now generally ice-free canals of Holland, for example, froze regularly (as painted by Pieter Brueghel the Younger). Currey began coring trees on Wheeler Peak, south of the Grant Range where John Muir had seen his bristlecones about a century earlier, when, as the story goes, he broke his increment borer. Because he would not have been able to get a replacement until the following field season, he decided to cut down the most promising tree and take it to his lab for study. He sought and was given permission for this "sectioning" of the tree, as it is called, from the Forest Service ranger in charge of the Snake Range. Thus it was that the 4,862-year-old tree—designated by Currey as WPN-114 and named Prometheus by some of its admirers—which "turned out to be the oldest known living Great Basin bristlecone pine . . . [was cut down by the Forest Service] during the summer the United States Congress debated and passed the Wilderness Act of 1964." [32] No older tree has been found to date.

In addition to causing a public controversy that helped propel the 1986 creation of Great Basin National Park, which moved Wheeler Peak from the jurisdiction of the Forest Service to the National Park Service, the dating of Prometheus clearly disproved Schulman's hypothesis that the oldest trees would all be in the White Mountains. Later work indicated that Inyo's mountains were one of *two* locations (eastern Nevada being the other) where bristlecones could live an estimated 5,000 years.

That work was done by Dana K. Bailey, a geophysicist, who demonstrated in 1970 that the California and Nevada trees—and the bristlecones in southern Utah which live about 3,000 years—exhibited significant enough differences to reclassify the bristlecone species into two varieties: *Pinus longaeva* D. K. Bailey, aptly named by Bailey to designate the variety that includes the oldest trees, those found in California, Nevada, and Utah, was added to the existing variety, *Pinus aristata* Engelmann, also no slouch in the age department with "individual trees reaching 1500 to 2000 years," [33] located in the remaining three southwestern states. The species' original scientific name *aristata* means "bristle," referring to the delicately curved "prickle at the end of each scale of the cone." [34]

What Bailey observed was that the needles of the *aristata* population, which he has suggested calling the Rocky Mountain bristlecone, have two distinguishing "externally observable features"; first, their tight little bundles spread open after they are "two or more years old," thus presenting a "soft brush" appearance; and second, they look "dandruffy" because they are liberally dotted with "resin exudations [that] exhibited a crusty, crazed surface that . . . made them whitish." [35] He also discovered differences in the chemical composition of the resins in the two populations and the fact that the Great Basin population holds onto its needles longest, a strategy for conserving much-needed energy in its harsher environment.

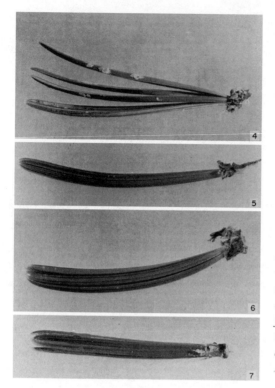

35. *Figures 4–7 show the fascicle and needle characteristics of bristlecone pine populations. Figure 4 shows the spread fascicle and resin-dotted "dandruffy" needles of the* Pinus aristata *population compared to the more tightly closed fascicle and shinier needles of* Pinus longaeva *in figures 5, 6, and 7. (Courtesy Dana K. Bailey)*

Another aspect of Schulman's work, the bristlecone chronology, also continued after his death. Today, following decades of gathering and dating living trees and dead bristlecone remains, the chronology has been pushed back to 6707 B.C.E., according to Rex Adams of the University of Arizona's Laboratory of Tree-Ring Research, very close to the 10,000-year span scientists have been hoping for—to the time of the last ice age.[36] When this precise history of weather patterns since the last glaciation at the end of the Pleistocene epoch is completed, climatologists believe they will be able to project future weather patterns more accurately.

The current chronology has, however, already yielded several significant results—among them the recalibration of carbon-14 dating and a historic understanding of water flow in the Colorado River basin. The bristlecone chronology was being extended further and further back in time at the same time that Willard Frank Libby was doing his Nobel Prize–winning work (awarded 1960) on carbon-14 dating, demonstrating that all living things assimilate carbon-14 (an unstable radioactive carbon isotope which deteriorates at a measurable rate), and therefore the age of organic remains can be calculated by measuring the amount of carbon-14 still present. However, when the dates produced by this process were measured against the highly accurate bristlecone chronologies, certain inaccuracies in carbon-14 dates were discovered. "At the time of the greatest deviation, about 4000 B.C. to 6000 B.C. the ^{14}C dates are about 800 to 900 years too young. At the present time, as a result of the combustion of fossil fuels, they are about 300 years too old."[37]

The consequences of this discovery were immediate and far-reaching. In England, for example, a young archaeologist named Colin Renfrew used "the tree-ring chronology as his base reference"[38] and challenged theories about the spread of European civilization—demonstrating conclusively that western European Megalithic cultures did not evolve from, but rather preceded the south-eastern Mycenaean culture.[39] The April 5, 1971, issue of *Newsweek* highlighted Renfrew's work, calling it the "stuff of high drama" and telling its readers that "according to Renfrew's calibrations, Stonehenge now becomes older than Mycenae. The megalithic tombs of Brittany and Iberia are a millennium older than the pyramids—and may even be the earliest of man's surviving monuments."

These ideas appeared at a time when cultural historians and others were already questioning models of culture change that relied on ideas of cultural diffusion—the idea that there was a single source for western civilization which had then spread outwards in a branching pattern—not unlike a tree. "Tree-rings dealt a particularly precise blow to [this] untenable picture of human history and reinforced the efforts of some scholars to create histories and literary canons that would include multiple human cultural responses to differing environmental circumstances."[40]

Trees living on a mountaintop in California have created such a highly sensitive record of the seasons of their lives that they have become a universal language of time, binding all life on earth in a single chronology. This new kind of evidence, the testimony of trees, continues to enlarge our understanding of the past. Recently tree-ring analysis (in this case using bald cypresses) untangled a persistent historical mystery, revealing that "the worst droughts of the last 800 years in that part of the country" were probably what doomed the so-called Lost Colony of Roanoake, settled in 1587.[41]

Trees are also providing commentary on regional development issues: "Reconstructions based on data from tree-ring sites in the Upper Colorado River Basin have shown that the river flow during the early part of the century, when political decisions were being made to allocate the river's water among the various states, was greater than at any other time during the past 400 years. In simple terms, the period of record represented above-average flow conditions, and Colorado River water has been overallocated."[42] The history and possible consequences of this "overallocation" have been treated in detail by Marc Reisner in *Cadillac Desert: The American West and Its Disappearing Water:* "The Colorado . . . has more people, more industry, and a more significant economy dependent on it than any comparable river in the world. If the Colorado River suddenly stopped flowing, you would have two years of carryover capacity in the reservoirs before you had to evacuate most of southern California and Arizona and a good portion of Colorado, New Mexico, Utah, and Wyoming."[43] Remembering the earlier records that Douglass called "lean years and fat years"[44] it is, in Yogi Berra's well-known words, like *déjà vu* all over again.

They are also hinting at contemporary climatic change—appropriately, since it was an interest in climate that had originally attracted dendrochronologists to the bristlecones in the first place. The timberline, as bristlecone pine forest manager John Louth reports, seems to be moving up, "based on evidence of young trees growing at higher altitudes than mature trees." The young trees are at a 100-to 150-foot higher elevation than the current 11,000-foot treeline, suggesting the "possibility that the warming trend from the Industrial Revolution may be allowing the treeline to move up." While Louth says his rationale for the upward movement is speculative, the movement is not.[45] "Because it is an edge, because it is sensitive to change, the timberline reveals the invisible flux of conditions that support lower-elevation terrestrial life, like humans."[46]

I imagine the bristlecone timberline as a series of dance patterns performed over the millennia: one step forward, two steps back, stand in place, and begin again. Or perhaps that isn't the correct choreography. Nonetheless, however the dance goes it is fair to say that we, and the entire span of our species, have experienced only a few of the moves.

Pines were firmly rooted in the Americas eons before humans began to roam the earth, and it is partially our recognition of that contrast—their rootedness with our wandering—that has placed trees so firmly within our imaginative landscape. As Alexandra Murphy writes in *Graced by Pines: The Ponderosa Pine in the American West:* "For more than 250 million years, pines and their conifer ancestors have survived and thrived on earth. *Homo sapiens* evolved a brief 300,000 years ago, and we have searched relentlessly ever since for satisfaction of our basic needs: food, shelter, water, community, and an understanding of our place and purpose on earth, what one might simply call rootedness."[47] Although some take the opposite view, seeing rootedness as merely confinement, John Muir speaks for me when he says:

> It has been said that trees are imperfect men, and seem to bemoan their imprisonment rooted in the ground. But they never seem so to me. I never saw a discontented tree. They grip the ground as though they liked it, and though fast rooted they travel about as far as we do. They go wandering forth in all directions with every wind, going and coming like ourselves, traveling with us around the sun two million miles a day, and through space heaven knows how fast and far![48]

According to Dana Bailey, "the geological period and region of origin of the genus *Pinus* will probably never be known precisely." What we do know, however, as Nicholas Mirov writes, is that "the earliest known pines of North America were those of the Jurassic period."[49] "Paleobotanists know largely from fossils that pines flowed first across what we now think of as the Bering land bridge and then southward, during the Jurassic but chiefly during the Cretaceous period, between 140 and 65 million years ago."[50]

But long before the pines appeared and even longer before the bristlecones evolved—about 500 million years ago when the continents were consolidating to form the supercontinent of Pangaea—the dolomite (limestone) soil favored by the Great Basin bristlecones was being laid down under the sea. Much later—after the continents as we know them began to take shape—beginning in the mid-Jurassic of about 150 million years ago, when dinosaurs and pines were living here side by side, two continental plates were colliding—the Pacific plate and the North American plate—creating such enormous heat and pressure that mineral-rich rock was first melted and then injected into the "cracks and faults,"[51] which developed, creating the famous Sierra Nevada gold deposits. And when the Cascade-Sierra Nevada-Penninsular cordillera was finally beginning to appear above water, about 65 million years ago—roughly 250 million years after the uplifting of the Appalachians—pines were widely dispersed across the continent. By then the pines and other conifers or gymnosperms (plants in which the so-called naked seeds are carried on scales, usually in cones) had to compete with the evolutionary newcomers, the flowering plants, or angiosperms, that enclose their seeds in the fleshy receptacles called fruits.

"By the Eocene [53–37 million years ago] a fossil pine . . . very similar to the present bristlecone pines, was growing in northeastern Nevada in what is now the northern Great Basin."[52] The Great Basin itself, so-named in 1844 by the explorer John Charles Frémont "because it seemed unnatural," was being formed by widespread volcanic activity during this epoch.[53] From then through the close of the last ice age 10,000 years ago, the Cascade-Sierra Nevada-Peninsular ranges continued to push upward to their present elevations, North America and Asia finally separated, and two distinct geographical flora evolved in the Great Basin region. One, which includes the bristlecones, was located in the southern Rockies and northern Sierra Madre mountains to withstand a warmer and drier climate. The other, which includes California's famous sequoias, ranged as far north as the Arctic and adapted to the moist, temperate climate that was more widespread before the last ice age. During and after the ice age plant populations moved to accommodate the fluctuations in precipitation and temperature. And "in the subsequent warming up and drying out, the . . . species that withdrew to southern California during the preceding cooler period regained former territory to the north and even expanded. The cone-bearing forests encroaching on the lowlands went back to high mountain retreats or were confined to the coastal strip. It was as though two great hands were at work," the naturalist Elna Bakker writes, "one keeping the Arcto-Tertiary [the sequoia group] elements on the cooler and moister mountain chains and along the shore, the other shoving the summer drought adapters [the bristlecone group] north and west from their interior and southern bases."[54]

It was the final elevation of the Cascade, Sierra Nevada, and Peninsular ranges that created the present topographical barrier to precipitation: "On the east side of the Sierra-Cascade crest, moisture drops immediately— from as much as 150 inches of precipitation on the western slope to as little as four inches on the eastern—and it doesn't increase much, except at higher elevations, until you have crossed the hundredth meridian, which bisects the Dakotas and Nebraska and Kansas down to Abilene, Texas, and divides the country into its two most significant halves—the one receiving at least twenty inches of precipitation a year, the other generally receiving less."[55] As Will Durant has said, "Civilization exists by geological consent, subject to change without notice."[56]

Bounded as it is by mountains on the east, deserts to the east and south, the Pacific Ocean on the west, and a colder climate to the north, California has developed a unique flora. Elna Bakker refers to this somewhat isolated floristic community as "an island called California."[57] It is an island especially rich in pines. One-fourth of the genus, *Pinus,* is native to California and many others—the Oriental, central European, and Mediterranean species—have been introduced as ornamentals. But the pines are only part of California's extraordinary population of conifers. Three world-record holders are native to California: "the tallest, coast redwood [*Sequoia sempervirens*]; the largest in diameter, big tree [*Sequoia gigantea*]; and the oldest, bristlecone pine [*Pinus longaeva*]."[58]

Like us, standing trees lead measured lives. They are measured for height, weight (or volume), and age. Volume is the most commonly taken measurement of a tree, because it is the measure used to determine its approximate board-foot content, or commercial value. It is calculated using the diameter of the tree at breast height (dbh), which is "defined in the United States as the stem diameter outside the bark at a point 4.5 ft. above the average ground line on the uphill side of the tree."[59] Height can be arrived at by standing at a fixed distance from a tree and using a hypsometer, a device based on trigonometric principles of triangulation. Nations and states measure and record the size of their trees, and California has won the contest hands down.

I have seen the sequoias and I know their impressive, unforgettable majesty. "The beauty of their forests, their great height and long lives, their hardiness and the quality and durability of their lumber have put these giants in a very special category. They evoke a kind of reverence accorded no other American tree."[60] All of that is true. The sequoias are natural wonders and national treasures. The discovery of the big trees caused such national and international excitement, in fact, that American and English botanists disputed their classification: the British named the tree *Wellingtonia gigantea,* after their famous hero, while Americans, not to be outdone, proposed *Washingtonia gigantea.* It was a French botanist, Joseph Decaisne, who finally resolved the matter. After examining specimens received from the French consul in California, Decaisne announced in 1854 that the big tree was similar enough to the coast redwood to be placed within the same genus *Sequoia*—"an eccentrically inappropriate label for either species," as Simon Schama writes in *Landscape and Memory,* "being the name of a half-blood Alabama Cherokee (a k a George Guess) who had invented a written language for the tribe"—and his classification has stood the test of time.[61]

But towering giants were not what drew me across the country to California. It was age, the idea of immortality as expressed by a tree. And it was a sense of wonder about survival under adversity: the "need," as Thoreau writes, "to witness our own limits transgressed, and some life pasturing freely where we never wander."[62] It was Inyo National Forest's Great Basin bristlecones that drew me. They were my destination trees.

THE CREATION OF THE MENTAL DOMAIN OF PHANTASY HAS A COMPLETE COUNTERPART IN THE ESTABLISHMENT OF "RESERVATIONS" AND "NATURE-PARKS" IN PLACES WHERE THE INROADS OF AGRICULTURE, TRAFFIC, OR INDUSTRY THREATEN TO CHANGE . . . THE EARTH RAPIDLY INTO SOMETHING UNRECOGNIZABLE. THE "RESERVATION" IS TO MAINTAIN THE OLD CONDITION OF THINGS WHICH HAS BEEN REGRETFULLY SACRIFICED TO NECESSITY EVERYWHERE ELSE; THERE EVERYTHING MAY GROW AND SPREAD AS IT PLEASES, INCLUDING WHAT IS USELESS AND EVEN WHAT IS HARMFUL. THE MENTAL REALM OF PHANTASY IS ALSO SUCH A RESERVATION RECLAIMED FROM THE ENCROACHES OF THE REALITY-PRINCIPLE.

SIGMUND FREUD, *General Introduction to Psychoanalysis* (1920)

36. Great Basin bristlecone. (Courtesy Eric A. Samuels)

IN 1989 IN CANTERBURY, ENGLAND, THE WORLD'S LEADING EXPERTS
ON FROGS AND OTHER AMPHIBIANS GATHERED FOR THEIR FIRST EVER
WORLD CONGRESS. . . . AT SOME POINT THEY REALIZED THAT THEY
WERE ALL SEEING THE SAME PROBLEM: THEIR FROGS AND TOADS WERE
DYING—NOT JUST IN DISTURBED HABITATS, BUT IN THE MOST PRISTINE
NATURE RESERVES—FROM BROWN TOADS IN YOSEMITE NATIONAL
PARK TO GOLDEN TOADS IN COSTA RICA. . . . IT . . . CALLS INTO
QUESTION THE DISTINCTION TOO OFTEN MADE BETWEEN HOME AND
AWAY, BETWEEN PROTECTED AREAS AND NONPROTECTED AREAS. . . .
BUT MAYBE THE FROGS . . . ARE TELLING US THAT THIS DISTINCTION
ISN'T VALID ANYMORE. MAYBE THEY'RE TELLING US THAT HOME IS
HOME AND AWAY IS HOME, AND IF YOU POLLUTE ONE YOU POLLUTE
THE OTHER.

THOMAS L. FRIEDMAN, *New York Times,* June 6, 1998

Inyo National Forest's 2 million acres are part of a national forest system that includes 155 national forests and comprises more than 191 million acres, more than double the 80 million acres managed by the National Park Service. But size is only the most obvious of the differences between the two agencies. They fit within a government structure that places the older one, the U.S. Forest Service, within the Department of Agriculture, and the National Park Service in the Department of the Interior. Beyond that, they operate under objectives that turn out to be quite different. The differences have been described by the environmental historian Alfred Runte as "esthetic as opposed to utilitarian conservation." [63] While each of our national parks has been designated by Congress to preserve specific natural, cultural, and/or historic features—hence, the transfer of the Wheeler Peak area to the National Park Service—the national forests have generally been created by presidential proclamation for both "consumptive and non-consumptive uses," [64] ranging from logging and mining to hiking and camping. The creation of Inyo National Forest is a case in point.

When the U.S. Forest Service was created in 1905, the agency was moved from the Department of the Interior to its present location along with the original forest reserves that had been established by Congress in 1891 plus the additional lands that had been set aside under the Harrison, Cleveland, and McKinley administrations. As Theodore Roosevelt took office in September 1901, in the wake of McKinley's assassination, the system included "approximately 46,000,000 acres . . . [b]y the end of his administration he had tripled the national forest system in the West to its present size of nearly 150,000,000 acres." [65] One of those additions was Inyo National Forest.

As U.S. Forest Service literature reports, "The original Inyo National Forest was a small area near the city of Bishop created by President Theodore Roosevelt in May of 1907. In 1908 President Roosevelt combined it with over a million acres of the Sierra Forest lying east of the Sierra divide in Mono and Inyo counties." Inyo's creation and expansion to include most of the Owens Valley followed Los Angeles' purchase of Owens River water rights (the major water source for the Owens Valley) and development of a plan for a 223-mile aqueduct that would divert that water to Los Angeles and the San Fernando Valley, the latter being almost worthless without irrigation. Roosevelt and his newly appointed chief of the Forest Service, Gifford Pinchot, supported this action, which was in keeping with their philosophy of utilitarian conservation—preserve now for use later—or economy before ecology (a field not formed until 1915, when the Ecological Society of America was founded).[66] In a letter supporting the diversion of the river, Rooosevelt wrote, "It is a hundred or a thousandfold more important to state that this water is more valuable to the people of Los Angeles than to the Owens Valley."[67] Land in the Owens Valley was not returned to the public domain for homesteading (which might have claimed some of the Owens River water that Los Angeles was hoping to receive) but instead turned into a portion of Inyo National Forest, a portion mostly devoid of trees.[68]

"With six inches of annual rainfall, the Owens Valley is too dry for trees."[69] The valley, at 4,000 feet, supports a plant community called Shadscale Scrub that includes shadscale, spiny salt bush, spiny sagebrush, squaw tea, and hopsage. But moving up from the valley floor, first, at around 7,000 feet, nut pines (*Pinus monophylla*) and Utah junipers (*Juniperus osteosperma*)—the same tree that perches on the edge of the Grand Canyon—emerge, followed at around 9,000 feet by the limber pines (*Pinus flexilis*) and the Great Basin bristlecones (*Pinus longaeva*). The bristlecones, as bristlecone pine forest manager John Louth explains, live within a "botanical reserve," a 28,000-acre protected area within Inyo called the Ancient Bristlecone Pine Forest. It was set aside in 1958, the same year that the Shulman Grove of bristlecones was named in memory of Edmund Schulman, and it includes the timberline Patriarch Grove, home of Alvin Noren's Patriarch, the bristlecone that had originally attracted Schulman to this place.

It is a place of beauty. It is also a place of science and, by extension, history. It is a place of recreation; a place to feel oneself created anew and to marvel at creation's amplitude. It is a resource, a nourisher of other species, including our own.

It is also, as Freud suggests, in some sense a fantasy. A place of national nostalgia. And, as Thomas Friedman reports, this particular fantasy may be about to collide with a reality we do not choose to see. The bristlecones, however, have a good record when it comes to endurance. And every park we create, every piece of land that we save and habitat that we protect preserves another piece of the whole. "The first rule of intelligent tinker-ing," as Aldo Leopold writes, "is to save all the parts."[70]

Standing, as they do, with their feet planted firmly in the earth and their heads in the heavens, mountains—from Sinai, to Olympus, to Fuji—have long been seen as places of godhead and wisdom. At its highest elevation of 14,246 feet—a mere 248 feet lower than nearby Mount Whitney, the highest point in the contiguous United States—the White-Inyo range has elicited similar reflections: "The word 'Inyo' is thought to be a Native American name of a mountain range which means 'the dwelling place of the great spirit.'"[71] Mountains are also widely used symbols of both chal-lenge and achievement. Borrowing from the languages of mountain climb-ing and topography we use phrases such as "climbing to the top," "pinnacle of achievement," and "peaks and valleys" to express our view of life-as-mountain.

But I had no experience with mountains. These were my first. Although I had skied and hiked, I had never been at what is called "altitude." Lacking experience, I also lacked expectations. I had not seen what the mountains demand: the adaptive lexicon of tree growth at or near the timberline where the bruisingly cold, windy, and snowy environment challenges life on a daily basis. Most obvious is the "flagging," a term used to describe the absence of limbs on the side of the tree facing the prevailing wind, thus leav-ing the remaining limbs looking like a flagpole with flaglike limbs fluttering behind. "Die-back or the death of most of the tree, leaving a minimum amount of foliage and bark to continue food making and transport, is an-other adjustment to the harsh environment."[72] Finally, *krummholz*, a Ger-man word meaning "crooked wood," is used to describe the "gnarled, stunted, and usually bush forms"[73] that many trees, including the fabu-lously contorted bristlecones, take in places where strong winds make upright growth difficult. *Krummholz* trees grow more horizontally than vertically to secure whatever protection is afforded by snow cover or nearby boulders or rock formations. Some of the older Great Basin bristle-cones are almost completely horizontal, magically hanging on to life by a narrow strip of living bark.

Like that of many Americans, my most physically adaptive behavior consists of my biannual closet cleaning—replacing summer clothes with winter ones and vice versa—and shifting the lever on the thermostat from heat to air-conditioning. Trees, of course, change leaves in a pattern that reverses our approach to cooler temperatures—they take off their clothes as we put on more of ours. "Do you know why deciduous trees lose their leaves?" Ken Cooper asked when we spoke by phone. Even though I knew it was not what he was asking, what little I remember of ninth-grade biology flashed through my mind before I said no. Then Cooper, a Native American spiritual and environmental storyteller, answered his own question. "The deciduous trees were so embarrassed at not being able to walk to the top of the mountain, that they dropped all their clothes."

Cause and effect may be reversed in the Native American story; in fact it is *because* deciduous trees drop all their leaves that they cannot walk to the top of the mountain. It takes an enormous amount of energy to create and maintain an entirely new wardrobe each spring, summer, and fall, and near the tops of mountains, at the timberline, the growing season is too short and the resources too scant to provide for such abundance. The Inyo bristlecones, for example, get only 8 to 10 inches of precipitation annually. Timberline trees, typically evergreens, reuse much of their foliage for many years, thus conserving the energy needed for survival in such inhospitable places. It is how they achieve the appearance of being always green, a sleight-of-hand produced by rotating rather than changing foliage. As in so many other areas, however, the Great Basin bristlecones are extraordinary in this regard as well: "exhibit[ing] needle retention for 25 to 30 years, and . . . a branch from a tree in the Snake Range, White Pine County, Nevada, [has] needles about 38 years old and still green and apparently capable of photosynthesizing." [74] Compare this with the nearby Jeffrey pine, which retains its needles from 5 to 8 years or the White pine (*Pinus strobus*) which, where I live in the East, keeps its needles for only about 15 to 16 months.

The Great Basin bristlecones have also adapted in another way—the way they establish a community. No upright, huddled eastern forests for the bristlecones, they grow in forests that more resemble a tree farm or a gym class asked to stand finger-length apart. This growth habit became clear about halfway into the Methuselah Walk—about the time I came to understand that it is called a walk because that is all most of us can manage

37. Hillside showing spacing of Great Basin bristlecones. (Courtesy
Eric A. Samuels)

over 10,000 feet and, corollarily, why it is necessary to allow two and a
half to three hours just to cover 4.2 miles, a distance I easily walk in an
hour and a half closer to sea level. Only then were my son and I able to see
further afield to the nearby hills, clearly dotted with their widely spaced
bristlecones.

And seeming to understand the three great tenets of real estate—location, location, location—the Great Basin bristlecones are also careful
where they choose to live, picking areas with dolomite soils rather than
the nearby sandstone. The reasons for this preference seem to be twofold:
"limestone and dolomite form relatively light colored soils which reflect
radiation better than granite and sandstones. As a result they possess lower

soil temperatures during the growing season and conserve water better. . . . Dolomites are also poorer in nutrients than granites and sandstones and thus discourage sagebrush, one of the important competitors of the bristlecones in the White Mountains."[75]

Besides having made many of the adaptations mentioned above, the ones who live the longest seem to have a few additional things in common. First, as Schulman discovered, "the trees of great longevity that have been found recently are all from environments strongly limited with respect to moisture or temperature or both,"[76] causing very, very slow growth. "A slow-growing White Mountains specimen at 10,500 feet grows one inch in radius for every 140 years of growth."[77] Second, their wood "contains more of the dense, hard latewood cells and probably a greater concentration of resin canals than does the wood of faster growing trees, hence is more resistant to decay."[78] It seems that adversity, not plenty, is responsible for longevity. Dana Bailey explains that "in regions where there is more abundant water, the trees grow rapidly and are more subject to heart rot."

Heart rot: what a fearsome-sounding death. And one inch in 140 years. It is almost too awesome to understand. As Thoreau writes, "at the same time that we are earnest to explore and learn all things, we require that all things be mysterious and unexplorable, that land and sea be infinitely wild, unsurveyed and unfathomable by us because unfathomable. We can never have enough of Nature."[79]

We can never have enough. So we plant trees in our communities and preserve trees in theirs. And when neither of these approaches seems adequate, we deed a tree to own itself. We tell their stories and they tell their stories and, when we look closely, we find our own stories are rooted in both. We do our own dance across the centuries—not the millennia of the bristlecones—sometimes harvesting the past, sometimes planting the future, and sometimes circling round the remnants of an earlier time to find the meanings that allow us to go on. We pack our bags with the seeds of memory and plant them liberally wherever we journey. And when those journeys make us fearful we plant a tree to guard our way. We plant trees to mark the happy days and the sad ones, to make a home, feed a family, and just to glory in their astounding beauty. Each one is a legacy, a gift of transformative power in life and of enduring beauty in death. As the internationally renowned woodworker George Nakashima writes:

We are left in awe by the nobility of a tree, its eternal patience, its suffering caused by man and sometimes nature, its witness to thousands of years of earth's history, its creations of fabulous beauty. It does nothing but good, with its prodigious ability to serve, it gives off its bounty of oxygen while absorbing gases harmful to other living things. The tree and its pith live on. Its fruits feed us. Its branches shade and protect us. And finally, when time and weather brings it down, its body offers timber for our houses and boards for our furniture. The tree lives on.[80]

NOTES

PREFACE

1. William Gilpin, *Remarks on Forest Scenery*, 1791.

1. TAKING ROOT: THE CHARTER OAK

1. Oliver Rackham, *Trees & Woodland in the British Landscape*, pp. 11–12.

2. William Barnes, "Trees Be Company," in Angela King and Susan Clifford, eds., *Trees Be Company*, pp. 139–140.

3. John Fowles, "Foreword" to King and Clifford, eds., *Trees Be Company*, p. xv; Ralph Waldo Emerson, from *Nature*, p. 19; and Annie Dillard, from *Teaching a Stone to Talk*, p. 55.

4. *Hartford Courant*, August 24, 1856.

5. Robert F. Trent, "The Charter Oak Artifacts," pp. 133–138.

6. Mark Twain, *Alta California*, February 1868.

7. In Carolyn Merchant, *Ecological Revolutions: Nature, Gender, and Science in New England*, p. 227.

8. Ibid., p. 231.

9. Perry Miller, *Nature's Nation*, pp. 11–12.

10. John F. Sears, *Sacred Places: American Tourist Attractions in the Nineteenth Century*, pp. 4–5.

11. Barbara Novak, *Nature and Culture*, pp. xxii, 9, 15.

12. Gerald L. Carr, *Frederick Edwin Church: Catalogue Raisonné of Works of Art at Olana State Historic Site*, pp. 93, 95, and 94.

13. Trent, "The Charter Oak Artifacts," pp. 129 and 127.

14. The first quote can be found in Anson T. McCook's address before the Society of the Founders of Hartford on the 250th Anniversary of the Hiding of the Charter, October 31, 1937, and the second in *The Connecticut Historical Society Bulletin* (July 1956): 67.

15. Michael Pollan, *Second Nature: A Gardener's Education*, p. 160.

16. William Cronon, *Changes in the Land*, p. 32.

17. Hazel R. Delcourt and Paul A. Delcourt, *Quaternary Ecology*, pp. 31, 57.

18. Jefferson's letter to Madame de Tesse can be found in Allen Lacy's *The American Gardener: A Sampler*, pp. 169–170.

19. Joseph Ewan, ed., *A Short History of Botany in the United States*, p. 12.

20. Charles Sprague Sargent, *The Silva of North America*, vol. 8, p. 19.

21. Quoted in ibid., p. 19, n. 1.

22. Donald Culross Peattie, *A Natural History of Trees of Eastern and Central North America*, pp. 195–196.

23. Whit Bronaugh, "National Register of Big Trees," *American Forests* (January/February 1994): 28.

24. Jan Murphy, "512-Year-Old Oak Tree Needs a Helping Hand," *Bucks County Intelligencer*, August 10, 1995, pp. A1, 8.

25. Ruth M. Miller and Linda A. Lennon, *The Angel Oak Story*, p. 9.

26. Sargent, *Silva*, vol. 8, p. 1.

27. Brayton F. Wilson, *The Growing Tree*, p. 45.

28. T. T. Kozlowski, *Growth and Development of Trees*, vol. 1, p. 201.

29. Ibid., p. 200.

30. Wilson, *The Growing Tree*, p. 46.

31. B. F. Graham, Jr., and F. H. Borman, "Natural Root Grafts," *The Botanical Review*, pp. 255, 274.

32. Ibid., pp. 274, 265.

33. Ibid., p. 259.

34. Carolyn Merchant, *Ecological Revolutions: Nature, Gender, and Science in New England*, p. 77.

35. W. L. Fletcher, *The Story of the Charter Oak*, pp. 34–35.

36. Raymond de Sebonde, "Natural Theology," in E.M.W. Tillyard, *The Elizabethan World Picture*, p. 27.

37. Cronon, *Changes in the Land*, p. 56.

38. Diana Ross McCain, "The Ol' Oak Tree," *Connecticut Magazine*, November 1987, pp. 164–166.

39. Pollan, *Second Nature*, p. 159.

40. F. E. Kuo and W. C. Sullivan, "Do Trees Strengthen Urban Communities, Reduce Domestic Violence?" *USDA Forest Service Southern Region, Technology Bulletin No. 4*, 1996.

41. Russell Page, *The Education of a Gardener*, p. 173.

2. FAMILY TREES

1. The information in this and the following paragraphs is drawn from a variety of sources: a letter from William Waldron to Richard Waldron, May 24, 1725; Samuel Penhallow, *History of the Wars of New England*, p. 112; Ellen Frye Barker, *Frye Genealogy*, p. 49; Clifford K. Shipton, *New England Life in the 18th Century: Representative Biographies from Sibley's Harvard Graduates*, pp. 213–215;

"Professions Followed by Harvard Men," *Harvard Alumni Bulletin*, October 16, 1912, p. 57; and Claude M. Fuess, *Andover: Symbol of New England*, pp. 131–132.

2. Leo Marx, *The Machine in the Garden*, p. 23.

3. Sarah Loring Bailey, *Historical Sketches of Andover*, p. 188.

4. Symmes's remarks can be found in Fuess, *Andover*, p. 132, and Bailey, *Historical Sketches*, pp. 187–188. The source for the Cotton Mather quote is Shipton, *New England Life*, p. 214.

5. Bailey, *Historical Sketches*, p. 192.

6. Nathaniel Hawthorne, "Roger Malvin's Burial," in *Young Goodman Brown and Other Tales*, pp. 56–57.

7. Charles Edgar Randall and Henry Clepper, *Famous and Historic Trees.*, p. 28; and Katharine Stanley Nicholson, *Historic American Trees*, pp. 88–89.

8. William T. Davis, ed., *Bradford's History of Plymouth Plantation*, p. 96.

9. Ralph Waldo Emerson, *Nature*, p. 6.

10. John R. Stilgoe, *Common Landscape of America, 1580 to 1845*, pp. 17–19. The quote is in Nathaniel Altman, *Sacred Trees*, p. 27.

11. James G. Frazer, *The Golden Bough*, p. 145.

12. Ibid., pp. 328–330; Alexander Porteous, *Forest Folklore, Mythology, and Romance*, pp. 182–183.

13. Porteous, *Forest Folklore*, p. 181.

14. Frazer, *Golden Bough*, p. 134.

15. Stilgoe, *Common Landscape*, p. 165.

16. Marx, *Machine in the Garden*, p. 73.

17. Frazer, *Golden Bough*, pp. 304–305.

18. *Greeley* [Colo.] *Tribune*, June 6, 1985.

19. Marx, *Machine in the Garden*, p. 365.

20. Porteous, *Forest Folklore*, pp. 188–189.

21. Jill Neimark, "Using Flows and Fluxes to Demythologize the Unity of Life," *New York Times*, August 11, 1998, p. F4.

22. Randall and Clepper, *Famous and Historic Trees*, p. 7.

23. William M. Harlow et al., *Textbook of Dendrology: Covering the Important Forest Trees of the United States and Canada*, p. 240; Bailey, *Historical Sketches*, p. 190; Donald Culross Peattie, *A Natural History of Trees of Eastern and Central North America*, p. 244.

24. Nicholson, *Historic American Trees*, p. 96.

25. Virginia Woolf, *Moments of Being: Unpublished Autobiographical Writings*, p. 70.

26. Randall and Clepper, *Famous and Historic Trees*, p. 70; Coolley family history; and *Tuscola Review*, February 7, 1974, p. 13.

27. Lillian Schlissel, *Women's Diaries of the Westward Journey*, pp. 58 and 47.

28. Keith Thomas, *Man and the Natural World: Changing Attitudes in England 1500–1800*, p. 218.

29. Esther B. Fein, "For Lost Pregnancies, New Rites of Mourning," *New York Times*, January 25, 1998, pp. 1, 34.

30. Virginia Cullen, *History of Lewes, Delaware,* p. 51.
31. Historic Woodburn brochure.
32. Iva Lillge, "Ash Nelson's Walnut Link," *American Forests* (January/February 1990): 47, 75.
33. Telephone conversation with Collin Proctor on March 31, 1998.
34. Marx, *Machine in the Garden,* p. 365.
35. Wallace Stegner, "Inheritance," in *American Places,* p. 12.
36. Wendell Berry, "Planting Trees," in King and Clifford, eds., *Trees Be Company,* pp. 100–101.
37. Harlow et al., *The Dendrology of Trees,* pp. 90, 134–138, 183–186, 239–241, 285–291, 416–418.
38. U.S. *Department of Commerce, Historical Statistics of the United States: Colonial Times to 1970,* part 1, p. 125.
39. John Ruskin, from *Seven Lamps of Architecture,* in *American Forests* 30 (April 1924): 242.
40. John Brinckerhoff Jackson, *Discovering the Vernacular Landscape,* p. 112.
41. Carolyn Merchant, *Ecological Revolutions: Nature, Gender, and Science in New England,* p. 227.
42. Terry L. West, *Centennial Mini-Histories of the Forest Service,* pp. 1–23.
43. *Plant Trees for America,* The National Arbor Day Foundation brochure.
44. Ellen Frankel, *The Classic Tales,* pp. 294–295.
45. Douglas T. Still and Henry D. Gerhold, "Motivations and Task Preference of Urban Forestry Volunteers," *Journal of Arboriculture* (May 1997): 116.
46. Talmud: Abot de Rabbi Nathan, II. Version, XXXI.
47. Steven A. Holmes, "U.S. No Longer a Land Steeped in Wanderlust," *New York Times,* September 12, 1995, pp. 1, 20.
48. Aldo Leopold, *A Sand County Almanac,* p. 81.
49. John Evelyn, *Sylva* (1664), in John Brinckerhoff Jackson, *A Sense of Place, a Sense of Time,* p. 102.

3. APPLES: CORE ISSUES

1. Robert C. Baron, ed., *The Garden and Farm Books of Thomas Jefferson,* p. 45.
2. Thomas Jefferson to James Madison, letter dated October 28, 1785, in ibid., pp. 178–179.
3. Roger Yepsen, *Apples,* p. 164.
4. Joan Morgan and Alison Richards, *The Book of Apples,* pp. 214–215.
5. Henry David Thoreau, *Wild Apples,* p. 1.
6. J. F. Basinger and D. L. Dilcher, "Ancient Bisexual Flowers," *Science,* pp. 511–513.
7. Ralph Austen, "To the Reader," in *A Treatise of Fruit-Trees,* p. 4.
8. N. W. Simmonds, *Evolution of Crop Plants,* pp. 247–250; and Beryl Brintnall Simpson and Molly Conner Ogorzaly, *Economic Botany: Plants in Our World,* pp. 79–82.

9. Lenore Loeb Adler, in *The Journal of Psychology* (January 1967): 15–21, and (May 1968): 53–61. In the first study, "drawings were collected from 2906 school children of both sexes in 13 countries on five continents" between the ages of 5 and 12 and "upon completion each child was asked individually to indicate the type of fruit tree pictured." The same approach was used in the second study, in which an additional 11 countries "yielded a total of 4314 pictures."

10. Simmonds, *Evolution of Crop Plants*, p. 248; Bayard Hora, ed., *Oxford Encyclopedia of Trees of the World*, p. 187; Peter Wynne, *Apples*, pp. 3–4.

11. Morgan and Richards, *Book of Apples*, pp. 9–10. I am very grateful to Joan Morgan and Alison Richards for their encyclopedic work, which has been extraordinarily useful in the preparation of this chapter.

12. Thomas F. Plummer, Jr. et al., *Landscape Atlas of the U.S.S.R.*, p. 126.

13. Morgan and Richards, *Book of Apples*, pp. 9–10; G. B. Masefield et al., eds., *The Oxford Book of Food Plants*, pp. 46–47.

14. Telephone conversation with Philip Forsline, USDA curator/horticulturalist at the National Plant Germ Plasm Repository, Geneva, N.Y., April 26, 1995.

15. Tom Christopher, *New York Times*, February 19, 1995, p. 50.

16. Alicia Amherst, *A History of Gardening in England*, p. 185.

17. Ralph Austen, *The Spirituall Use of an Orchard*, p.2.

18. Thoreau, *Wild Apples*, pp. 25–26.

19. Perry Miller, *Errand into the Wilderness*, p. 208.

20. *From Seed to Flower, Philadelphia 1681–1876: A Horticultural Point of View*, p. 19.

21. Morgan and Richards, *Book of Apples*, pp. 201, 244, 199.

22. For information on Emerson's interest in orchards see Robert D. Richardson, Jr., *Emerson: The Mind on Fire*, pp. 433–434.

23. Thomas Jefferson to Ellen Randolph Coolidge, letter dated March 19, 1826, in Baron, ed., *Garden and Farm Books*, pp. 209–210.

24. George L. Scheper, "Apple," in David Lyle Jeffrey, ed., *A Dictionary of Biblical Tradition in English Literature*, p. 50.

25. Quotes are in Morgan and Richards, *Book of Apples*, p. 23; Henning Cohen and Tristram Potter Coffin, eds., *The Folklore of American Holidays*, p. 310; Charles Skinner, *Myths and Legends of Flowers, Fruits, and Plants*, p. 44.

26. Morgan and Richards, *Book of Apples*; the quote about Alexander the Great is on p. 14, the reference to Pliny is on p. 16, and the information on grafting and pruning is on p. 23.

27. H. R. Loyn and John Percival, *The Reign of Charlemagne: Documents on Carolingian Government and Administration*, pp. 64–73.

28. Alicia Amherst, *A History of Gardening in England*, pp. 98–99.

29. U. P. Hedrick, *A History of Horticulture in America to 1860*, p. 95.

30. Rosalind K. Marshall, *Henrietta Maria: The Intrepid Queen*, pp. 67–70.

31. Roy Strong, *The Renaissance Garden in England*, p. 188.

32. Mary Anne Everett Green, *Letters of Queen Henrietta Maria*, p. 19.

33. Strong, *Renaissance Garden*, p. 197.
34. Marshall, *Henrietta Maria*, p. 14.
35. Diodorus Siculus, Book II. 10 (English trans. C. H. Oldfather).
36. Green, *Letters of Queen Herietta*, pp. 110 and 121.
37. Wallace Stegner, *The Spectator Bird*.
38. Amherst, *History of Gardening*, pp. 315–328.
39. Morgan and Richards, *Book of Apples*, p. 55.
40. Ibid., p. 57.
41. Amherst, *History of Gardening*, p. 181.
42. Shirley Abbott, *Womenfolks*, p. 149.
43. Morgan and Richards, *Book of Apples*, p. 28.
44. James E. Ivey, *In The Midst of a Loneliness: The Architectural History of the Salinas Missions*, p. 27.
45. Ibid., p. 27.
46. Quote from the diary of Ezra Stiles, president of Yale College, included in the entry on Blackstone or Blaxton in *The Dictionary of National Biography (DNB)*, vol. 2, pp. 594–595.
47. Hedrick, *History of Horticulture*, p. 30.
48. *DNB*, p. 595.
49. Hedrick, *History of Horticulture*, p. 38.
50. John R. Stilgoe, *Common Landscape of America, 1580–1845*, pp. 200–201.
51. Quoted in Hedrick, *History of Horticulture*, pp. 19, 105, 56, 79–80, 6–8, and 305.
52. Robert Price, *Johnny Appleseed: Man and Myth*, p. 38.
53. Hedrick, *History of Horticulture*, p. 302.
54. Morgan and Richards, *Book of Apples*, p. 69.
55. Hedrick, *History of Horticulture*, p. 340.
56. Fred Lape, *Apples and Man*, p. 20.
57. Hedrick, *History of Horticulture*, pp. 315, 330, 376–377, 386–388.
58. Lape, *Apples and Man*, p. 21.
59. Morgan and Richards, *Book of Apples*, p. 107.
60. Price, *Johnny Appleseed*, pp. 199, 38–39.
61. Frederick Jackson Turner, *The Frontier in American History*, pp. 3–4.
62. Price, *Johnny Appleseed*, p. 102.
63. Carolee Michener, "Six Cents Was Price per Tree," *The News Herald*, March 24, 1981.
64. W. D. Haley, "Johnny Appleseed—A Pioneer Hero," *Harper's New Monthly Magazine*, p. 832.
65. Price, *Johnny Appleseed*, p. 139.
66. Haley, "Johnny Appleseed," p. 835.
67. Price, *Johnny Appleseed*, p. 141.
68. Ibid., p. 49.
69. Thoreau, *Wild Apples*, p. 15.
70. Richard M. Dorson, *American Folklore*, pp. 107–110.

71. Haley, "Johnny Appleseed," p. 830.

72. Richard M. Dorson, *American Folklore and the Historian*, p. 214.

73. Ibid., p. 226.

74. Daniel Hoffman, *Paul Bunyan: Last of the Frontier Demigods*, pp. 162, 40.

75. National Arbor Day Foundation Press Release, "Chief Jake Swamp to Receive Arbor Day Foundation Media Award," April 15, 1998.

76. Letter from Jake Swamp to Gayle Samuels, December 30, 1997.

77. Robert Hendrickson, *Ladybugs, Tiger Lillies, and Wallflowers*, p. 10.

78. International Apple Institute, fact sheet, *Apple Facts: The U.S. Industry*.

79. Diane Ackerman, *A Natural History of the Senses*, p. 57.

4. THREE CHERRIES

1. L. H. Bailey, *Manual of Cultivated Plants*, p. 493.

2. Henry M. Cathey, "Foreword," in Roland Jefferson and Kay Kazue Wain, *The Nomenclature of Cultivated Japanese Flowering Cherries (Prunus): The Sato-Zakura Group*.

3. All quotes attributed to Paul Downs are from a March 14, 1997, interview at Downs's Bala Cynwyd, Pa., showroom and studio.

4. George Nakashima, *The Soul of a Tree: A Woodworker's Reflections*, p. 94.

5. Charles Sprague Sargent, *The Silva of North America*, vol. 4, p. 46.

6. François A. Michaux, *The North American Sylva*, intro., vol. 1, p. 1.

7. Ibid., vol. 2, p. 207.

8. Nakashima, *The Soul of a Tree*, p. 94, and quoted in Derek E. Ostergard, *George Nakashima: Full Circle*, p. 91.

9. Sargent, *Silva*, vol. 4, p. 46.

10. Donald Culross Peattie, *A Natural History of Trees of Eastern and Central North America*, p. 386.

11. Sargent, *Silva*, vol. 4, p. 9.

12. Sacvan Bercovitch, ed., *A Library of American Puritan Writings: The Seventeenth Century*, vol. 9, p. 20.

13. Ernest H. Wilson, *Aristocrats of the Trees*, pp. 194–195, 205, 206.

14. Sargent, *Silva*, vol. 4, pp. 46–47.

15. *The New Encyclopaedia Britannica*, vol. 3 Micropaedia, s.v. "cherry."

16. U. P. Hedrick, *A History of Horticulture in America*, p. 157.

17. Charles M. Skinner, *Myths and Legends of Flowers, Trees, Fruits, and Plants*, pp. 81–82.

18. Peter Conn, "Paternity and Patriarchy: *The Last Puritan* and the 1930s," p. 286.

19. B. A. Botkin, ed., *A Treasury of American Folklore*, pp. 256–257.

20. Samuel Eliot Morison and Henry Steele Commager, *The Growth of the American Republic*, vol. 2, p. 273.

21. Ernest H. Wilson, *The Cherries of Japan*, p. ix.

22. H. M. Cathey and F. S. Santamour, Jr., "Significance of Research," in U.S. National Arboretum Plant Exploration and Research Proposal, "Introduction

and Documentation of Superior Japanese Cherry Selections into the United States," October 29, 1981, p. 2.

23. Collingwood Ingram, *Ornamental Cherries*, p. 55.

24. Ernest H. Wilson, *China, Mother of Gardens*, pp. 288–291.

25. Ingram, *Ornamental Cherries*, p. 56.

26. Wilson, *Cherries of Japan*, p. ix.

27. Jefferson and Wain, *The Nomenclature of Cultivated Japanese Flowering Cherries*, p. 3.

28. National Park Service News Release, revised February 20, 1997, press contact (202) 260–3282.

29. Roland Jefferson, note to author, August 12, 1998.

30. *Washington Herald*, "Koreans Claim Cherry Trees," April 5, 1942.

31. Roland M. Jefferson and Alan E. Fusonie, *The Japanese Flowering Cherry Trees of Washington, D.C.*, p. 2.

32. This information is drawn from Eliza Ruhamah Scidmore's article, "The Cherry-Blossoms of Japan," in *Century Magazine*, p. 644; Christopher Thacker, *The History of Gardens*, p. 63, also related in Skinner, *Myths and Legends*, p. 80; and Jefferson and Fusonie, *The Japanese Flowering Cherry Trees of Washington, D.C.*, p. 1.

33. Paul Russell, *The Oriental Flowering Cherries*, p. 2; and Donald L. Philippi, trans., *Kojiki*, pp. 144–147.

34. Philippi, trans., *Kojiki*, p. 145.

35. Ibid., p. 145.

36. Koichi Oshida, *Newsletter of the Japan Program of the University of Alabama*, vol. 4, p. 2.

37. Scidmore, "Cherry-Blossoms of Japan," p. 644.

38. Oshida, *Newsletter*, pp. 1–3.

39. Nakashima, "At One with Nature," in Ostergard, *George Nakashima*, p. 91.

40. Ingram, *Ornamental Cherries*, pp. 59 and 97.

41. Donald Keene, ed., *Anthology of Japanese Literature*, p. 439.

42. Manabu Miyoshi, *Sakura: Japanese Cherry*, pp. 11–20.

43. Philip J. Pauly, "The Beauty and Menace of the Japanese Cherry Trees," *Isis* (March 1996): 61.

44. Roland M. Jefferson, "Boxwood Round the Lincoln Memorial," p. 6.

45. Roland M. Jefferson, "The History of the Cherry Blossom Trees in Potomac Park," p. 33.

46. Ibid., pp. 33–34.

47. Pauly, "The Beauty and Menace," pp. 66–67.

48. Jefferson and Fusonie, *Japanese Flowering Cherry Trees*, pp. 4–6.

49. Ibid., p. 7.

50. David Fairchild, "How United States and Japan Entered into a League of Flowers," p. 5.

51. Jefferson and Fusonie, *Japanese Flowering Cherry Trees*, p. 7; and "Behind the

Scenes," *National Geographic*, April 1997. Scidmore's role is verified in David Fairchild's *The World Was My Garden: Travels of a Plant Explorer*, p. 412.

52. Fairchild, *The World Was My Garden*, p. 412.
53. First Indorsement, Office of Public Buildings and Grounds, Washington, D.C., April 6, 1909, Record Group 42, Entry 97, File 52, Potomac Park: General, National Archives, Washington, D.C.
54. Pauly, "Beauty and Menace," p. 51.
55. Col. Cosby to Hoopes Bros. & Thomas Company, April 12, 1909, Record Group 42, Entry 97, File 52, Potomac Park: General, National Archives, Washington, D.C.
56. Russell, *Oriental Flowering Cherry Trees*, p. 3.
57. Jefferson and Fusonie, *Japanese Flowering Cherry Trees*, p. 9.
58. Ibid., pp. 10–15, 53; and Pauly, "Beauty and Menace," pp. 51–52.
59. Pauly provides an excellent treatment of the link between the development of policies regulating human and nonhuman species in the first decades of the twentieth century. See ibid., pp. 60 and 68 for quotes.
60. Keene, ed., *Anthology*, p. 247.
61. Jas. J. Thomas, Mayor, to the Secretary of State and to the Mayor of Tokio, both November 17, 1925, Record Group 59, Box 438, File 093.941 W 27, National Archives, Washington, D.C.
62. *Washington Star*, April 3, 1927, Record Group 42, Entry 109, Newspaper Clippings, National Archives, Washington, D.C.
63. Jefferson, "History of the Cherry Blossom," p. 36; and Ingram, *Ornamental Cherries*, p. 59.
64. Letter to: Secretary, USDA through: N. C. Brady, Director of Science and Education, from: George W. Irving, Jr., Administrator, April 12, 1965, Record Group 16, General Correspondence 1965, Trees, Box 4393, National Archives, Washington, D.C.
65. Jefferson and Fusonie, *Japanese Flowering Cherry Trees*, pp. 24 and 28; and National Park Service News Release, p. 7.
66. Jefferson, "History of the Cherry Blossom," p. 37.
67. Lewis Hyde, *The Gift: Imagination and the Erotic Life of Property*, dedication.
68. Roland Jefferson, note to author, August 12, 1998.
69. Isabel S. Cunningham, "The U.S. National Arboretum: Leader in Ornamental Plant Germplasm Collection."
70. Ibid.
71. Jefferson, "History of the Cherry Blossom," p. 38.
72. Roland Jefferson, note to author, August 12, 1998.
73. Peattie, *A Natural History*, p. 505.
74. Miyoshi, *Sakura*, p. 6.
75. Hyde, *The Gift*, p. 3.
76. Ibid., p. 11.
77. Lafcadio Hearn, *Glimpses of Unfamiliar Japan*, pp. 20–21.

78. National Park Service sign, West Potomac Park, Washington, D.C.
79. National Cherry Blossom Festival 1997 brochure.
80. John Brinckerhoff Jackson, *A Sense of Place, a Sense of Time*, p. 193.
81. Eleanor Perényi, *Green Thoughts*, p. 137.
82. Pauly, "Beauty and Menace," p. 59.
83. Ibid., p. 69.
84. Telephone conversation with Robert DeFeo, May 28, 1997.

5. RETURNING NATIVES

1. O. E. Rölvaag, *Giants in the Earth*, p. 413.
2. Carl Ubbelohde, Maxine Benson, Duane A. Smith, *A Colorado History*, pp. 29–30.
3. Carl Abbott, Stephen J. Leonard, David McComb, *Colorado: A History of the Centennial State*, p. 6; also in Carl Ubbelohde et al., *Colorado History*, pp. 28–29.
4. Abbott et al., *Colorado*, pp. 6–7.
5. Ibid., p. 6.
6. Reed F. Noss and Robert L. Peters, *Endangered Ecosystems: A Status Report on America's Vanishing Habitat and Wildlife*, p. 63.
7. Phillip L. Sims, "Grasslands," in *North American Terrestrial Vegetation*, p. 266.
8. Richard Manning, *Grassland*, p. 138.
9. Sims, "Grasslands," p. 266.
10. Ubbelohde et al., *Colorado History*, p. 27.
11. Sims, "Grasslands," p. 268.
12. Paul E. Collins, *The "Siberian Elm" Slippery Elm Hybrid*, Technical Bulletin No. 39, p. 5.
13. Sims, "Grasslands," p. 282.
14. Conversation with Ann F. Rhoads, chair of botany, Morris Arboretum, University of Pennsylvania, February 20, 1998.
15. John R. Stilgoe, *Common Landscape of America, 1580 to 1845*, p. 99.
16. Ibid., pp. 99–107.
17. Ibid., pp. 98, 133.
18. Works Projects Administration [WPA], *Colorado: A Guide to the Highest State*, pp. 68–69.
19. Abbott et al., *Colorado*, p. 172.
20. Patricia Nelson Limerick, *The Legacy of Conquest: The Unbroken Past of the American West*, p. 60.
21. Glenn R. Scott, "Historic Trail Maps of the Sterling 1° × 2° Quadrangle," text to accompany USGS map I-1894, p. 1.
22. Manning, *Grassland*, pp. 83–89.
23. Willa Cather, *O Pioneers!*, p. 13; Rölvaag, *Giants*, p. 227.
24. Gen. James S. Brisbin, *Trees and Tree-Planting*, p. xxvi.
25. Abbott et al., *Colorado*, p. 159.
26. Ubbelohde et al., *Colorado History*, p. 133.
27. Abbott et al., *Colorado*, p. 159.
28. David Boyd, *A History: Greeley and the Union Colony of Colorado*, pp. 79–80.

29. Ibid., p. 81.
30. Ibid., pp. 61, 56, 57.
31. Abbott et al., *Colorado*, p. 21.
32. Ibid., pp. 23, 169.
33. Ibid., p. 172.
34. Telephone conversations with Dr. George Ware, November 1997.
35. Jonathan Raban, *Bad Land*, p. 7.
36. Conversation with Lucy Price at Lucy's Cafe, Sedgwick, Colo., November 3, 1997.
37. Theodore Roosevelt, Arbor Day Proclamation, 1907.
38. Conversation with Gary Lancaster, extension agent, Sedgwick County, Colo., November 3, 1997.
39. Collins, *"Siberian Elm" Slippery Elm*, p. 5.
40. Clyde M. Brundy, "The Cottonwood Retreat," p. 20.
41. Walter E. Webb, "A Report on Ulmus Pumila in the Great Plains Region of the United States," p. 274.
42. Collins, *"Siberian Elm" Slippery Elm*, p. 5.
43. Webb, "Report on Ulmus Pumila," pp. 275, 274.
44. Ibid., p. 274.
45. Donald J. Leopold, "Chinese and Siberian Elms," p. 175.
46. Isabel S. Cunningham, *Frank N. Meyer: Plant Hunter in Asia*, pp. 5–6.
47. Manning, *Grassland*, p. 173.
48. Cunningham, *Frank N. Meyer*, p. 261.
49. Donald Culross Peattie, *Flowering Earth*, pp. 17–18.
50. Harold E. Engstrom and Lewis S. Matthew, "Effects of the 1940 Armistice Day Freeze on Siberian Elm in the Plains Country," p. 707.
51. Ibid.
52. Ibid., pp. 706–707.
53. C. G. Bates, "Comment," p. 708.
54. Telephone conversation with George H. Ware, January 16, 1998.
55. Ron Gosnell, "A Halloween Tree Killer," p. 36.
56. Peattie, *A Natural History of Trees*, p. 244.
57. Dennis Cauchon, "The Great Elm Returns," p. 1.
58. WPA, *Colorado*, p. 15.
59. *Greeley Tribune*, June 16, 1976.
60. John Seelmeyer, "Cotton-Bearing Tree Controversy Revived," *Greeley Tribune*, July 7, 1976.
61. *Greeley Tribune*, March 22, 1977.
62. Article I, in General, Sec. 22–28, Sale, Planting of certain trees prohibited. Sterling [Colo.] City Ordinances.
63. Randy Marshall, "Tree Removal Hacks off Weld Farmer," *Greeley Tribune*, June 14, 1990.
64. James Brooke, "Pollen Police and Arboreal Outlaws," *New York Times*, December 22, 1996, p. 12.

65. Gosnell, "Halloween Tree Killer," p. 34.

66. Report by Colorado State Extension Service, provided by Philip J. Hoefer, Colorado State Forest Service, November 7, 1997.

67. *Greeley Tribune,* November 1, 1991.

68. Bill Jackson, "Winterkill Destroying Greeley Trees," *Greeley Tribune,* May 13, 1992.

69. Gosnell, "Halloween Tree Killer," p. 36.

70. Jim Nighswonger, "A Report of Streetside Losses of Siberian Elm in Western Kansas Resulting from Freeze Damage on October 31, 1991," p. 1.

71. Halloween Freeze Recovery Initiative, Council of Western State Foresters, Supplemental Budget Request "White Paper" for FY94, p. 1.

72. Bill Scanlon, "Tree Loss Stands at $425 Million," *Rocky Mountain News,* November 17, 1992.

73. Ibid.

74. Brayton F. Wilson, *The Growing Tree,* p. 124.

75. Gary Gerhardt, "Tree Die-off Makes Some Spots Look Like Florida after Andrew," *Rocky Mountain News,* September 24, 1992.

76. Included in Report by Colorado State Extension Service, provided by Philip J. Hoefer, Colorado State Forest Service, November 7, 1997.

77. Emily Dickinson, *Complete Poems,* ed. Thomas Johnson, poem 873.

78. Telephone conversation with Nolan Doesken, November 7, 1997.

79. Peter Farb, *The Forest,* p. 10.

80. "Tree Damage Drastic This Year," *Holyoke Enterprise,* May 28, 1992.

81. City of Sterling Ten-Year Urban Forestry Management Plan, p. 5.

82. Gerhardt, "Tree Die-off."

83. Nighswonger, "Report of Streetside Losses."

84. Interview with Joe Lohnes in Greeley, Colo., November 4, 1997, and by telephone, January 21, 1998.

85. City of Sterling Ten-Year Urban Forestry Management Plan, p. 5.

86. Interview with Mike Jackson in Sterling, Colo., November 5, 1997.

87. Interview with Mark Brown in Holyoke, Colo., November 5, 1997.

88. Gosnell, "Halloween Tree Killer," pp. 34–35.

89. Interview with Leroy "Butch" Blockowitz in Julesburg, Colo., November 3, 1997.

90. Interviews with Lucy Price, Gary Lancaster, and Katherine Mills in and around Julesburg, Colo., November 3, 1997.

91. *Oxford English Dictionary,* s.v., "experience," and "experiment."

92. John Dixon Hunt and Peter Willis, *The Genius of the Place: The English Landscape Garden 1620–1820,* p. 212.

93. Cauchon, "Great Elm Returns," p. 2.

94. Peattie, *Natural History of Trees,* p. 240.

95. Thomas J. Schlereth, "The Above-Ground Archaeology of Trees," p. 41.

96. Berton Roueché, "A Great Green Cloud," *The New Yorker,* July 15, 1961, p. 36.

97. Cauchon, "Great Elm Returns," p. 2.

98. Quote in Lancaster, Pa., *Intelligencer Journal*, June 3, 1997, p. A-5; a photo of the design for the bombing memorial is in the *New York Times*, July 2, 1997, p. A20.

99. *Elm Leaves*, publication of the Elm Research Institute, July 1998.

6. THE TREE THAT OWNED ITSELF

1. Deed of Conveyance, Knott County, Kentucky, August 30, 1918.

2. Richard Lowitt, "Alice Spencer Geddes Lloyd," *Notable American Women: The Modern Period*, p. 423.

3. P. David Searles, *A College for Appalachia*, p. 42.

4. David E. Whisnant, *All That Is Native and Fine*, p. 19.

5. Lowitt, "Alice Spencer Geddes Lloyd," p. 423.

6. Ibid., p. 424.

7. Cindy Fassnacht, "June Buchanan at ALC," *Knott County News*, November 6, 1975.

8. Nevyle Shackelford, *Robinson Substation: A Short History*, p. 6.

9. Kirk Johnson, "Sycamore, 110 Million Years in the Making," pp. 4–5.

10. F. Kevin Simon, ed., *WPA Guide to Kentucky*, p. 22.

11. Donald Culross Peattie, *A Natural History of Trees of Eastern and Central North America*, pp. 318, 316.

12. Julia Ellen Rogers, *The Tree Book*, p. 282.

13. Johnson, "Sycamore," p. 5.

14. Thomas Pakenham, *Meetings with Remarkable Trees*, p. 69.

15. François A. Michaux, *The North American Sylva*, vol 2, pp. 58–59.

16. Norman Taylor, *The Guide to Garden Shrubs and Trees*, p. 189.

17. Harriet L. Keeler, *Our Native Trees*, p. 265.

18. Brayton F. Wilson, *The Growing Tree*, p. 27.

19. D. W. Meinig, ed., *The Interpretation of Ordinary Landscapes*, p. 44.

20. Simon, ed., *WPA Guide*, p. 3.

21. Paul Camplin, ed., *Forestry in Kentucky*, p. 6.

22. Simon Schama, *Landscape and Memory*, p. 107.

23. Camplin, ed., *Forestry*, p. 6.

24. Ibid., pp. 51, 6.

25. Simon, ed., *WPA Guide*, p. 51.

26. Susan Cooper, *Rural Hours*, pp. 213–214.

27. Camplin, ed., *Forestry*, p. 6.

28. W. B. Webb, "Retrospect of the Lumber Industry in Eastern Kentucky: Story of Fifty Years of Progress."

29. Rick Bragg, "Termites Haunt, and Topple, Mighty Oaks in Leafy New Orleans," *New York Times*, June 30, 1996, p. 14.

30. John Fowles, *The Tree*, pp. 41–42.

31. Schama, *Landscape and Memory*, p. 15.

32. National Public Radio, "Morning Edition," transcript of October 16, 1995, broadcast, pp. 11–13.

33. Joseph Berger, "A Tree Survives; Foes Do Not," *New York Times*, September 27, 1995, pp. B1 and B7.

34. William T. Davis, ed., *Bradford's History of Plymouth Plantation*, 1908. p. 96.

35. William Cronon, *Changes in the Land*, p. 75.

36. *From Seed to Flower, Philadelphia 1681–1876: A Horticultural Point of View*, pp. 17–18.

37. Ralph Waldo Emerson, *Nature*, pp. 10–11.

38. Laws of the Town of Summerville, [S.C.], Chapter 20, "Tree Protection," modified May 10, 1995.

39. Henry H. Tryon, "A Town That Owns Its Trees," pp. 209ff.

40. Alfred Runte, *National Parks: The American Experience*, pp. 29–30.

41. Conversation with Paul Meyer, Morris Arboretum, Philadelphia, Pa., November 6, 1995.

42. Christopher D. Stone, *Should Trees Have Standing?: Toward Legal Rights for Natural Objects*, p. 47.

43. Ibid., pp. xii–xiii.

44. Robert Frost, "The Gift Outright."

45. T. C. McLuhan, ed., *Touch the Earth: A Self-Portrait of the Indian Existence*, p. 6.

46. Ibid., p. 99.

47. Aldo Leopold, *A Sand County Almanac*, p. viii.

48. John Donne, "Devotions Upon Emergent Occasions," XVII.

49. Garrett Hardin, "Foreword," in Stone, *Should Trees Have Standing?*, p. xvi.

50. William K. Stevens, "One in Every 8 Plant Species Is Imperiled, a Survey Finds," *New York Times*, April 9, 1998, p. 1.

51. Gretchen C. Daily, ed., *Nature's Services: Societal Dependence on Natural Ecosystems*, p. 366.

52. Edward O. Wilson, "Back from Chaos," *The Atlantic Monthly*, March 1998, p. 54.

53. Harold A. Mooney and Paul R. Ehrlich, "Ecosystem Services: A Fragmentary History," in Daily, ed., *Nature's Services*, p. 17.

7. METHUSELAH'S WALK

1. H. D. Thoreau, *Journal*, November 1, 1853, quoted in Eliot Porter, *"In Wildness Is the Preservation of the World,"* p. 92.

2. Michael Cohen, *A Garden of Bristlecones: Tales of Change in the Great Basin*, p. 133.

3. Ibid., p. 157.

4. N. T. Mirov, *The Genus Pinus*, p. 419.

5. Hugh Mozingo, *Shrubs of the Great Basin: A Natural History*, p. 19.

6. Brian Miller and Edwin Rockwell, *Methuselah Walk*, brochure produced by the Eastern Sierra Interpretive Association.

7. Nathaniel Altman, *Sacred Trees*, p. 167.

8. Emily Dickinson, *Complete Poems*, ed. Thomas H. Johnson, poem 987.

9. Joseph Wood Krutch, "Introduction," in Porter, *"In Wildness Is the Preservation of the World,"* p. 9.

10. John Muir, *The Mountains of California*, p. 154.

11. Edmund Schulman, "Bristlecone Pine, Oldest Known Living Thing," *National Geographic*, March 1958, p. 366.

12. Ibid., p. 355.

13. William R. Boggess, "Dendrochronology," *McGraw-Hill Encyclopedia of Science & Technology*, vol. 5, pp. 100–101.

14. Fritz Hans Schweingruber, *Tree Rings: Basics and Applications of Dendrochronology*, p. 256.

15. Ibid.

16. Ibid., pp. 2–3, 256–257.

17. Thomas E. Graedel and Paul J. Crutzen, *Atmosphere, Climate, and Change*, p. 81.

18. "Andrew Ellicott Douglass 1867–1962," *Tree-Ring Bulletin* 24 (May 1962): 3.

19. Boggess, "Dendrochronology," p. 101.

20. C. W. Ferguson, "Bristlecone Pine: Science and Esthetics," *Science* 159 (February 23, 1968): 840.

21. Andrew Ellicott Douglass, "The Secret of the Southwest Solved by Talkative Tree Rings," *National Geographic*, December 1929, pp. 750, 737, 743.

22. Cohen, *Garden*, p. 32.

23. Douglass, "Secret of the Southwest," p. 770.

24. Schweingruber, *Tree Rings*, p. 153.

25. Douglass, "Secret of the Southwest," p. 739.

26. "Edmund Schulman 1908–1958," *Tree-Ring Bulletin* 22 (December 1958): 3.

27. David Muench and Darwin Lambert, *Timberline Ancients*, p. 62.

28. Schweingruber, *Tree Rings*, p. 42.

29. Schulman, "Bristlecone Pine, Oldest Known Living Thing," p. 361.

30. Muench and Lambert, *Timberline Ancients*, p. 63.

31. Schulman, "Bristlecone Pine," p. 361.

32. Cohen, *Garden*, p. 63.

33. William M. Harlow, Ellwood S. Harrar, James W. Hardin, and Fred M. White, *Textbook of Dendrology: Covering the Important Forest Trees of the United States and Canada*, pp. 90–91.

34. Cohen, *Garden*, pp. 5–6.

35. D. K. Bailey, "Phytogeography and Taxonomy of *Pinus* Subsection *Balfourianae*," pp. 221, 217.

36. From telephone conversations with Gary Funkhouser on July 30 and August 6, 1997, and Rex Adams on October 12, 1998.

37. Schweingruber, *Tree Rings*, p. 248.

38. "Pyramids from France?" *Newsweek*, April 5, 1971, p. 50.

39. Schweingruber, *Tree Rings*, p. 251.

40. Cohen, *Garden*, p. 54.

41. William K. Stevens, "Drought May Have Doomed the Lost Colony," *New York Times*, April 24, 1998, pp. 1, 14.

42. Boggess, "Dendrochronology," pp. 102–103.

43. Marc Reisner, *Cadillac Desert: The American West and Its Disappearing Water,* p. 127.

44. Douglass, "Secret of the Southwest," p. 741.

45. Telephone conversation with John Louth, bristlecone pine forest manager, Inyo National Forest, September 2, 1997.

46. Cohen, *Garden,* p. 114.

47. Alexandra Murphy, *Graced by Pines: The Ponderosa Pine in the American West,* p. 25.

48. John Muir, *John of the Mountains,* p. 313.

49. Bailey, "Phytogeography," p. 237; Mirov, *The Genus Pinus,* p. 30.

50. Cohen, *Garden,* pp. 153–154.

51. Elna Bakker, *An Island Called California: An Ecological Introduction to Its Natural Communities,* p. 183.

52. Bailey, "Phytogeography," p. 238.

53. Cohen, *Garden,* p. 11.

54. Bakker, *An Island Called California,* p. 100.

55. Reisner, *Cadillac Desert,* p. 3

56. Will Durant, in Graedel and Crutzen's *Atmosphere, Climate, and Change,* p. 1.

57. Bakker, *An Island Called California.*

58. Ibid., pp. 88–89.

59. *McGraw-Hill Encyclopedia of Science & Technology,* vol. 7, p. 366.

60. Bakker, *An Island Called California,* p. 106.

61. Simon Schama, *Landscape and Memory,* p. 187; Francis P. Farquhar, *History of the Sierra Nevada,* p. 87.

62. Henry D. Thoreau, *Walden,* p. 212.

63. Alfred Runte, *National Parks: The American Experience,* p. 83.

64. Telephone conversation with John Louth, bristlecone pine forest manager, Inyo National Forest, August, 29, 1997.

65. Runte, *National Parks,* p. 70.

66. Terry L. West, *Centennial Mini-Histories of the Forest Service,* p. 53.

67. Reisner, *Cadillac Desert,* pp. 85–86.

68. For a more complete treatment of this subject see ibid., pp. 54–86.

69. Ibid., p. 86.

70. Aldo Leopold in Graedel and Crutzen, *Atmosphere, Climate, and Change,* p. 89.

71. Inyo National Forest Map, U.S. Forest Service, 1993.

72. Bakker, *An Island Called California,* pp. 243–244.

73. Michael Allaby, ed., *The Concise Oxford Dictionary of Botany,* p. 221.

74. Bailey, "Phytogeography," p. 224.

75. Ibid., p. 327.

76. Edmund Schulman, "Longevity under Adversity in Conifers," p. 397.

77. Cohen, *Garden,* p. 83.

78. Muench and Lambert, *Timberline Ancients,* p. 67.

79. Thoreau, *Walden,* pp. 211–212.

80. George Nakashima, *The Soul of a Tree: A Woodworker's Reflections,* p. 81.

BIBLIOGRAPHY

Abbott, Carl; Stephen J. Leonard; and David McComb. *Colorado: A History of the Centennial State*. Revised edition. Boulder: Colorado Associated University Presses, 1982.

Abbott, Shirley. *Womenfolks: Growing Up Down South*. New York: Ticknor & Fields, 1983.

Ackerman, Diane. *A Natural History of the Senses*. New York: Vintage Books, 1991.

Adler, Lenore Loeb. "A Note on Cross-Cultural Preferences: Fruit-tree Preference in Children's Drawings." *The Journal of Psychology* (January 1967): 15–21.

———. "A Note on the Cross-Cultural Fruit-Tree Study: A Test-Retest Procedure." *The Journal of Psychology* (May 1968): 53–61.

Allaby, Michael, ed. *The Concise Oxford Dictionary of Botany*. Oxford and New York: Oxford University Press. 1992.

Altman, Nathaniel. *Sacred Trees*. San Francisco: Sierra Club Books, 1994.

Amherst, The Hon. Alicia. *A History of Gardening in England*. 2d edition. London: Bernard Quaritch, 1896.

Austen, Ralph. *A Treatise of Fruit-Trees*. Oxford: Tho. Robinson, 1653.

Bailey, D. K. "Phytogeography and Taxonomy of *Pinus* Subsection *Balfourianae*." *Annals of the Missouri Botanical Gardens* 57 (1970): 210–249.

Bailey, L. H. *Manual of Cultivated Plants*. New York: Macmillan, 1949.

———. *The Standard Cyclopedia of Horticulture*. Vol. 2. New York: Macmillan, 1950.

Bailey, Sarah Loring. *Historical Sketches of Andover (comprising the present towns of North Andover and Andover) Massachusetts*. Boston: Houghton, Mifflin and Company, 1880.

Bakker, Elna. *An Island Called California: An Ecological Introduction to Its Natural Communities*. 2d edition. Berkeley, Los Angeles, London: University of California Press, 1972.

Barker, Ellen Frye. *Frye Genealogy*. New York: Tobias A. Right, Printer, 1920.

Baron, Robert C., ed. *The Garden and Farm Books of Thomas Jefferson*. Golden, CO: Fulcrum, 1987.

Basinger, J. F., and D. L. Dilcher. "Ancient Bisexual Flowers." *Science* 224 (1984): 511–513.

Bates, C. G. "Comment." *Journal of Forestry* 40 (1942): 708.

Bercovitch, Sacvan, ed. *A Library of Puritan Writings: The Seventeenth Century.* Vol. 9. New York: AMS Press, Inc., 1986.

Berger, Joseph. "A Tree Survives; Foes Do Not." *New York Times,* September 27, 1995.

Bickford, Christopher P. "Connecticut and Its Charter." *The Connecticut Historical Society Bulletin* (summer 1984): 111–122.

"Big Cherry Blossom Pageant Will Be Presented Saturday." *Washington Star.* April 3, 1927, Record Group 42, Entry 109, Newspaper Clippings, National Archives, Washington, DC.

Bixby, William. *Connecticut: A New Guide.* New York: Charles Scribner's Sons, 1974.

Blackmore, Stephen, ed. *The Facts on File Dictionary of Botany.* Aylesbury, U.K.: Market House Books Limited, 1984.

Boggess, William R. "Dendrochronology," s.v. In *McGraw-Hill Encyclopedia of Science and Technology.* Volume 5. 7th edition. New York: McGraw-Hill, 1992. pp. 100–103.

Botkin, B. A., ed. *A Treasury of American Folklore.* New York: Crown Publishers, 1944.

Boyd, David. *A History: Greeley and the Union Colony of Colorado.* Greeley, CO: The Greeley Tribune Press, 1890.

Bragg, Rick. "Termites Haunt, and Topple, Mighty Oaks in Leafy New Orleans." *New York Times,* June 30, 1996.

Brisbin, Gen. James S. *Trees and Tree-Planting.* New York: Harper & Brothers, 1888.

Bronaugh, Whit. "National Register of Big Trees." *American Forests* (January/February 1994): 26, 28, 48.

Brooke, James. "Pollen Police and Arboreal Outlaws." *New York Times,* December 22, 1996, p. 12.

Brundy, Clyde M. "The Cottonwood Retreat." *Empire Magazine,* November 25, 1973.

Camplin, Paul, ed. *Forestry in Kentucky.* Frankfort: Kentucky Department of Natural Resources, 1966.

Carr, Gerald L. *Frederick Edwin Church: Catalogue Raisonné of Works of Art at Olana State Historic Site.* Vol. 1. Cambridge: Cambridge University Press, 1994.

Cather, Willa. *O Pioneers!* New York: Bantam Books, 1989.

Cathey, H. M., and F. S. Santamour, Jr. "Significance of Research" Section. U.S. National Arboretum Plant Exploration and Research Proposal "Introduction and Documentation of Superior Japanese Cherry Selections into the United States," October 29, 1981.

Cato, Marcus Porcius. *On Agriculture.* Cambridge, MA, London: Harvard University Press, 1954.

Cauchon, Dennis. "Great Elm Returns." *USA Today,* November 6, 1997, pp. 1–2.

City of Sterling Ten-Year Urban Forestry Management Plan, 1993.

Christopher, Tom. "Grafting: Playing Dr. Frankenstein in the Garden." *New York Times,* February 19, 1995, p. 50.

Cohen, Hennig, and Tristram Potter Coffin, eds. *The Folklore of American Holidays.* Detroit: Gale Research Company, 1987.

Cohen, Michael P. *A Garden of Bristlecones: Tales of Change in the Great Basin.* Reno: University of Nevada Press, 1998.

Compact Oxford English Dictionary. 2d edition. Oxford: Clarendon Press, 1991.

Collins, Paul E. *The Siberian Elm Slippery Elm Hybrid.* Technical Bulletin No. 39. Brookings: South Dakota State University, Agricultural Experiment Station, November 1971.

Conn, Peter. "Paternity and Patriarchy: *The Last Puritan* and the 1930s." In *Critical Essays on George Santayana,* ed. Kenneth M. Price and Robert C. Leitz III. Boston: G. K. Hall, 1991.

Cooley family papers. "Fairfield." Undated manuscript given to author by Jane Waldbillig.

Cooper, Susan. *Rural Hours.* Philadelphia: Willis P. Hazard, 1854.

Cosby, Spencer. First Indorsement, Office of Public Buildings and Grounds, Washington, April 6, 1909, Record Group 42, Entry 97, File 52, Potomac Park: General, National Archives, Washington, DC.

————. Letter to Hoopes Bros. & Thomas Company, April 12, 1909, Record Group 42, Entry 97, File 52, Potomac Park: General, National Archives, Washington, DC.

Cronon, William. *Changes in the Land: Indians, Colonists, and the Ecology of New England.* New York: Hill and Wang, 1983.

Cullen, Virginia. *History of Lewes, Delaware.* Lewes and Rehoboth: Daughters of the American Revolution, Colonel David Hall Chapter, 1956.

Cunningham, Isabel S. "The U.S. National Arboretum: Leader in Ornamental Plant Germplasm Collection." *Diversity,* No. 14 (1988): 28–29.

————. *Frank N. Meyer: Plant Hunter in Asia.* Ames: The Iowa State University Press, 1984.

Cutright, Paul Russell. *Lewis and Clark: Pioneering Naturalists.* Urbana: University of Illinois Press, 1969.

Daily, Gretchen C., ed. *Nature's Services: Societal Dependence on Natural Ecosystems.* Washington, DC: Island Press, 1997.

Davis, William T., ed. *Bradford's History of Plymouth Plantation.* New York: Charles Scribner's Sons, 1908.

Deed of Conveyance. Knott County, Kentucky, August 30, 1918.

Delcourt, Hazel R., and Paul A. Delcourt. *Quaternary Ecology: A Paleoecological Perspective.* London: Chapman & Hall, 1991.

DeMao, Lisa. "Historic Tree Can Be Felled." *Albany Herald,* September 21, 1995.

Dillard, Annie. *Teaching a Stone to Talk: Expeditions and Encounters.* New York: Harper & Row, 1982.

Diodorus of Sicily in Twelve Volumes. Books I and II. C. H. Oldfather, trans. Cambridge MA: Harvard University Press, 1933.

Dorson, Richard M. *American Folklore and the Historian.* Chicago: University of Chicago Press, 1971.

Douglass, Andrew Ellicott. "The Secret of the Southwest Solved by Talkative Tree Rings." *National Geographic Magazine,* December 1929, pp. 737–770.

Elm Leaves. Publication of the Elm Research Institute, July 1998.

Emerson, Ralph Waldo. *Nature.* New York: Penguin Books, 1995.

Engstrom, Harold E., and Lewis S. Matthew. "Effects of the 1940 Armistice Day Freeze on Siberian Elm in the Plains Country." *Journal of Forestry* 40 (1942): 704–707.

Ewan, Joseph, ed. *A Short History of Botany in the United States.* New York and London: Hafner Publishing Company, 1969.

Fairchild, David. "How United States and Japan Entered into a League of Flowers." *Sakura* 1, no. 4 (April 1921): 4–6.

———. *The World Was My Garden: Travels of a Plant Explorer.* New York and London: Charles Scribner's Sons, 1938.

Farb, Peter. *The Forest.* New York: Time Incorporated, 1963.

Farquhar, Francis P. *History of the Sierra Nevada.* Berkeley and Los Angeles: University of California Press, 1966.

Fassnacht, Cindy. "June Buchanan at ALC." *Knott County News,* November 6, 1975.

Fein, Esther B. "For Lost Pregnancies, New Rites of Mourning." *New York Times,* January 25, 1998, pp. 1, 34.

Ferguson, C. W. "Bristlecone Pine: Science and Esthetics." *Science* 159 (1968): 839–846.

Fletcher, W. I. *The Story of the Charter Oak: Compiled under the Direction of the Late Marshall Jewell.* Hartford: The Case Lockwood & Brainard Co., 1883.

Formigari, Lia. "Chain of Being." In *Dictionary of the History of Ideas,* ed. Philip P. Weiner. New York: Charles Scribner's Sons, 1973, pp. 325–335.

Fowles, John. *The Tree.* The Nature Company, 1994.

Frankel, Ellen. *The Classic Tales: 4,000 Years of Jewish Lore.* Northvale, NJ: Jason Aronson Inc., 1989.

Frazer, James G. *The Golden Bough: The Roots of Religion and Folklore.* New York: Avenel Books, 1981.

Friedman, Thomas L. "Mr. Toad's Last Ride." *New York Times,* June 6, 1998, p. 11.

From Seed to Flower, Philadelphia 1681–1876: A Horticultural Point of View. Philadelphia: The Pennsylvania Horticultural Society, 1976.

Frost, Robert. "The Gift Outright." In *Robert Frost: A Tribute to the Source.* New York: Holt, Rinehart and Winston, 1979.

Fuess, Claude M. *Andover: Symbol of New England, the Evolution of a Town.* The Andover Historical Society and The North Andover Historical Society, 1959.

Gerhardt, Gary. "Tree Die-off Makes Some Spots Look Like Florida after Andrew." *Rocky Mountain News,* September 24, 1992.

Gosnell, Ron. "A Halloween Tree Killer." *American Forests* 99 (January/February 1993): 34–36.

Gould, Stephen Jay, gen. ed. *The Book of Life*. New York and London: W. W. Norton & Company, 1993.

Graedel, Thomas E., and Paul J. Crutzen. *Atmosphere, Climate, and Change*. New York: Scientific American Library, 1995.

Graham, B. F., Jr., and F. H. Borman. "Natural Root Grafts." *The Botanical Review* 32 (July–September 1966): 255–292.

Green, Mary Anne Everett. *Letters of Queen Henrietta Maria Including Her Private Correspondence with Charles the First*. London: Richard Bentley, 1857.

Haley, W. D. "Johnny Appleseed—A Pioneer Hero." *Harper's New Monthly Magazine* 43 (November 1871): 830–836.

Halloween Freeze Recovery Initiative, Council of Western State Foresters, Supplemental Budget Request "White Paper" for FY94.

Hamil, Laura Cooley; Dorothy Burres Woods; Carmen Church Akers; Marion F. Cooley; and Ruhama Louise McIntyre. *A Story of Pioneering*. [Danville]: Illinois Printing Company, 1955.

Harlow, William H., Ellwood S. Harrar; James W. Hardin; and Fred M. White. *Textbook of Dendrology: Covering the Important Forest Trees of the United States and Canada*. 7th edition. New York: McGraw-Hill, Inc., 1991.

Harris, Edward Moseley. *Andover in the American Revolution: A New England Town in a Period of Crisis, 1763–1790*. Marceline, MO: Walsworth Publishing Company, 1976.

Harris, James G., and Melinda Woolf Harris. *Plant Identification Terminology: An Illustrated Glossary*. Spring Lake, UT: Spring Lake Publishing, 1994.

Hartford Courant, August 22 and 24, 1856.

Hawthorne, Nathaniel. *Young Goodman Brown and Other Tales*. Oxford, New York: Oxford University Press, 1987.

Hearn, Lafcadio. *Glimpses of Unfamiliar Japan*. Vermont and Tokyo: Charles E. Tuttle Company, 1993.

Hedrick, U. P. *A History of Horticulture in America to 1860*. New York: Oxford University Press, 1950.

Hendrickson, Robert. *Ladybugs, Tiger Lillies and Wallflowers: A Gardener's Book of Words*. New York: Macmillan, 1993.

"Historic Woodburn" brochure from Delaware Governor's Mansion, undated.

Hoffman, Daniel. *Paul Bunyan: Last of the Frontier Demigods*. Philadelphia: Temple University Press, 1952.

Holmes, Steven A. "U.S. No Longer a Land Steeped in Wanderlust." *New York Times*, September 12, 1995, pp. 1, 20.

Hora, Bayard, ed. *The Oxford Encyclopedia of Trees of the World*. Oxford, Toronto, New York, Melbourne: Oxford University Press, 1981.

Hunt, John Dixon, and Peter Willis. *The Genius of the Place: The English Landscape Garden 1620–1820*. Cambridge, MA: The MIT Press, 1988.

Huxley, Anthony. *Green Inheritance*. Garden City, NY: Anchor Press/Doubleday, 1985.

Hyde, Lewis. *The Gift: Imagination and the Erotic Life of Property*. New York: Vintage Books, 1983.

Ingram, Collingwood. *Ornamental Cherries*. London: Country Life Limited; New York: Charles Scribner's Sons, 1948.

International Apple Institute. "Series of Fact Sheets." 6707 Old Dominion Drive, Suite 320, PO Box 1137, McLean, VA, 22101.

Irving, George W. Letter to: Secretary, USDA through: N. C. Brady, Director of Science and Education, from: Administrator [George W. Irving], April 12, 1965, Record Group 16, General Correspondence 1965, Trees, Box 4393, National Archives, Washington, DC.

Ivey, James E. *In the Midst of a Loneliness: The Architectural History of the Salinas Missions*. Southwest Cultural Resources Center, Professional Papers No. 15, Santa Fe, NM, 1988.

Jackson, Bill. "Winterkill Destroying Greeley Trees." *Greeley Tribune*, May 13, 1992.

Jackson, John Brinckerhoff. *Discovering the Vernacular Landscape*. New Haven and London: Yale University Press, 1984.

———. *A Sense of Place, a Sense of Time*. New Haven and London: Yale University Press, 1994.

Jefferson, Roland M. "Boxwood Round the Lincoln Memorial." *American Horticulturist* 54, no. 4 (summer 1975): 6–10.

———. "The History of the Cherry Blossom Trees in Potomac Park." In *Introducing Modern Japan*. Lecture Series, vol. 4. Publication of the Japan Information & Culture Center, Embassy of Japan, 1995.

Jefferson, Roland M., and Alan E. Fusonie. *The Japanese Flowering Cherry Trees of Washington, D.C.: A Living Symbol of Friendship*. Washington, DC: National Arboretum Contribution No. 4, Dec. 1977.

Jefferson, Roland M., and Kay Kazue Wain. *The Nomenclature of Cultivated Japanese Flowering Cherries (Prunus): The Sato-Zakura Group*. Washington, DC: United States Department of Agriculture, National Arboretum Contribution No. 5, 1984.

Jeffrey, David Lyle, gen. ed. *A Dictionary of Biblical Tradition in English Literature*. Grand Rapids, MI: William B. Eerdmans Publishing Company, 1992.

"John Ruskin on Tree Planting." *American Forests* 30 (April 1924): 242.

Johnson, Kirk. "Sycamore, 110 Million Years in the Making." *Morris Arboretum Newsletter* 14, no. 2 (March–April 1985): 4–5.

Johnson, Thomas H., ed. *The Complete Poems of Emily Dickinson*. Boston: Little, Brown and Company, 1960.

Keeler, Harriet L. *Our Native Trees*. New York: Charles Scribner's Sons, 1913.

Keene, Donald, ed. *Anthology of Japanese Literature: From the Earliest Era to the Mid-Nineteenth Century*. New York: Grove Press, Unesco Collection of Representative Works, 1955.

King, Angela, and Susan Clifford, eds. *Trees Be Company: An Anthology of Poetry.* Bedminster, Bristol, UK: The Bristol Press, 1989.

Kozlowski, T. T. *Growth and Development of Trees.* Vols. 1 and 2. New York and London: Academic Press, 1971.

Kuo, F. E., and W. C. Sullivan. "Do Trees Strengthen Urban Communities, Reduce Domestic Violence?" *United States Department of Agriculture Forest Service Southern Region, Technology Bulletin No. 4,* Forestry Report R8-FR 55, Athens, GA, 1996.

Lacy, Allen. *The American Gardener: A Sampler.* New York: The Noonday Press, Farrar Straus Giroux, 1988.

Lape, Fred. *Apples and Man.* New York: Van Nostrand Reinhold Company, 1979.

Laws of the Town of Summerville. Chapter 20, "Tree Protection," modified May 10, 1995.

Le Dantec, Denise, and Jean-Pierre Le Dantec. *Reading the French Garden: Story and History.* Trans. Jessica Levine. Cambridge, MA, and London: The MIT Press, 1990.

Leopold, Aldo. *A Sand County Almanac: and Sketches Here and There.* London: Oxford University Press, 1968.

Leopold, Donald J. "Chinese and Siberian Elms." *Journal of Arboriculture* 6, no. 7 (July 1980): 175–179.

Lillge, Iva. "Ash Nelson's Walnut Link." *American Forests* (January/February 1990).

Limerick, Patricia Nelson. *The Legacy of Conquest: The Unbroken Past of the American West.* New York: W. W. Norton & Co., 1987.

Loyn, H. R., and J. Percival. *The Reign of Charlemagne: Documents on Carolingian Government and Administration.* London: Edward Arnold (Publishers) Ltd., 1975.

McCain, Diana Ross. "The Ol' Oak Tree." *Connecticut Magazine,* November 1987, pp. 164–165.

McCook, Anson T. "The Saving of the Charter." An Address before the Society of the Descendants of the Founders of Hartford, on the 250th Anniversary of the Hiding of the Charter, October 31, 1937.

McLuhan, T. C., ed. *Touch the Earth: A Self-Portrait of Indian Existence.* New York: Outerbridge & Dienstfrey, 1971.

Manning, Richard. *Grassland.* New York: Penguin Books, 1995.

Marshall, Randy. "Tree Removal Hacks off Weld Farmer." *Greeley Tribune,* June 14, 1990.

Marshall, Rosalind K. *Henrietta Maria: The Intrepid Queen.* Owings Mills, MD: Stemmer House Publishers, Inc., 1990.

Marx, Leo. *The Machine in the Garden: Technology and the Pastoral Ideal in America.* London: Oxford University Press, 1964.

Masefield, G. B.; M. Wallis; S. G. Harrison, eds. *The Oxford Book of Food Plants.* London: Oxford University Press, 1969.

Meinig, D. W., ed. *The Interpretation of Ordinary Landscapes.* New York: Oxford University Press, 1979.

Merchant, Carolyn. *Ecological Revolutions: Nature, Gender, and Science in New England*. Chapel Hill and London: The University of North Carolina Press, 1989.

Michaux, François A. *The North American Sylva, or a Description of the Forest Trees of the United States, Canada and Nova Scotia*. Paris: C. D'Hautel, 1819.

Michener, Carolee. "Six Cents Was Price per Tree." *The News Herald*, March 24, 1981.

Miller, Brian, and Edwin Rockwell. *Methuselah Walk*. Brochure for Inyo National Forest. Bishop, CA: Eastern Sierra Interpretative Association, n.d.

Miller, Perry. *Errand into the Wilderness*. Cambridge, MA: The Belknap Press of Harvard University Press, 1956.

———. *Nature's Nation*. Cambridge, MA: The Belknap Press of Harvard University Press, 1967.

Miller, Ruth M., and Linda A. Lennon. *The Angel Oak Story*. Charlestown, SC: Tradd Street Press, 1994.

Mirov, N. T. *The Genus Pinus*. New York: The Ronald Press Company, 1967.

Miyoshi, Manabu. *Sakura: Japanese Cherry*. [Tokyo]: Board of Tourist Industry, Japanese Government Railways, 1934.

Morgan, Joan, and Alison Richards. *The Book of Apples*. London: Ebury Press, 1993.

Morison, Samuel Eliot, and Henry Steele Commager. *The Growth of the American Republic*. Vol. 2. New York: Oxford University Press, 1962.

Mozingo, Hugh. *Shrubs of the Great Basin: A Natural History*. Reno: University of Nevada Press, 1987.

Muench, David, and Darwin Lambert. *Timberline Ancients*. Portland, OR: Charles H. Belding, 1972.

Muir, John. *John of the Mountains*. Ed. Linnie Marsh Wolfe. Boston: Houghton Mifflin Company, 1938.

———. *The Mountains of California*. New York: Penguin Books, 1985.

Murphy, Alexandra. *Graced by Pines: The Ponderosa Pine in the American West*. Missoula, MT: Mountain Press Publishing Company, 1994.

Murphy, Jan. "512-Year-Old Oak Tree Needs a Helping Hand." *Bucks County Intelligencer*, August 10, 1995.

Murtaugh, William J. *Keeping Time: The History and Theory of Preservation in America*. Pittstown, NJ: The Main Street Press, 1988.

Naipaul, V. S. *A Way in the World*. New York: Alfred A. Knopf, 1994.

Nakashima, George. *The Soul of a Tree: A Woodworker's Reflections*. Tokyo and New York: Kodansha International, 1989.

National Park Service News Release. "Washington's Cherry Blossoms." Revised 2/20/97, press contact (202) 260–3282.

National Public Radio. "300-Year-Old Oak Loses Out to Progress." *Morning Edition*. Transcript of October 16, 1995, broadcast, pp. 11–13.

"National Register of Big Trees." *American Forests* (spring 1998).

Neimark, Jill. "Using Flows and Fluxes to Demythologize the Unity of Life." *New York Times*, August 11, 1998, p. F4.

The New Encyclopaedia Britannica. Vol. 3. 15th edition, 1993.

Nicholson, Katharine Stanley. *Historic American Trees.* New York: Frye Publishing Company, 1922.

Nighswonger, Jim. "A Report of Streetside Losses of Siberian Elm in Western Kansas Resulting from Freeze Damage on October 31, 1991." Urban and Community Forestry [State of Kansas].

Noss, Reed F., and Robert L. Peters. *Endangered Ecosystems: A Status Report on America's Vanishing Habitat and Wildlife.* Washington, DC: Defenders of Wildlife, 1995.

Novak, Barbara. *Nature and Culture: American Landscape Painting 1825–1875.* New York: Oxford University Press, 1995.

Oshida, Koichi. *Newsletter of the Japan Program of the University of Alabama.* Vol. 4, issue 1, 1997.

Ostergard, Derek E. *George Nakashima: Full Circle.* New York: Weidenfeld & Nicholson, 1989.

Pakenham, Thomas. *Meetings with Remarkable Trees.* London: Weidenfeld & Nicholson, 1996.

Page, Russell. *The Education of a Gardner.* New York: Random House, 1983.

Pauly, Philip J. "The Beauty and Menace of the Japanese Cherry Trees." *Isis* 87, no. 1 (March 1996): 51–73.

Peattie, Donald Culross. *Flowering Earth.* New York: G. P. Putnam's Sons, 1939.

———. *A Natural History of Trees of Eastern and Central North America.* Boston: Houghton Mifflin Company, 1991.

Perényi, Eleanor. *Green Thoughts.* New York: Vintage Books, 1981.

Philippi, Donald L., trans. *Kojiki.* Tokyo and Princeton: University of Tokyo Press and Princeton University Press, 1969.

Phillips County Historical Society, compilers. *Those Were the Days.* Phillips County Historical Society, 1988.

Plummer, Thomas F., Jr., et al. *Landscape Atlas of the U.S.S.R.* West Point, NY: United States Military Academy, 1971.

Pollan, Michael. *Second Nature: A Gardener's Education.* New York: The Atlantic Monthly Press, 1991.

Porteous, Alexander. *Forest Folklore, Mythology, and Romance.* New York: The Macmillan Company, 1928.

Porter, Eliot. *"In Wildness Is the Preservation of the World."* New York: Sierra Club/ Ballantine Books, 1962.

Preston, Dickson J. *Wye Oak: The History of a Great Tree.* Cambridge, MD: Tidewater Publishers, 1972.

Price, Robert. *Johnny Appleseed: Man and Myth.* Bloomington: Indiana University Press, 1954.

"Professions Followed by Harvard Men." *The Harvard Alumni Bulletin,* October 16, 1912.

"Pyramids from France?" *Newsweek,* April 5, 1971, p. 50.

Raban, Jonathan. *Bad Land: An American Romance.* New York: Vintage Books,1996.

Randall, Charles Edgar, and Henry Clepper. *Famous and Historic Trees.* Washington, DC: American Forestry Association, 1977.

Raphael, Sandra. *An Oak Spring Pomona.* Upperville, VA: The Oak Spring Garden Library, 1990.

Reisner, Marc. *Cadillac Desert: The American West and Its Disappearing Water.* New York: Viking Penguin, 1986.

Richardson, Robert D., Jr. *Emerson: The Mind on Fire: A Biography.* Berkeley and Los Angeles: University of California Press, 1995.

Rodman, John. "The Liberation of Nature." *Inquiry* 20 (1977).

Rogers, Julia Ellen. *The Tree Book.* New York: Doubleday, Page & Co., 1908.

Rölvaag, O. E. *Giants in the Earth.* Trans. Lincoln Colcord. New York: Harper-Collins, 1991.

Roueché, Berton. "A Great Green Cloud." *The New Yorker,* July 15, 1961, pp. 35–53.

Runte, Alfred. *National Parks: The American Experience.* 3rd edition. Lincoln and London: University of Nebraska Press, 1997.

Russell, Paul. *The Oriental Flowering Cherry Trees.* Washington, DC: United States Department of Agriculture, Circular No. 313, March 1934.

Salwen, Bert. "Indians of Southern New England and Long Island: Early Period." In *Handbook of North American Indians,* ed. William Sturtevant. Vol. 15. Washington, DC: Smithsonian Institution, 1978.

Sargent, Charles Sprague. *Manual of the Trees of North America.* Boston and New York: Houghton, Mifflin and Company, 1905.

———. *The Silva of North America.* 14 vols. Boston and New York: Houghton, Mifflin and Company, 1891–1902.

Scanlon, Bill. "Tree Loss Stands at $425 Million." *Rocky Mountain News,* November 17, 1992.

Schama, Simon. *Landscape and Memory.* New York: Alfred A. Knopf, 1995.

Schlereth, Thomas J. "The Above-Ground Archaeology of Trees." *Orion* (autumn 1984).

Schlissel, Lillian. *Women's Diaries of the Westward Journey.* New York: Schocken Books, 1982.

Schulman, Edmund. "Bristlecone Pine, Oldest Known Living Thing." *National Geographic Magazine,* March 1958, pp. 355–372.

———. "Longevity Under Adversity in Conifers." *Science* 119 (1954): 396–399.

Schweingruber, Fritz Hans. *Tree Rings: Basics and Applications of Dendrochronology.* Dordrecht, Boston, Lancaster, Tokyo: D. Reidel Publishing Company, 1988.

Scidmore, Eliza Ruhamah. "The Cherry-Blossoms of Japan: Their Season a Period of Festivity and Poetry." *The Century Magazine* 79, no. 5 (March 1910): 643–653.

Scott, Glenn R. "Historic Trail Maps of the Sterling 1° × 2° Quadrangle." Text for USGS Map I–1894.

Searles, P. David. *A College for Appalachia: Alice Lloyd on Caney Creek.* Lexington: The University Press of Kentucky, 1995.

Sears, John F. *Sacred Places: American Tourist Attractions in the Nineteenth Century.* New York and Oxford: Oxford University Press, 1989.

Seelmeyer, John. "Cotton-Bearing Tree Controversy Revived." *Greeley Tribune,* July 7, 1976.

Shackelford, Nevyle. *Robinson Substation: A Short History.* University of Kentucky, College of Agriculture, Cooperative Extension Service, n.d.

Shipton, Clifford K. *New England Life in the 18th Century: Representative Biographies from Sibley's Harvard Graduates.* Cambridge, MA: The Belknap Press of Harvard University Press, 1963.

Simmonds, N. W., ed. *Evolution of Crop Plants.* London and New York: Longman, 1984.

Simon, F. Kevin, ed. *The WPA Guide to Kentucky.* Lexington: The University Press of Kentucky, 1996, reprint.

Simpson, Beryl Brintnall, and Molly Conner Ogorzaly. *Economic Botany: Plants in Our World.* New York: McGraw-Hill Book Company, 1986.

Sims, Phillip L. "Grasslands." In *North American Terrestrial Vegetation,* ed. Michael G. Barbour and William Dwight Billings. Cambridge: Cambridge University Press, 1988, pp. 265–286.

Skinner, Charles M. *Myths and Legends of Flowers, Fruits, and Plants.* Philadelphia and London: J. B. Lippincott Company, 1925.

". . . a special breed of men . . ." *The Tuscola Review,* February 7, 1974.

Stegner, Wallace. *The Spectator Bird.* New York: Penguin Books, 1990.

Stegner, Wallace, and Page Stegner. *American Places.* Ed. John Macrae III. New York and Avenel, NJ: Wings Books, 1993.

Stephen, Sir Leslie, and Sir Sidney Lee, eds. *The Dictionary of National Biography.* Vol. 2. London: Oxford University Press, 1921–1922.

Sterling (Colorado) City Ordinances, Article I. In General, Sec. 22–28. Sale, Planting of Certain Trees Prohibited.

Stevens, William K. "Drought May Have Doomed the Lost Colony." *New York Times,* April 24, 1998, pp. 1, 14.

———. "One in Every 8 Plant Species Is Imperiled, a Survey Finds." *New York Times,* April 9, 1998, pp. 1, 24.

Stilgoe, John R. *Common Landscape of America, 1580 to 1845.* New Haven and London: Yale University Press, 1982.

Still, Douglas T., and Henry D. Gerhold. "Motivations and Preferences of Urban Forestry Volunteers." *Journal of Arboriculture* 23, no. 3 (May 1997): 116–130.

Stone, Christopher D. *Should Trees Have Standing? Toward Legal Rights for Natural Objects.* Los Altos: William Kaufmann, 1974.

Strong, Roy. *The Renaissance Garden in England.* London: Thames and Hudson Ltd., 1979.

"Sycamore." *American Forests* 42 (August 1936).

Talmud: Abot de Rabbi Nathan, II. Version, XXXI.

Taylor, Norman. *The Guide to Garden Shrubs and Trees: Their Identity and Culture.* Boston: Houghton Mifflin Company, 1965.

Taylor's Guide to Trees, Boston: Houghton Mifflin Company, 1988.

Thacker, Christopher. *The History of Gardens.* Berkeley and Los Angeles: University of California Press, 1979.

Thomas, Jas. J. (mayor of Columbus, Ohio). Letters to [U.S.] Secretary of State and to the Mayor of Tokio [Japan], both November 17, 1925. Record Group 59, Box 438, File 093.941 W27. National Archives, Washington, DC.

Thomas, Keith. *Man and the Natural World: Changing Attitudes in England 1500– 1800.* London: Penguin Books, 1984.

Thoreau, Henry D. *Selected Journals of Henry David Thoreau.* Edited by Carl Bode. New York: Signet, 1967.

———. *Walden* and *Resistance to Civil Government.* 2d edition. New York & London: W. W. Norton & Company, 1992.

———. *Wild Apples.* Old Saybrook, CT: Applewood Books, undated reprint.

Tillyard, E.M.W. *The Elizabethan World Picture.* London: Chatto & Windus, 1960.

The Torah, The Five Books of Moses. Philadelphia: The Jewish Publication Society of America, 1962.

"Tree Damage Drastic This Year." *Holyoke Enterprise,* May 28, 1992.

Tree-Ring Bulletin. Vol. 22 (December 1958); and vol. 24 (May 1962).

Trent, Robert F. "The Charter Oak Artifacts." *The Connecticut Historical Society Bulletin* (summer 1984): 125–139.

Tryon, Henry H. "A Town That Owns Its Trees." *American Forests* 33 (April 1927): 209.

Turner, Frederick Jackson. *The Frontier in American History.* Tucson: University of Arizona Press, 1986.

Twain, Mark. "Charter Oak." In *Alta California,* March 3, 1868.

Tymn, Marshall B., ed. *Thomas Cole's Poetry.* York, PA: Liberty Cap Books, 1972.

Ubbelohde, Carl, Maxine Benson, and Duane A. Smith. *A Colorado History: Revised Centennial Edition.* Boulder, CO: Pruett Publishing Company, 1976.

U.S. Department of Commerce. *Historical Statistics of the United States: Colonial Times to 1970, Part 1.* Washington, DC, 1975.

Waldron, William, to Richard Waldron. Dana Mss. Massachusetts Historical Society. May 24, 1725.

[Warren, William L.] "The Charter Oak." *Connecticut Historical Society Bulletin,* July 1956.

Webb, W. B. "Retrospect of the Lumber Industry in Eastern Kentucky: Story of Fifty Years of Progress." *Southern Lumberman,* December 22, 1923.

Webb, Walter E. "A Report on Ulmus Pumila in the Great Plains Region of the United States." *Journal of Forestry* 46 (1948): 274–278.

West, Terry L. *Centennial Mini-Histories of the Forest Service.* United States Department of Agriculture, Forest Service FS-518, July 1992.

Whisnant, David E. *All That Is Native and Fine: The Politics of Culture in an American Region.* Chapel Hill: University of North Carolina Press, 1983.

Whittle, C. A. "The Sycamore's Ancient Family Tree." *American Forests* 36 (May 1930).

Wilson, Brayton F. *The Growing Tree*. Amherst: The University of Massachusetts Press, 1984.

Wilson, Edward O. "Back From Chaos." *The Atlantic Monthly,* March 1998.

Wilson, Ernest H. *Aristocrats of the Trees*. New York: Dover Publications, Inc., 1974.

———. *The Cherries of Japan*. Cambridge, MA: Harvard University Press, Publications of the Arnold Arboretum, No. 7, March 30, 1916.

———. *China, Mother of Gardens*. Boston: The Stratford Company, 1929.

"Winter Storm Punches Area a Third Time." *Greeley Tribune,* November 1, 1991.

Woolf, Virginia. *Moments of Being: Unpublished Autobiographical Writings*. New York and London: Harcourt Brace Jovanovich, 1976.

The Work Projects Administration in the State of Colorado, Workers of the Writers' Program. *Colorado: A Guide to the Highest State*. New York: Hastings House, 1941.

Wyman, Donald. *Trees for American Gardens, Third Edition,* New York: Macmillan Publishing Company, 1990.

Wynne, Peter. *Apples*. New York: Hawthorn Books Inc., 1975.

Yepsen, Roger. *Apples*. New York: W. W. Norton &. Co., 1994.

Zerubavel, Yael. *Recovered Roots: Collective Memory and the Making of Israeli National Tradition*. Chicago: University of Chicago Press, 1995.

INDEX

ABOUT THE
AUTHOR

Gayle Brandow Samuels is a lifelong gardener and lover of trees. She is the principal author of *Women in the City of Brotherly Love . . . and Beyond* and an editor of *Past and Promise: Lives of New Jersey Women.* Samuels has written for newspapers and magazines, including the Pennsylvania Horticultural Society's *Green Scene.*